Betrothed

A COLLECTION OF

LOVE STORIES

REFLECTING AN ANCIENT FAITH

Presented by

HaYovel Inc. and the Waller family

(www.hayovel.com)

Betrothed, A Collection of Love Stories Reflecting an Ancient Faith
ISBN: 978-1-941173-05-3
Third edition, copyright © 2015 by HaYovel

Published by
Olive Press Messianic and Christian Publisher
olivepresspublisher.com

Printed in the USA.

Messianic & Christian Publisher

Cover design by Heather Meyers (www.heathermeyers.com)
Cover photos of Caleb and Kendra Waller © 2014 by Heather Meyers
Photos on page 85, photographer Lydia Taylor, © 2014 by Nate and Katie Waller
Photos on page 84 © 2014 by A-Team Photography
    (www.a-teamphotography.com)

I go to prepare a place for you.
John 14:2

I will come again and receive you to Myself.
John 14:3

Acknowledgements

A huge thank you goes to everyone who
contributed to this *Betrothed* project:

- Heather Meyers, for spending time out of her busy life to design an
  artistically beautiful cover;

- All of the individual couples, for sharing their stories with us for
  this book;

- The Ellison family, for spending a huge amount of time editing all
  of the stories;

- Ken Groat and Amy Mucklestone, for acting as our proof-readers
  and for contributing to the editing process;

- All of the other individuals, for all the little but important
  contributions to the book;

- And all of our parents, for heeding the call and courageously
  leading us to walk the ancient paths.

If you have any questions when you are finished reading this book,
feel free to write to Brayden and Tali Waller at
brayden@hayovel.com

The Kingdom of Heaven is like a king
who prepared a wedding banquet for his son.
Matthew 22:2 NIV

Foreword

By Tommy and Sherri Waller

The Beauty of Holiness

"Oh, worship the LORD in the Beauty of Holiness!" (Psalm 96:9)

Is it conceivable within the walls of our faith to define the "Beauty of Holiness?" Have we seen it? Have we experienced it? Can we rightly worship God without understanding the Beauty of His Holiness?

It may sound absurd, but there were years in my life when I desperately sought to find beauty in unholiness. I was told and taught that the beauty of unholiness was found in God's grace—His unmerited favor. Since it is "impossible for me or anyone to walk in holiness," my only hope was to abandon myself to God's grace. "I am a wretched sinner, desperately wicked, and through 'God's unmerited favor,' I can stay that way for the rest of my life...and feel good about it." After all, Yeshua said in John 8:7 (NIV), *"If any one of you is without sin, let him be the first to throw a stone..."* In 1 John 1:8 we are taught that, *"If we say that we have no sin, we deceive ourselves, and the truth is not in us."*

Is this truly the "good news" Yeshua came to deliver–to merely cover our sins like a beautiful cloth can cover an old and rotten piece of furniture? Yeshua's "good news" message to the woman who was about to be stoned for her sin was, "Go and sin no more." He goes on to say, *"I am the light of the world* [The Beauty of Holiness]. *He who follows Me shall not walk in darkness* [sin], *but have the light of life* [The Beauty of Holiness]" (brackets mine).

As we read further in 1 John, he writes in chapter three verse eight, *"He who sins is of the devil.... for this purpose the Son of God was manifested, that He might destroy the works of the devil."*

The truth is that there never has been and there never will be beauty in unholiness. The Bible, God's word and instruction, specifically teaches us that unholiness, which may also be defined as unrighteousness, always has a destructive end. If, today, a person makes a decision to be unfaithful (unholy/unrighteous) to his or her spouse, it will lead to a devastating wound—one that may never heal. I have heard magnificent testimonies from men and women boasting of God's grace over the sin of unfaithfulness (adultery). Each time I am encouraged by the person's desire, after hitting bottom, to rise again to the place of faithfulness. However, as I am listening to the remarkable testimony, my mind drifts to the question of how the spouse is doing in all this? How are the children? How is the "other" person entangled in this affair?

It may be difficult to create a box office hit or to sell magazines at Walmart without unfaithful (unholy) content, but out of all the people I know desiring to get married—to start a family—I have never met the person whose heart longs to find an unfaithful spouse. There is no beauty in unholiness.

The betrothal accounts in this book are to me an epic picture of the "Beauty of Holiness." These accounts tell of couples who chose to stay away from the destructive path of unfaithfulness and defraudment even before marriage. Many of these accounts are written by my own children. Their testimonies are the result of God's mercy in making a presentation to me and my wife, Sherri, many years ago. He enabled us to see clearly that our children were at great risk and under the plan of unfaithfulness and defraudment. Which of our children would make it and which ones would fall?

At this writing we have five married children. All of them have chosen to walk through the beautiful process of betrothal. There has never been a time in my life when I have witnessed anything close to the intensity of love birthed from two undefiled hearts

9

as I have in betrothal. Every betrothal I witness confirms in me the Father's true grace—the unmerited favor He desires to lavish on all of us. After experiencing the "Beauty of His Holiness," I would be a fool to ever look back.

Tommy Waller

Executive Director, HaYovel Inc.

Be Prepared to Enter into a Different World.

These accounts open up the heart of God for His people. His ways are high and lofty, set apart...unlike anything common or natural. They are holy.

It is the responsibility of the people of God to make His ways known to the world, to separate the clean from the unclean, the profane from the holy. This is what betrothal is all about!

Tommy and I set out on a quest to bring our children to marriage pure. We didn't have a model, but we had the Guidebook, and we knew that God had a perfect plan. Unbeknownst to us, we entered a paradigm shift. When we embraced the ways of the God of Israel, betrothal opened up to us. The thought was deep in our spirits and we were committed to protect and direct our children, and not to be intimidated by our own past failures or other's attempts to discourage us. We would fight for it! God birthed the zeal in us to carry us all the way step by step. We are humbled to see how God has honored our simple faith and blessed us past our wildest dreams! We couldn't see the end; you never can. We only need the faith to trust for the beginning.

Sherri Waller

Helpmeet to Tommy Waller and mother of eleven

*And I John saw
the holy city, new Jerusalem,
coming down from God out of heaven,
prepared as a bride
adorned for her husband.*

Revelation 21:1

TABLE OF CONTENTS

Introduction

The Beauty of Betrothal

The bridegroom heart of God is a recurring theme throughout Scripture. The Bible actually begins and ends with a wedding: first, Adam and Eve in the garden, and last, the marriage supper of the Lamb. Betrothal is an essential key to this whole story. To understand this ancient and Biblical way of marriage is to better understand the relationship we have with God. My hope in this introduction is to show how betrothal paints a vivid picture of the covenant relationship we have with Yeshua (Jesus).

What my Dad told me growing up is especially true of betrothal: God loves object lessons. He loves them because they speak directly to our hearts. Like marriage, betrothal is an object lesson or parable reflecting our covenant with God. In Ephesians we see Paul calling the parable of marriage a "great mystery." Ephesians 5:31-33 says, "'For this reason a man shall leave his father and mother and be joined to his wife, and the two shall become one flesh.' This is a great mystery but I speak concerning [Messiah] and the church." This symbolic picture of marriage is most likely not a new idea to you; however, maybe the picture of betrothal is. Our prayer is that the testimonies in this book will give you greater understanding and appreciation of this ancient path.

Unlike engagement, betrothal is an actual covenant that is made prior to the wedding day. Biblical betrothal can basically be defined as a covenant that unites a man and woman in marriage, but is not physically consummated until the day of the wedding. Establishing a covenant before the wedding is the very thing God has done with us! He has made a covenant with us by the blood of Yeshua, and the wedding is yet to come. Revelation 19:7 tells us of this coming wedding, "Let us be glad and rejoice and give Him glory, for the marriage of the Lamb has come, and His wife has made herself ready." Yeshua loves us as a man loves his bride! When we embrace His love in this way it becomes real and pulsing with life.

Betrothal is much further reaching than the confines of a culture. It is something that the LORD Himself participates in. He says in Hosea 2:19-20, "*I will betroth you to Me forever; yes I will betroth you to Me in righteousness and justice, in loving kindness and mercy; I will betroth you to Me in faithfulness, and you will know the LORD.*" In verse sixteen of this same chapter, God says, "*You will call Me 'My Husband,' And no longer call Me 'My Master.'*" Do you hear the heartbeat of God? He wants to be an intimate husband to His people. Even in His appeal for us to come back to Him, listen to God's compassionate voice, "*Return O backsliding children,*" says the LORD, "*for I am married to you*" (Jeremiah. 3:14). Exposed and vulnerable, God lays His broken heart before His people. He is the faithful husband who cries out for us to return to Him. In full assurance, God waits, knowing that one day His Bride will turn to Him in wholehearted love. He sees the end already and has foretold it. One day the Bride will be enamored with her Bridegroom King. Along with the Spirit, she will cry "Come!" (Revelation. 22:17). So may the cry of our hearts intensify as we long to be with Yeshua. In answer to a question about fasting, Yeshua replied, "*Can the friends of the bridegroom mourn as long as the bridegroom is with them? But the days will come when the bridegroom will be taken away from them, and then they will fast*" (Matthew 9:15). Here, Yeshua identifies himself as a bridegroom. He said when He is taken away, then they will fast. We are in that season now. Our betrothed bridegroom is not physically with us, therefore we fast as an expression of the ache in our hearts for Him to come. Come, Yeshua come!

In this book we show what a modern-day betrothal can look like. You will encounter stories as broad in scope as the personalities of those who wrote them. Each story will have its own unique sparkle of divine authorship shining through the couple's testimony. While some like a small intimate gathering for the betrothal ceremony, others prefer to include many to witness their vows. Some separate after the betrothal, not seeing each other until the wedding. Others choose to spend time together leading up to the wedding. Some have a long period of time between the wedding and betrothal, while others like to keep the waiting time to a minimum and have the wedding just weeks after the betrothal. The details are just like the wedding dress, tailor-designed to meet the desires of the couple.

First, let's turn our attention to God's covenant faithfulness through history. As clouds are made amazingly beautiful when the sun shines through them, so the pages of the Bible come alive with beauty when they are illuminated with God's love. Jeremiah 2:2: *"Thus says the LORD: 'I remember you, the kindness of your youth, the love of your betrothal, when you went after Me in the wilderness, in a land that was not sown.'"* From the context of this verse, we see that the people whom God is speaking to about betrothal are the Israelites in the wilderness. It was there, far away from the slavery and distractions of Egypt, that God made a covenant with Israel. Sometimes God does the same with us. He strips away what is familiar and comfortable to show us our great need for Him.

There are four primary love stories in the Bible that reflect the bridegroom heart of God. I will list them and give a brief summary of how they reflect the Bridegroom.

Adam and Eve—The need for a bride.

God brought all the animals before Adam, but none was found to be a helper for him. Adam was alone and incomplete until God made Eve. Just as there was a void in Adam's heart until Eve was brought to him, so there is a void in the heart of Yeshua until His Bride is prepared and the wedding takes place.

<u>Isaac and Rebecca—The Holy Spirit, The Helper, seeks out a bride.</u>

Abraham sends out his servant to seek a bride for his son. This unnamed servant is most likely Eliezer (Genesis 15:2), whose name means "God is my helper"! Rebecca's willingness to go with this servant is a picture of the Bride's willingness to be led by the Holy Spirit (The Helper) in preparation to meet her Beloved.

<u>Boaz and Ruth—The Redeemer purchases a bride from the nations.</u>

Boaz redeems (buys) Ruth from a life of poverty and shame even though she is a Moabitess. The undeserved favor that Ruth receives from Boaz is a picture of the undeserved favor that Yeshua shows to us.

<u>King Ahasuerus and Esther—The Bride reigning with the King.</u>

In this beautiful story, God favors a lowly orphan girl, Esther, by raising her up to be the queen of a vast kingdom. Fasting and intercession play a major role in Esther fulfilling her divine destiny. The Bride in the last days will also be engaged in fasting and prayer to see the Kingdom of God established on earth.

Every one of these stories is loaded with revelation about Yeshua and The Bride. I encourage you to read these accounts and ask the Father to give you deeper understanding into His heart.

The two most significant parts of a betrothal ceremony are the drinking of the cup and the bride price. The climax of a betrothal is when the groom signifies his vows by drinking from a cup of wine and then hands the cup to the bride. If she drinks, the covenant is sealed. Without understanding this concept that was familiar to the people of Yeshua's day, the significance of "the cup" is not fully grasped. *"Then He took the cup and gave thanks, and gave it to them saying, 'Drink from it all of you. For this is My blood of the new covenant, which is shed for many for the remission of sins. But I say to you, I will not drink of this fruit of the vine from now on until that day when I drink it new with you in My Father's kingdom"* (Matthew 26:27-29). That night when the disciples drank the cup, they in essence were agreeing to the covenant Yeshua proposed to them. They were spiritually entering into a betrothal, just as we in a spiritual way become betrothed to Yeshua when we say yes to Him and "drink the cup." For Yeshua, the cup was symbolic of His shed blood, the price he paid to redeem us. This "cup" that Yeshua drank was a point of great turmoil for Him as He wrestled in the garden with the immense suffering He would endure as He poured His life out on the tree. He begged that if it could be the Father's will, that the cup would pass from Him. In the end, Yeshua embraced the Father's will and paid the price. *"For you were bought at a price"* (1 Corinthians 6:20). *"Knowing that you were not redeemed with corruptible things, like silver or gold, from your aimless conduct received by tradition from your fathers, but with the precious blood of Christ, as of a lamb without blemish and without spot."* (1 Peter 1:18-19) Here are a few Bible references where the practice of paying a "bride price" is mentioned: Exodus 22:16, and 2 Samuel 3:14. Because of its rich symbolic meaning, many incorporate the "bride price" into their betrothal.

At the set time when the Father says "Go!," Yeshua will come for His Bride and the marriage will be complete. When we take on the magnitude that we are preparing for a wedding feast, we no longer view holiness as a burdensome lifestyle, but rather as pure white linen on a beautiful bride.

Joseph and Mary's betrothal story is found in Matthew 1:18-19. *"Now the birth of Yeshua Messiah took place in this way. When His mother Mary had been betrothed to Joseph, before they came together she was found to be with child from the Holy Spirit. And her husband Joseph, being a just man and unwilling to put her to shame, resolved to divorce her quietly*" (RSV). This account gives us a window of understanding into what first century betrothal would have looked like. First we see that Joseph and Mary were betrothed before they came together (before they were fully married). Secondly, we see that the betrothal covenant was so strong it would require a divorce to end it.

Whether you are reading this book for the spiritual application of being betrothed to Yeshua, or you are interested in betrothal as the way you want to start your covenant with your future spouse, know that entering into covenant with someone is no small matter. "*For I am jealous for you with godly jealousy. For I have betrothed you to one husband, that I may present you a chaste virgin to [Messiah]*" (2 Corinthians 11:2). One day the Bride will be presented to Messiah pure and spotless! What a glorious truth! Yeshua desires us so much that He paid the price of His own blood to redeem us. May your love for Him be stirred to new heights as you read this book.

Brayden Waller

The Love Stories

"His Banner over Me is Love"

Brayden and Tali Waller

Brayden's Story

When I was growing up, Dad and Mom set a vision before me of only being romantically involved with one person. I remember Mom telling me not to kiss her on the lips because that was the kiss I should save for my future wife. When I would see my parents lovingly linger at the door before Dad went to work, giving one another that special kiss, it only served to reinforce my young heart's resolve to wait for the "one."

By the time I was sixteen or so, Dad began having discussions with my younger brother Zac (14) and me on what he called the "game plan." The game plan consisted of the real life process of pursuing a wife without having to wrestle through the entangling nets of youthful lust. Paul tells us to flee youthful lust (2 Timothy 2:22). The world promotes the exact opposite of this by encouraging young people to stir up youthful lust at every chance. Dad encouraged us to do something different than the status quo—something that, with God's help, would protect and prepare us to enter into marriage with our emotional and physical purity still intact. One thing Dad would ask us was, "If you knew that your future wife was with (i.e. dating) another guy, how would you feel about that?" Our obvious answer was that we wouldn't like it. Dad then turned it around and said, "Well, she probably wouldn't want you to be involved with another girl that way either." It made sense. Dad envisioned something that would spread the weighty decision of marriage and a lifetime partner onto more shoulders than just the emotional guy and girl. The plan was for Dad and Mom (along with me and each of my

22

brothers) to prayerfully seek God about who the "one" was to be. If we felt confident that God was leading toward a particular young lady, I would then proceed to talk to her father. If her dad felt peace to continue the process, he would present the possibility to the young lady, who would then either say "yes," "no," or "give me time to think about it." If she said yes, then we would get to know each other better. If the answer was no, any further pursuit of her would be halted. These talks provided great structure for the adventure that lay ahead of us. If we intend to go forward living in the culture that surrounds us, we must have a plan of action. Can you imagine embarking on a trip down the Amazon River, only to realize a short way downstream that your canoe is full of holes? Instead of enjoying the ride, you would constantly be trying to keep your canoe from sinking.

God intends for marriage to be a life of adventure, one that becomes more and more engaging with every bend in the river! If you are an unmarried person, make it your goal to keep your canoe hole-free, prepared for the adventure of a lifetime. For those reading who have regrets in regard to purity, don't lose heart. Start now to repair the broken areas of your life by repenting and accepting the forgiveness of Yeshua. He is a faithful restorer!

Primarily, it was my dear parents who spoke truth into my life. There was, however, a young man whom God divinely placed in my life as well, one who dramatically rocked my spiritual world. We had only lived in Russell Creek (a plain, homesteading community) for a few months, when a family from Bolivia moved in next door to us. In this family was a sixteen-year-old son named Noah. I remember as a twelve-year-old going down for the first time to meet the new neighbors. Before I knew it, Noah had begun to show me pictures of the exotic world of Bolivia. The mountain lions, jungles, and hunting stories were enough to impress a boy like me. Adventures like that were pretty distant from my farm-boy experiences. Little did I know when I left that day, that God was about to fascinate Noah with more than creation, but with the Creator Himself. Not long after our first meeting, Noah got born again. With this event I noticed a marked difference in Noah's life. I saw a delight in holiness and a genuine hunger for God burning in his heart. Seeing this transformation take place before my eyes had a profound effect on me. In the ensuing years, Noah's friendship would continue to challenge and bless me. Once, while I was in the barn working on a project, Noah came riding up on his bicycle with an urgent prayer request. He had received news that a friend of his was sick with a life-threatening illness. After telling me the need for prayer, Noah then posed one of the most pointed questions I had ever been asked. In a tone of simple curiosity, he asked, "Do you ever pray?" I was convicted. I knew prayer was important, but somehow it had found little place in my personal life.

Another time I remember being challenged was one night during a weekly prayer meeting. One of the men we were praying with fervently cried out to God, "Lord, reveal the secret sins!" I was cut to the heart.

If I was going to make any progress pursuing God, I knew there was no alternative but to face the hidden sin in my life. Not until I began confessing my sin did I see the light of Yeshua scatter the darkness. The effect was often instantaneous. After confessing an area of sin I was struggling with, I would feel on top and no longer underneath the sin that was trying to wield its influence over me. My brother, Zac, was a great accountability partner over the years. Confessing our faults to one another (James 5:16) became a powerful weapon against the enemy, leaving no room for sin to fester in the darkness.

At 19 years old I crossed paths with another young man who would impact my life. He is a Canadian named Yisrael. While pruning grapevines on the Mountains of Samaria, Yisrael and I exchanged stories of how the Father had worked in our lives.

We soon realized that our stories had a lot in common. A friendship was born. Yisrael's love for Hebrew was an inspiration that sparked something in my own heart to delve into the language. Also, his deep-rooted faith encouraged me to keep pressing on for all that God had in store for me. A few years after our meeting, he became betrothed and married. Yisrael was the first person that I knew who had decided to do betrothal. Later when I was preparing for Tali and my betrothal ceremony, Yisrael was a great person to get ideas from.

Once while we were staying at a friend's house in Colorado, Yisrael and his wife paid us a surprise visit. It had been quite awhile since Yisrael and I had seen each other and, as far as I knew, he was several hundred miles away. A lot had happened since we had last talked. The father of the family we were staying with runs a window washing business and asked me if I wanted to join him to work for the day. It was an enjoyable day learning the ins and outs of the window washing trade. When we got home my family was all sitting in the living room and I began to tell them about what we had done. What I didn't notice right away was that Yisrael was sitting right in the middle of them. I did a double take or two before realizing who it was. In times of great joy or surprise I am known to be on the exuberant side. So upon finally seeing him, I fell to the floor in shock, beating my cap on the floor at random intervals and laughing. I was overcome with happiness. Soon we began speaking Hebrew as we caught up on each other's lives.

I reflect with a thankful heart for the friendships and experiences that God used to challenge and prepare me to be wed to Tali.

The first time I remember hearing about Tali was in Ariel, Israel, in 2006. She had written us an email with a few links attached. One of these links led to a site where there were pictures of her and her sisters' music band. Upon seeing the pictures, my brother, Nate, humorously called out to me, "Brayden, I have found your wife!" I was probably the most influenced by our time in Russell Creek, so artsy photos and vintage fashion had little appeal to me. Nevertheless, thanks to Nate, the first time I heard of Tali was of her being my wife! We saw each other for the first time in person at a Passover gathering my family held in Tennessee. At that time, being around Tali and her family was uneventful, but even then God was laying a foundation for the future. It was during this trip that Tali's parents bought a piece of property in Tennessee. This was very uncharacteristic for Mr. Kenny, Tali's father, a man who had lived in the same area in Pennsylvania since his childhood. The Lupinaccis (Tali's maiden name) had their house in Pennsylvania on the market with the intentions of moving to Tennessee as soon as it sold, but no one ended up buying it until a few years later. This left the property in Tennessee available for a young newly-married couple that needed a place to stay—and that was Tali and me!

About a year before I got married, I started to feel restless about my future. With no money-generating job (I was full-time in the family ministry), no house or car, and no way of obtaining these without going into debt (which I was opposed to), I felt that if any young woman was going to be interested in marrying me something had to change. With these thoughts weighing on me, I went with Dad on a little road trip to pick up something. Dad patiently listened as I described how I was not prepared to get married because of all the things I was lacking.

Once I was through, Dad asked, "What about me? I have eleven children." It was true; Dad's income was just as much by faith as mine was. I left that conversation feeling much more at peace. After we had sold our farm in Russell Creek to start working in Israel, life took on a new degree of dependency on the Father. The Almighty had proven Himself faithful in every way. Trusting Him was the best place to be. Little did I know, He was working behind the scenes, and He already had the house question answered.

Tali and I only saw each other sporadically after our first meeting, due to the distance between us. When we did see each other, something that really blessed me about Tali was her non-flirtatious character. This spoke to me that she was content in the Father's timing.

Because of flights to Israel being cheaper out of northern airports than out of Tennessee, my family would often travel north en route to Israel. One of our favorite stopping places on the way was the Lupinacci's home in Pennsylvania. Their gift of making someone feel perfectly at home in their house was only accented by the talent of Tali's mom, Diane, as an Italian cook. Ms. Diane would start preparing food weeks before our arrival. Plus, there was a grand piano nicely situated in their living room, making an ideal place for praise times together.

Tali had been to Israel once before, and since that trip, she had always dreamed of returning. In 2008, when my family left for the airport from the Lupinacci's house, Tali was visibly emotional that she was not able to go with us. As I later found out, my parents were very impacted by how heartfelt Tali was in her love for Israel. They were so impressed that, during the harvest that year, Dad and Mom took me aside one night and asked me what I thought of Talitha Lupinacci. They were feeling that she could possibly be the one for me. Initially I was hesitant to believe that it could be true. For the time I was content to commit the idea to prayer but I had no real assurance that I should pursue Tali as a potential wife. In God's plan though, my hesitations were about to disappear.

After that harvest season was over in the mountains of Israel, we flew back into New York, and the Lupinaccis were there to welcome us. We made our way from the airport to the Lupinacci home, got settled in, and everything was going as usual until I laid my travel-worn body down to sleep. Immediately after falling asleep I had a vivid dream in which Tali told me she wanted to be married. The dream had such a sense of authority to it, that I had little doubt that God was speaking to me. Could it be that after all the years of waiting and praying, God had now revealed who my wife was to be? The next morning, I excitedly went to the room my parents were staying in to let them know about the dream. Later on Mom and Dad told me how amused they were at the possibility of Tali's very artistic world coming together with my very simple, Amish-influenced world.

Tali's room was a work of art. An oversized, gaudy, gold clock contrasted sharply with the wall she had painted bold red. Peacock feathers and rose petals added their own unique touch as well. In some ways our upbringing could not have been more opposite. While I was out under the Tennessee sun plowing behind a team of horses, Tali was in New York City attending fashion school. By this time, however, God was divinely intersecting our paths and neither of us were on such opposite ends of the spectrum as we had been just a few years before. For me, even though I loved the homesteading lifestyle, I knew that God had taken us to Israel where things were much different. For Tali, God had been directing her away from the fashion scene and giving her a heart to pursue purity. I so admire her for walking away from the things aspired to by the world. Needless to say, I was more aware of Tali during the remainder of our time in Pennsylvania.

About four days later, back in Tennessee, I made my way out to the privacy of our little office to make the call to Tali's father. Ms. Diane answered the phone, and when I asked for Mr. Kenny she, with wide-eyed curiosity, handed the phone to him (this was the first time I remember calling the Lupinaccis). Her inquisitiveness only rose, I'm sure, when I asked to talk to Mr. Kenny alone. So Mr. Kenny left the room to talk while Ms. Diane and Tali, full of restless curiosity, waited for him to return. To my surprise, he acted like he had expected my call. His easygoing nature quickly set all my pent-up emotions at ease. I told him how I respected Tali, and asked what he thought of me pursuing her as a wife. Mr. Kenny was positive about the idea. I left the conversation encouraged but at the same time in suspense. What would Tali think when her dad told her? I wasn't sure when Mr. Kenny was planning to tell her. I didn't expect he would tell her right away. Three days later I got an answer. Mr. Kenny had told Tali right away and she was interested. I was ecstatic! I remember joyously dancing in our living room with some of my younger siblings after hearing the news. I had gone from (1), not knowing whether it was God's will for me to pursue Tali as my wife; to (2), knowing I should pursue her; to (3), finding out she was interested in me, all in a matter of days. It was too good to be true. On top of all this, we were only getting green lights from our parents to keep things going. The agreement that everyone shared in these early stages of the relationship between Tali and me was a major confirmation that we were on the right track.

Thanksgiving was just a few weeks away at the time, so it was planned that the Lupinaccis would join us, along with our extended family, for our traditional Thanksgiving get-together. Our purpose during that Thanksgiving visit was focused. We went on walks together, and we shared our testimonies with each other. We were very honest with one another about our past and also about what we felt God calling us to in the future. Our goal was to find out one thing: was it God's will for us to be married? If the answer was yes, then we wanted to embrace our destiny and move forward. If the answer was no, we wanted to be ready to lay it down without any hurt between us. If there was going to be romance between us, I desired that it would be pure and permanent.

By the end of our time together, there was little doubt in my mind that Tali was the one. As a reminder to her that I was serious about seeking God for the next step in our relationship, I sent my tallit (a rectangle cloth with tzit-tzit attached to each corner) home with her. Over the following weeks, we continued to pray for God's will to be done concerning us. We had a few talks by phone. We both came to a place of deep peace about the direction we were going, and we began planning the betrothal during this time. Things were happening fast, but if God was the author of it we were more than willing to hold on tight and enjoy the ride. Our next time together in person was a few weeks later during Hanukkah. Here is a journal entry from the trip:

12/17/08: "I'm going north, destined for the Lupinacci's house with Mama Jo and Pa Bill [my grandparents]. They were wanting to visit some relatives up this way, so Zac and I are traveling together with them. There are many unknowns for me about this trip, one being how Talitha's extended family is going to react to me."

We arrived at the Lupinacci's after a full day's drive. The snow-packed driveway was too slick to drive on so we parked on the road, about seventy-five feet from the house. Nearly running across the icy yard, I made a beeline for the front door. Once inside, I exuberantly greeted the family. Until now I had felt reserved around Tali. This time though, I felt at liberty to really express my excitement.

We were thinking of doing the betrothal in mid-January, which was only a few weeks away. So the primary purpose of this trip was to begin working on the plans for the betrothal. It was soon realized during our five days together, however, that a big decision had to be made before we could move forward with our plans. The decision was whether or not Tali would finish nursing school. Was she going to finish the three months it would take to get her degree, or would we have the betrothal in January? To do both would be too much, because we wanted the time between the betrothal and the wedding to be devoted to preparation. If

Tali was going to finish school we would postpone the wedding until early summer. The prospects of waiting didn't appeal to me, but I was ready to submit to whatever decision was made.

At a certain point Mr. Kenny, Ms. Diane and Tali met to come to a conclusion. While they were talking, I went to the room Zac and I were staying in, to pray. For what seemed like a very long time I waited attentively for someone to bring the news. Finally, Mr. Kenny came to the door. I could hardly believe my ears when he told me that they had decided that Tali wouldn't go back to school. To Mr. Kenny's shock, I lunged through the doorway into his arms with one of the most excited hugs I had ever given. Then with ecstatic leaps of joy I bounced down the hallway toward the kitchen where the rest of the family was. Once in the kitchen, Ms. Diane had to caution me not to hit my head on the ceiling, I was jumping so high! Bursting out the door into the icy cold, I ran and jumped while freely expressing my thankful heart to God. Back in the kitchen, I told Tali, who was also beaming with joy, "This changes everything!" Now we could start doing what we were originally thinking, planning for a mid-January betrothal. When Ms. Diane wanted to get a picture of us, I was standing about four feet away from Tali, so with one big stride I stood right by her. Even though we didn't touch each other, it was nonetheless amazing just to stand next to each other.

Right away I shared an idea of something we could do leading up to the betrothal. I asked, "What do you think about us seeing how many ways we can say how much we appreciate each other without saying 'I love you?'" Tali liked the idea and so began a season that I believe even Noah Webster would have approved of. We took advantage of every complimentary word we could think of. You're amazing, you're beautiful, you're wonderful, you're smart, you're extravagant, you're fabulous, you're graceful, etc. etc. We were thoroughly in love.

The excitement of entering into covenant with one another was mounting. Only a few short weeks and we would be betrothed! I would wake up in the morning with ideas filling my mind of new ways to show Tali my love for her. One morning I wrote a message for her in the snow. It was an unforgettable moment, standing there in the early morning sunlight and seeing Tali's face light up as she read what I had written. It was in this season that I understood what it means for love to be awakened as it says in Song of Songs 3:5. We enjoyed reading the love stories of the Bible together—Isaac and Rebecca, Boaz and Ruth. We were also able to read other passages pertaining to marriage. It was good to have a biblical foundation to build on.

Leaving each other was not something we were looking forward to as the trip wound to an end. Nevertheless, we were excited about what lay ahead of us. The plan was that in a few weeks, Tali would come down to Tennessee and we would finish writing our ketubah (vows) and finish planning the betrothal ceremony. As we exchanged parting words we both laughed and felt blessed beyond measure to see how the Father had grown our friendship in such a short period of time. I waved a kiss to Tali as we drove off; so ended a beautiful chapter in our journey toward betrothal.

As I waited for Tali's upcoming trip to Tennessee, my mind percolated with ways to bless her. One of the ideas came from Song of Songs 2:4, "He brought me to his house of wine and his banner over me is love." This Scripture had impacted me greatly in my walk with Yeshua. The truth of Yeshua's love being over me as a banner was something that had really softened and transformed my heart. Now I wanted Tali to know that my banner over her was love. Thus began the making of a love banner. It was made of a cloth about two feet wide and six feet long with the Hebrew letters written on it that spell "Ahavah" (love). It just so happened that there was also some glow-in-the-dark paint in the shed, so I outlined the letters with it and hung it in a wide doorway inside the house. When Tali and her family arrived, we turned all the lights out to get the full glow-in-the-dark effect. She loved it. Our time together in Tennessee was full. We prayed, read the Word, and prepared for the betrothal. To emphasize the seriousness of the covenant we were about to enter into, we decided to get legally married. There was no hesitation in doing this; we both knew we were walking in the destiny God had laid before us.

A week before the betrothal, we had what we called an engagement party. This was a time for people to come and meet Tali and for us to share some about how God had brought us together.

Despite the inevitable ebb and flow of emotions that come with a romantic relationship, we felt secure being surrounded by family who supported us and held us accountable. If there is one thing the devil is out to destroy today, it is solid marriages. The enemy of your soul would like nothing more than to seduce you like the bird in Proverbs 7:23 who hastened to the snare, not knowing it would cost him his life. There is a life and death battle being fought when it comes to relational purity. We must be able to give a message of hope. Recently, a friend of mine told me the story of a large church that was teaching the importance of physical purity in their youth group. One of the young people asked the group leader, "Can you tell me of one couple in this church who kept themselves physically pure before marriage?" The leader was at a loss. Tragically, he could not think of a single couple who had saved themselves for each other.

A testimony has power. It gives strength to those who are seeking to resist the devil. Happily married couples are one of the best witnesses that can be given to our generation. We must understand the reason God wants healthy marriages and their importance to Him. The prophet Malachi says, "But did He not make them one, having a remnant of the Spirit? And why one?

He seeks godly offspring" (2:15). As the enemy makes an all-out assault on biblical faith being passed from generation to generation through godly offspring, we must be aware of his tactics and fight to win. God desires healthy marriages because He desires godly offspring. The two are inseparable.

The day of the betrothal, we were still working on the ketubah. A few hours before the ceremony we finished it. I was greatly helped in getting an idea of what goes into ketubah-making from my dear friend, Yisrael, since he and his wife were the only couple I knew who had been betrothed, other than one other couple who were not yet wed. Their counsel was a great blessing to Tali and me. One of the ideas we got from Yisrael was to incorporate the Ten Commandments into the ketubah. Under each command we wrote how we would aspire to live it out in our marriage.

Based on Jeremiah 2:2, Jewish people see Mount Sinai as the place where Israel became betrothed to God. The verse says, "Go and cry in the hearing of Jerusalem, saying, 'Thus says the Lord, "I remember the kindness of your youth, the love of your betrothal, when you went after Me in the wilderness, in a land not sown."'" In this understanding, the Ten Commandments are seen as the ketubah or vows that Israel was to agree to in order to enter into covenant with God.

Tali and I split our ketubah into two halves; one side is the Ten Commandments, including our commitments to each one, and the other side is our personal vows to one another. We also had a place on the ketubah where Tali and I, along with our parents, signed as witnesses. It felt so momentous as we approached the evening of our betrothal. Soon we were going to share a full-on covenant. Up until the betrothal, there was always that slim outside chance that something would come up that would interfere. After the betrothal there would be no turning back. I sang this song for Tali that night:

My heart is full of passion as it finds this new
expression, my beloved and my friend; to you
I pledge my hand and this promise will endure,
for I promise I am yours.

I am yours; today I want you to know to you I
am pledged in faithfulness all my days in joy and
in sorrow; I am yours.

Today I enter into this covenant with you. May
our love for one another serve to be a picture of
Yeshua and His bride. He's calling us, saying
I am yours.

Come what may, we were in agreement to be covenantal
friends from that day forward. A shofar sounded to begin the
betrothal ceremony. The setting was intimate, with no more than
thirty people present as witnesses. We read this beautiful passage from Hosea, "I will betroth you to Me forever; yes, I will
betroth you to Me in righteousness and justice, in loving kindness and mercy; I will betroth you to Me in faithfulness, and you
shall know the LORD" (Hosea 2:19-20). We also read a passage
from Exodus 19:16-20 speaking of the Sinai betrothal of God
to Israel. Then we had a time of worship. After Dad and Mom
prayed for me, I offered Mr. Kenny the bride price and read
1 Corinthians 6:20, "For you were bought with a price; therefore
glorify God in your body and in your spirit, which are God's." We
decided to do the bride price because of the symbolic picture it
gives of the price Yeshua paid for us. Next, Mr. Kenny was asked
if he would give Tali to me in marriage, and then he asked Tali if
she would go with me (Gen. 24:58). Tali responded wholeheartedly, "I will go!" Mr. Kenny and Ms. Diane prayed for Tali, and
then she joined me under the chuppah (pronounce *khoopah*, the
"kh" making a guttural sound).

My brothers constructed the chuppah (a wooden frame holding my tallit that we stood under as we read our vows) on the

day of the betrothal. It was beautifully crafted from freshly cut cedar poles taken from the nearby forest. This is the point where we held hands for the first time. It was an exhilarating moment! It was also at this time that we first said "I love you" to each other. (Tali had picked up some Hebrew so we were able to say "I love you" in the resurrected language of the Bible!) I imagine you could have powered a nuclear plant from the energy produced between us during those first few seconds! We read our ketubah and then shared a cup of wine as a confirmation of our commitments. First I drank, and then offered the cup to Tali. When Tali drank there was much rejoicing, because like the bride of Yeshua who accepts His offer of the cup (Matthew 25:27-28), Tali and I were now covenantally betrothed. We then exchanged rings, broke bread together, and were pronounced husband and wife. Next the parents, grandparents and elders who were present gathered around Tali and me and prayed for us. Tali and I then anointed one another with oil, prayed, and washed each other's feet. Our brothers and sisters shared some things they had prepared for us. Some were emotional and some were funny. They were all priceless.

After a little singing, we proceeded to have a feast. To remember Israel we decided to include what is known as the seven species in the meal. These are wheat, barley, grapes, figs, pomegranates, olives, and dates (Deut. 8:8). One more prayer time followed the meal. We finished praying, and while I was not looking forward to letting go of Tali's hand, I knew it was time. I told Tali, "I am going to prepare a place for you" (John 14:2). We lingered at the door, hand in hand, trying to stretch out those last few moments as long as we could. Then I left, not knowing the day or hour when we would see each other again. "But of that day and hour no one knows, not even the angels of heaven, but my Father only" (Matthew 24:36). This was a radical decision, but Tali and I were in total agreement: from the time of the betrothal we wanted to separate until the undisclosed wedding day. We knew the general season, just not the day and hour. Dad agreed to be the one to announce the time for the wedding. Our goal was to portray the heartbeat of Yeshua as He waits for His bride.

Soon after the betrothal I began work on "the place," while Tali returned to Pennsylvania to begin work on her wedding dress. We were separated by many miles physically, but our hearts were being irrevocably knit together with every love letter and every phone conversation we shared. The separation time turned out to be two and a half months. Early on, during that two and a half months, it was decided that the wedding would take place at some point over a set weekend, a three-day window of time.

With the help of many faithful friends and hardworking brothers, work on the house was steadily progressing. Miraculously, after weeks of focused effort to build the house, I received its final inspection the day before I left for the wedding! God's timing is perfect! An unexpected blessing came when my childhood friend Noah came to help. I was so happy to share this season of my life with him. The week before the wedding, Noah and I were able to put some of the finishing touches on the house. Once we were through, we traveled to the wedding grounds together.

The trip turned out to be a memorable one. Here is a little background to help understand the following story. Noah is an amazing carpenter. His carpentry skill is even more remarkable when one knows all the obstacles he has overcome to develop it. As a young man, meningitis severely damaged Noah's hearing and eyesight. At one point during the sickness, we were unsure whether Noah would even live, so we are thankful to God that He delivered Noah from death and also brought partial recovery to his body. So even though Noah knew how to drive, he only did so when necessary. We were only a few miles from the campground when suddenly my cell phone stopped working, and I had no way of knowing where Tali was. I knew she was at the campground; just where was the question. I certainly did not want to be casually going through the campground and end up seeing her after waiting two-and-a-half months to reach the climax of the wedding. Therefore, the only option was for Noah to drive and for me to hunker down in the floorboard of the truck. We did end up passing Tali on the road, but thankfully, I was nowhere to be seen. The moral of the story is that when presented with two risks at once, a person must choose the one that will least likely spoil his dreams. The dream was still intact.

Now we waited: I for the release from my dad, and Tali for the sound of the shofar. We were in two different locations. Tali and most of the wedding guests were at the campground where the wedding would take place. Dad, my oldest brothers, and I were at a campground a few miles away. The one I was at was a campground specifically designed for people to bring their horses to ride trails. This happened to be a divine setup. The idea of riding in on a horse to meet Tali was one I really liked but had laid down, thinking it was an impossibility. Well, thanks to persistent brothers who went from site to site through the campground seeing if anyone would let us borrow their horse, what seemed impossible became reality. After several failed attempts, they came up to one site where a couple agreed to let us use their white horse. Amazingly, they were even leaving the campground at the time we would need the horse! There was nothing to worry about. It felt like God already had everything, even the smallest details, under complete control. Blessed be His glorious Name! At this point I knew the day, but was still waiting to know the hour. After spending some time in the Word, and being encouraged by Dad, we prepared to leave the little cabin we were staying in. The time had come. With the energy of broncos let out of a chute, my brothers took off to spread the news. First they told Tali and then proceeded to let everyone else know. After a loud shofar blast, the announcement rang throughout the campground, "The bridegroom is coming!" Everyone knew from the time of the shofar's blast they had one hour to get dressed and ready for the wedding.

The people with the horse showed up as they had said at a place less than half a mile from where Tali and the wedding guests were. Getting accustomed to the horse, I rode him around for a few minutes before going to meet Tali. Dad and I exchanged a few words, and then with his approval, I took off. My brothers ran alongside me as we went. With a round of shofar blasts, everyone was alerted to our advance. Nearing the place where everyone was assembled, I dismounted, and with joy full of glory, made quick strides toward Tali. She was so beautiful in her pure white linen dress! It felt like a dream. After all the weeks of waiting, we had finally reached this moment. We embraced, and with a sense of wonder, gave each other our first kiss. We were very preoccupied with one another for those fantastic first seconds. Then, pulling our eyes off each other, I greeted the family and friends who were all around us. Their loving and happy faces only added to the joy we already felt. The time had come; the procession was ready to begin.

"Are you ready to go?!" I shouted.

"Yes!" came the response.

Energetically I replied, "Let's go!" With worship songs being lifted up, we began the procession to the gazebo where the ceremony would take place. Previously I had hung the "Ahavah" banner over the path between two trees. Once we reached and stood directly beneath the banner, I kissed Tali again. We were thoroughly in love! We arrived at the gazebo situated near a sparkling lake.

Once everyone got settled, the ceremony began. Dad shared an inspiring message on the importance of covenant. Our sisters did a dance to a beautiful song Tali had written called "In Love." Tali and I reaffirmed our vows by reading our ketubah. We also did a salt covenant, which is mentioned a few times in the Bible (Leviticus 2:13; 2 Chronicles 13:5). What we did was combine two bags of salt; one was mine, and the other was Tali's. The symbolic meaning was that as hard as it would be for us to put the grains of salt back into their original sacks, so it would be just as hard to separate Tali and me. After the ceremony, we had a time of joyous dancing. Our families joined us as we danced around in a circle. It was an all-out celebration!

Then there was the reception where we were able to greet our friends and family. It was wonderful to share our joy with so many we loved. Exhausted, Tali and I left before most everyone else. We heard the next morning that people kept dancing until nearly midnight. We were glad to be by ourselves after such an action-packed day. The drive was only a few miles to the place where we spent our first few days together. After that, we came back to Kenlake (the campground where the wedding took place) and stayed in a cabin. In between spending quality alone time, we were also able to participate in the family event that was going on the week after our wedding. I remember reading through the Song of Solomon that first week together. The book's poetic language of love began to find its way into our vocabulary. I would call Tali "Ahuvi" (my beloved) and she would call me "Khatani" (my bridegroom).

By the time the campout came to an end, Tali and I were eager to head off to the place I had prepared in Tennessee. Tali had not yet seen any of the work on the house, so I was very excited to see how she would like it. On the drive down, I taught Tali how to say most of the colors in Hebrew. That proved to be the first of many Hebrew lessons we would do over the following year. We arrived at the house late in the afternoon. Before carrying Tali over the threshold, I asked her to close her eyes. I carried her inside and then sat down on the couch in the living room. The surprise on Tali's face when she opened her eyes was priceless. The last time she had seen the house, it was nothing more than an empty shell. Now it was a home. My goal was to spend as much time as possible at home during our first year. We desired to do this based on Deuteronomy 24:5 that says, "When a man has taken a new wife, he shall not go out to war or be charged with any business; he shall be free at home one year, and bring happiness to his wife whom he has taken." In order to do this, we decided to live as frugally as possible. This was not too hard. We did very little traveling, raised a garden, and had a good neighbor whom I did some work for in trade for milk and eggs. Plus, there was a creek running through the valley that was full of watercress!

The watercress became a point of mild contention between us after Tali became pregnant with our daughter, Yael. I found out very quickly that cooking breakfast only wins points when the food tastes good. Watercress, no matter how much I tried to promote its great health benefits, was intolerable to Tali's pregnant taste buds. Unable to convince Tali to appreciate the food that I liked, we ended up going to the store and stocking up on "mommy food." That year, thanks to a patient and loving wife, I learned some of the basics of what it means to "make your wife happy." It was quite an adventure. We continually learned new things about one another and found our love ever deepening. Five years later I can truly say that it only gets better. We are more in love today than ever. At this time we are blessed with three children. Yael (Jael) is four and is growing into a lovely little lady. She is becoming a big helper to Mommy. Keturah is two and keeps us thoroughly amused with her quirky sense of humor. Zephaniah is eight months. He is such a bundle of joy. We love them all so much, and we can hardly wait for news that we are expecting another!

At the end of that first year, the Father opened doors for us to study Hebrew in Jerusalem. Since then we have had many opportunities to teach others. When we look back at how the Father has led us, we know that He is the Author of our story. To Him be all glory and honor and praise! If you are single, may you be strengthened to wait on the One who already knows the "one" you are to become one with. His plan for you is more romantic and exciting than anything you could ever come up with on your own. His way is the best!

Tali's Story

It seems to me that our story begins way before the wedding, before the betrothal, even before Brayden and I met. Our Heavenly Father had a plan as He spoke the world into existence, and He knew that we would be a part of that plan. The miracle of how He brought us together increases our hope and gives us the faith to believe that His plan is truly good.

Kenneth and Diane Lupinacci, my amazing parents, have also experienced the goodness of God's plan. My parents both grew up in Italian Catholic households in Pennsylvania, but with very differing lifestyles. My father lived on a farm most of his life; my mother was born to a radiologist. They both led pretty average lives, doing what most other people around them did; hanging out with friends, dating, going to movies, going to parties, and going to church on Sundays. The Catholic church was a pretty defining part of both of their lives, but the emptiness of their lifestyles and the Catholic religion left my parents spiritually hungry for more. In the late 1970s God revealed more of Himself to each of them separately, and He brought them both out of the Catholic church.

My dad was thirty-five years old and single when he felt that he had his first major encounter with God. He left the Catholic church and began attending a home group Bible study where he made relationships that would build him up and encourage him in his faith. Before this time God was a distant thought, but now the Father was in the forefront of his life. The Bible study he attended was also special in that there was a major focus on Israel. As a thirty-eight-year-old lovable, sweet, single Christian man, my father had many friends working to find him a wife. He attended a 1982 New Year's Eve party at which he was introduced to a flamboyant Italian Christian talk show host in a gold sequin shirt named Diane DeLuise.

My mom graduated from college with a performing arts degree in the 70s and headed straight for Hollywood to try to "make it big" in acting. She experienced there a lifestyle that led to very dark places. Toward the end of the 70s, a friend of hers, who was an actress in a famous soap opera, took my mom to Jack Hayford's church where she experienced God's love and she gave her life to Him. She went through a radical change in a short amount of time. Her mother died of alcoholism shortly after that experience, so she left the Hollywood area and moved back to Pennsylvania. She was glad to be out of the Hollywood scene but didn't know what to do outside of entertainment, so she and a friend of hers began a Christian talk show on a local TV channel. My mom was twenty-eight and single at the time, and she was fervently looking for a husband. She thought she was looking for a charismatic, charming man who would host the TV show with her, but the mention of any single man sparked her interest. The mention of a single Christian man is what inspired my mom to go to the New Year's Eve party wearing her gold sequin shirt.

Their personalities were about as opposite as could be. My dad was quite shy and felt comfortable staying in the background. My mom, on the other hand, did not know what the background looked like. She spent quite a bit of time right in the middle of whatever was going on. My dad was intrigued by my mom's enthusiasm for God; my mom was probably a little less impressed with my dad's quiet demeanor. Despite the differences, they decided to give it a shot. Their first date was at the Messianic Jewish synagogue in Philadelphia with a group of friends. They had little time to converse between themselves, so they had their second date a week later. My mom says that during the drive on that second date, my dad did not say a single word for the entire two-hour ride! Thankfully, my mom was a seasoned talker and was able to fill up the silence just fine. They returned home from the restaurant they went to and decided to watch a Christian TV show. They felt led to begin praying afterward and immediately went into some powerful prayers. Those prayers led to my father being filled with the Holy Spirit. Despite the major personality differences, they knew that God was doing something, and by the end of the night they knew that it was the Father's will for them to get married. The news came as a shock to both of their families. Their parents thought that, after waiting all these years to be married, their children were marrying strangers. My parents had confidence that this was God's will and they got married on June 5th, 1982.

This was the story we grew up with and it had a pretty big effect on me, especially as I walked through this betrothal process. While I am sure they did not do everything perfectly, they laid a foundation that I could build on. I hope that our story does the same for you.

I was born on July 16th, 1983 and two sisters followed behind me: Angela (1986), and Kendra (1989). After the long wait, our parents finally had a family and were overflowing with love for each other and love for us. Family life was very sweet. My earliest memories were reading Christian picture books with Mom and Dad before bed, memorizing Bible verses, having home group meetings, etc. We made many visits to see our grandparents, but most of our time was spent with our church family. Playing "house" was a common game in our children's church group and I remember getting a plastic engagement ring from one of the little boys. There was another little boy I remember dancing with at a church wedding. Our moms took pictures and talked jokingly about the potential match.

When I began school, my parents decided to send me to a Christian school. My mom visited the school regularly and got a job driving her Chevy Suburban "school bus" to my school with other students. All of my friends knew my mom. My parents were more involved in my activities than most of my friends' parents, but my friends became a bigger and bigger part of my life. In third grade, a group of us students thought it would be fun to pair off and pretend to be couples off of a popular TV show everyone watched. It was all a game. The game probably lasted a couple weeks before everyone moved on to the next game, but my little match seemed to stick more so than the other ones. In third grade the match was obviously looked at as childhood innocence. We would write through the summer and hang out in school together. We both came from strong Christian homes, so our parents didn't think it was a bad idea. It was probably just looked at as childish fun. As the years went on, the relationship impacted my mind more and more. We rarely held hands and never went on "dates," but we definitely had each other's attention and were a known pair in class. By the time I got to eighth grade (twelve years old), my mind and heart were pretty involved. In my mind it didn't seem like it would ever change. Much to my surprise, during the eighth grade school year, the attention that I was so used to getting began shifting to another girl in the class. I didn't know what to do with this new situation. At first it wasn't too big of a deal. This other girl was funnier and tougher than I was, so I thought maybe if I tried to be tougher and funnier I would be able to win back his attention. That tactic did not work, even though I tried it for another year or so. At this point I lost hope, and my attention was drawn to someone else during my freshmen year.

He went to my youth group and was a musician in a "Christian" band. The style of music that he played was new to me, so I quickly became acquainted with a number of new bands that I never knew existed before. His older sister was a professional model and was well known for her latest "fashions" wherever she went. I was introduced to many new worlds at this time— fashion, art, theatre, music. My parents watched me go through many changes at this time, and they probably got a bit worried.

I dressed very differently, listened to different music, and hung out with different people, but I was still very close to my sisters and parents and everything that I was involved in still had the "Christian" label. Eventually my parents were convinced not to get too worried because they had heard that teenagers go through these "stages" and it is normal.

The young man and I began dating while I was still a freshman (fourteen to fifteen years old). We decided that we were "not going to kiss until we got married." The idea to keep physical distance sounded like a "safe" call, but even the talk about marriage put my heart in a very vulnerable position. Our parents were involved, as most of our "dates" were at each other's houses or spent at shows with his older sister. I can't say my parents were too thrilled by the match, but again, he was from a good Christian family and we were still young. The whole time we dated I was scared of the rejection that I had faced earlier, therefore, my personality was quite inhibited. Much to my dismay, my fears were realized when he wrote a letter to me six months later, breaking off the relationship. This one caused tears, but I again held on to some hope that he would change his mind even though I probably only saw him a handful of times over the following years. At this point, my life took an even more major turn.

My mom found out that I could sing when I was in fourth grade, and due to her performing arts background, she encouraged me to pursue it. Although this was uncomfortable to my shy personality, I ended up being in every school musical from that time on. The first community theatre play I took part in was when I was about fifteen, and it was a whole new ball game. I did well and enjoyed the attention I got from it, so I talked with my parents about transferring to public high school for my junior and senior year because they offered more opportunities in the performing arts area. Public school also had many art classes, which was another subject I was becoming more involved in.

Family finances were tight because Mom had just lost her job as a school bus driver, so we agreed it would be a good idea. I began public school in my junior year.

The year began with me making many observations of this new world, but I didn't work up the courage to engage too much. As the year progressed, I became heavily involved in choir. I got a lead role in the yearly school musical, and was involved in many art classes. I gradually made friends in school who shared common interests; art, music, and theatre. Before long, I was completely immersed in this new world. In that same year, I became much more involved in community theatre musicals. I took dance classes and went to art shows and music shows. The music I listened to was no longer only Christian, and the people I spent most of my time with in school were no longer only Christians. As the music I listened to went from strange to stranger and from dark to darker, so did the movies I watched. My hair went through many changes at this time with different colors and cuts and I even wore wigs from the theatre to school a couple times. The clothing I wore was pretty different and got more immodest as time went on. My dad quietly stated his opinion during my high school years. I knew he didn't like my dyed and cut hair and a lot of my clothing, but they weren't major objections. He hung a picture of me with my natural hair on the wall and would tell people when they came to our house, "This is what she REALLY looks like." I thought he didn't understand my "creative" personality. It did not take long for me to stick out in school. I was always a quiet personality but my clothes spoke loudly and so did the characters I played in the school musicals. The yearbook for my senior year shows Talitha Lupinacci voted by the entire senior class as "Most unique" and "Most likely to be in show business."

Our family had found our church "home" back in 1986 when I was three. It was/is a small non-denominational congregation in Quakertown, Pennsylvania. Although the names and the meeting places changed regularly, the same core group of people hung in there through the shifting. To this day we have a very special relationship with this core group, even though many of us have moved to different places.

My sister and I joined the church's worship team when I was about twelve (my sister was nine). We grew up on the worship team at church. We began with singing, but eventually learned to play guitar, piano, bass, and drums, and sing harmony as there was need. Folks at the church watched me go through changes: first as I entered Christian high school, and then as I entered public school. Some lighthearted comments were made every once in a while about my clothing or about the movies I was watching, but unfortunately, I did not take them to heart. I think my heavy involvement in church kept my parents from worrying too much. Our church also had a big emphasis on outreach, so when I entered public school and began acting in community plays, I thought it was a perfect opportunity to be a light to the world. I held on to this goal for many years, but I had no idea about the kind of darkness that was out there. Two years of public school brought much confusion into my life. At fifteen, I thought that it would be a neat idea to save my first kiss until marriage. I held onto the idea for a short time, but I had no encouragement to walk it out and definitely didn't have an example to follow. By the time I turned seventeen, I was an oddball to everyone around me, even my friends in church. As I tried my best to be a light, I ended up in some foolish situations on my own, and, in the midst of the confusion, I reluctantly gave up my first kiss. At this point one of my youth leaders, Christy, saw the burden I was bearing, and she came to my side to help. She had a strong salvation testimony, and she began witnessing to my friends. I brought a vast variety of friends to church around this time and my two best friends became Christians. I was repentant for getting physically involved with someone. At this point church became an even bigger focus. I felt an urge to seek God more seriously, but as I sought Him I also became even more heavily involved in theatre and the arts. I couldn't understand the confusion and darkness that I felt in my spirit even though I was seeking God more. I did not see the influence the world had on my life until I came out from it years later. My senior year of high school was probably one of the darkest years of my life. I was confused, and I didn't feel like I could get out from under it. I looked forward to the end of high school and a chance for a new beginning.

As my involvement in theatre grew, so did my interest in New York City. My dad plainly stated his thoughts on NYC: "I wouldn't go there if you paid me to go!" That did not stop me, however, as I blamed his opinion on his farm upbringing. In high school, I began taking regular trips to visit New York and see Broadway shows, either with my mom and sisters or with friends. Talk began about college and we began discussing the options of majoring in performing or visual arts. I auditioned for a few professional musicals in New York, but there was too much competition, so we decided it would be better to go to a school for the visual arts. Because of my "artsy" clothing, my art teacher encouraged me to look into fashion design and maybe eventually get into costume design. It sounded like a good idea, so I ended up starting college in Philadelphia to major in Fashion Design, but after three semesters I decided to make the move to a college in New York. It was a dream-come-true at the time, to be living in the middle of this massive city.

During my years in college, I was heavily involved in school but I always made sure to have a three-day break so I could make the two-hour trip to Pennsylvania every weekend to see my family and play on the worship team at church. I stayed pretty distant from other students because of the experience I had gone through in high school, but I made one very important friend. She was from Israel, and we connected very quickly as she taught me the Hebrew alphabet while we waited for subways together. I ended up moving into an apartment with her and another Israeli friend for my last semester. I graduated from fashion design school with an Associate Degree and began looking for a job. As I went job hunting, I became less and less impressed with New York and the fashion world. I decided to move back to my Pennsylvania home.

My uncle and his family had started a restaurant/resort on Nevis, an island in the West Indies, many years before. My cousin was in town soon after I moved back to Pennsylvania, and he asked me if I would be interested in coming down for a few months to make uniforms for their workers. I had no job, I was done with school, and I thought it would be a good opportunity to spend time with family that I rarely saw, so I decided to take him up on the offer. This would be the longest stretch of time that I would be separated from my family and our church. We had begun reading about the pagan roots of Christianity right before I left, and I went down knowing that I could no longer celebrate Easter and Christmas. However, it left me with many questions about my faith and put me in a very vulnerable position.

In Nevis, I was introduced to people from many countries all over the world and heard many stories. The main resort manager was an agnostic man from Scotland, and the general atmosphere there was very humanistic. From the day I arrived, I was showered with questions about my faith and Christianity. The questions were challenging, but again I took this on as an opportunity to be a light. I gave witnessing my best shot, but my own list of questions about Christianity became longer and longer as time continued. My belief in God and the Bible did not wane, but I was discouraged to find that I didn't know a whole lot about either one. It had a wearing effect on me as the months went on, and I again found myself in the midst of confusion and foolish situations. I again got into bad relationships and made even more major compromises on my convictions. I left the island and returned home in the darkest place spiritually I had been in my whole life. I was ready for change.

I was glad to return home and be free from the many temptations that were on the island. I was repentant for all the compromises I had made, but I felt the weight of all my bad decisions. On top of it all, I felt a total lack of direction. I had already wasted several years and a lot of money on school for a career I decided wasn't for me. I had also pretty much walked away from theatre and performance after a bad experience. My parents encouraged me to be able to support myself as they were both getting older, so we decided that a nursing career would be the most practical choice. During my first semester of prerequisites, I got a call from my Israeli friend from New York, inviting me to go to Israel with her to visit family. Excitement built as I discovered that the time frame happened to be right over my spring break. My parents were a little hesitant and needed a bit of encouragement from some Israel-loving friends. In the end, they felt like it was the Father's will for me to go. Because traveling to Israel was a lifelong dream, I couldn't believe it was actually happening, and I had no idea what was in store for me there.

The plane landed at Ben Gurion Airport and I met my friend at the greeters' hall. We boarded a *sheroot* (taxi) to Jerusalem, and I sat next to an elderly Jewish woman. Something incredible happened to me as I was talking to her. The conversation itself was of no real significance, but it was in that moment that I felt like God gave me His heart for His Land and His people. Would I be a part of what God was doing on this earth, or would I try to keep chasing my own ideas and worldly dreams? Throughout the whole trip, I felt that God was making a presentation to me, and even though I spent most of the trip with non-religious Jews, it was a spiritual awakening for me. The two weeks went by, and I flew back to the States with direction. I knew that God would bring me back.

This first trip to Israel was the biggest turning point of my life. Major shifting started taking place. Back home, I returned to school, but in my heart I seriously wondered if that was what God had in store for me. I talked to my parents about quitting school, but all I had to offer was a new excitement to learn about the Jewish people and the Land of Israel. The next practical step I was to take was very unclear. Maybe I would volunteer for the Israeli army as a nurse? We decided it would be best to keep pursuing a nursing career, but I was on a mission. I visited local Messianic congregations and attended conferences, trying to get in contact with anyone and everyone that had been to Israel. At the same time, my friend, Christy, shared her heart with me about modesty and introduced me to the *Above Rubies* magazine. I began getting a vision for being a wife and mother. How was Israel going to work in with all of that? An excitement to see God's plan unfold in my life began to grow in me. Movies and music that I used to listen to began to make me feel spiritually slimed, and I realized that investing my time in them was counterproductive. God's plan was going to take every bit of my life, and He had brought me to a place where I was not only ready for it—I was excited about it.

One very important issue of *Above Rubies* came out that had a picture of a little boy praying at the Western Wall. I was so excited to read about the Waller family's ministry called HaYovel, and I immediately ordered a documentary about them called *A Journey Home*. Tears streamed down my face as I watched the story of their fight for purity and their love for Zion. Out of all the ministries and Israel connections I had made, my heart made an immediate connection to this family and this work. I wrote an email to Mrs. Sherri Waller, sharing my heart to return to the Land, and I stated in the email, "I would love to be a part of what you are doing." HaYovel sent out an email shortly after, inviting people to come to Tennessee to celebrate Passover with the family and friends. We already had planned a trip to Texas around that time, so I talked to my whole family about making the trip to Tennessee instead to celebrate Passover. The plan worked out perfectly, and my family was also very excited about meeting the Wallers. As the plans came together for the trip, I also got an idea to look at property in Tennessee. I sent emails to each member of my family, advocating why it would be a good choice to relocate to that state. My whole family agreed that the Father was leading us into a new season.

Several families gathered for the Passover Seder that year, but we had traveled farther than any of them. One sweet family offered to house us for the weekend and we became good friends. The excitement escalated as we pulled into the parking lot filled with fifteen-passenger vans. Members of the Waller family came out to greet us, and one by one we met them all through the night. As I walked in the building, I remember noticing Brayden praying with one of the elders present. It was a big weekend. We met with the Wallers at three separate occasions and also ended up looking at a property that we all felt we should make an offer on.

There was no doubt that I immediately fell in love with the Waller family. From that point on I looked for every excuse possible to meet them wherever they were in the States, and I knew for sure I would be with them one day in Israel. I kept in contact with Tommy and Sherri by email, and I also received the family and ministry updates.

The next opportunity arose to see the Wallers in July at a CUFI (Christians United for Israel) conference in Washington, D.C. While we were in D.C., our families decided to visit the Holocaust museum. As we moved through the museum, Brayden and I had our first conversation, which included subjects like farm animals, Israel, and music. I had a hard time paying attention to the exhibits. I was twenty-three years old at the time and everyone knew I wanted to be married, so everyone was doing their best to match me up. When the *Above Rubies* article had first come out, Christy had said to me, "Maybe one of those guys is your husband!" The picture in the magazine showed most of the Waller boys wearing cowboy hats, so I laughed it off, thinking that they didn't really match my artsy flair. Also, one of the ladies from that first Passover weekend with the Wallers had mentioned that I might be a nice match for Brayden and emailed me later, asking if I had gotten a chance to talk to him. I replied that we hadn't been able to talk, and to be honest, I didn't feel inclined to be the one to initiate a conversation. However, now in D.C., it was Brayden who initiated the conversation, and I was all ears. Brayden also led the group, mainly his brothers, in prayer as we walked around the capital and as we worshiped in the 24/7 prayer room there. I had never met any other young man like him, and I was very impressed. On the ride home I informed my parents that I would love to marry someone like Brayden Waller. The thought of marrying Brayden, or even someone like him, also made me a little scared. I had not walked in the purity that Brayden had fought for all of his life.

After the CUFI conference, the Wallers began preparing for sending a team to Israel for the 2007 harvest. They invited me to come and help because they knew that I wanted to come, and the team that year was small. I tried everything I could to get days off from my job in the hospital and to take off some days from nursing school, which I was just starting. After many tears and weeks of trying, I finally had to give up and accept that it might not be the Father's will. I was devastated and even talked again with my parents about quitting school, but my parents still felt like I should continue. My concerns grew because nursing school didn't seem to be the path that would lead me to being a wife, mother, and help to Israel. However, honoring my parents' leading seemed to be the place of blessing.

The next opportunity to spend time with the Wallers was in the Winter of 2007/2008. They had invited us to come and stay with them for a few days. By this time we had already purchased the house we had looked at during our Passover visit and were making steps to move down. My expectation in this visit was quite high as I was wondering if Brayden would show any further interest in getting to know me. Three days went by, and I don't think we shared more than the few words that were exchanged during the Hebrew lesson Brayden gave while we were there. Despite the lack of interest shown on his part, he was becoming more and more interesting to me.

Shortly after our trip to Tennessee, we hosted a family from Israel that was visiting the States. I was given a book that introduced the word "betrothal" to me. This particular novel was written to cast a vision to single people to not only remain pure physically, but to guard yourself emotionally and mentally as you wait for your mate. The book threw me a bit of a curve ball because I was enjoying thinking more and more about the possibility of marrying Brayden. So, as the Holy Spirit convicted me through this story, I entered into battle. Fantasizing is a common weakness of most girls, never mind an artistic, post-actress, and former avid movie watcher. I fought to stay in a place, mentally and emotionally, where I could bless his future wife if there would be an announcement that day. I did not always succeed.

This all happened during a season of about two years where the Father brought me through intense sanctification boot camp. Little did I know that He was leading me as a bride who was making herself ready for her bridegroom. There was much work to be done.

Over the year 2008, there were two more occasions that brought our families together. You could probably count on one hand the number of conversations Brayden and I had together during this time, but I clung to Tommy and Sherri at every chance

I could. They walked in the fullness of life, purity, and victory that I wanted to see in own my life. Apart from my parents, they became my dearest counselors. During this time, I also observed Brayden's character and saw that there was a great calling on his life.

The whole Waller family made preparations for the 2008 harvest and had booked their tickets to leave out of New York. An invitation was offered again to join them, but harvest dates happened to start right as nursing classes started up again. We offered to drop them off at the airport and pick them up again three months later when they flew back. They came up a week before their flight to speak at a local congregation and spend time with us before they left. Having them there for a week, singing Hebrew songs and participating in Hebrew lessons helped me to stay positive even though it was hard to face the fact that I wasn't going to make it on that plane again. The day before they flew out, Tommy stood up and triumphantly read the list of names off the flight itinerary. I made it through about half the names before bursting into tears. Between the sobs I assured them I was very happy for them and apologized for the disruption. Tommy and Sherri gave me big hugs and assured me I would be with them in the Land one day. Several more tears came in the days after seeing them all go. I was willing to accept that this was the will of God, but for me this was a time of intense battle. It seemed like God was giving me a vision for one thing, but the path He had me on seemed to be taking me in a totally opposite direction. Every day at nursing school I faced the worldly culture I was so wanting to escape. I found myself singing Brayden's song, "More of You in Me," over and over.

More of You in Me

In the cleanliness of Your covering protect my
mind and keep me safe

Encompass the thinking of every thought with
the knowledge of my faith

So that even though I'm tempted there's escape
for my desperate mind

And even through the struggle there's a Presence
pressing me to find

Through the fire a blazing victory

And through it all more of You in me

May it be that I find more of You in me

The darkness that sees us a threat and worthy of
a fight

Must be met wisely with a soul clad in armor
fashioned in might

No earthly armor is comparable as the young
giant-killer learned

And the weapons that win the victory

Are heavenly, and for them I've yearned.

During the three months that the Wallers were gone, our family decided to visit a local congregation that was celebrating the Feast of Tabernacles. There were many sweet people gathered at the campground, but we couldn't help but notice that there was a nice young man there who was my age. We hit it off right away with his family. My parents encouraged me to get to know him, and it was fairly easy to do because I loved hanging out with his sisters. The first major red flag was that he didn't know much at all about Israel, and he didn't seem too interested in searching it out. However, we shared other interests such as music and art. I expressed to my parents my doubts, but it was a rarity at that point to find someone my age within our circles. He ended up showing some interest in me, so both our parents thought it might be something to consider. Within this same time frame, I was at a family party when one of my dad's longtime Christian friends looked at me very seriously while I was expressing my desire to have a family, and he said, "The time is soon." I laughed it off but he looked straight at me and said that he was serious. So now I was in a bit of a quandary. The only person who seemed to be an option was this young man who had no vision of going to Israel.

The time came for the Wallers to return to the States, so we picked them up in New York and they stayed with us for a few days before heading back to Tennessee. I was desperate to talk to Tommy and Sherri about my situation. The day after they arrived I sat Sherri down and poured out my heart. I was not at all excited about this potential match, so I asked Sherri if my expectations were too high and asked her if this could be the Father's will. She heard me through the tears, and the short story of her counsel to me was an enthusiastic "WAIT!" The Wallers pulled their big red bus out of the driveway and I again wound up in tears. After that conversation with Sherri, I vetoed the option of this other guy and assumed that if Brayden had any interest in me he would have talked to my dad by now. The next night I lay in bed, pouring my heart out to God in tears. I cried out in a climax of frustration and confusion, but I also declared I would trust Him and wait for His perfect plan. Little did I know...

The following Saturday morning I sat brushing my teeth in my parents' bedroom. Both of my sisters had moved down to Tennessee for a season while Angela did an internship at a Nashville recording studio, so it was just my parents and me in our Pennsylvania house. The phone rang, and the caller ID said it was the Wallers. My mom picked it up nonchalantly, thinking they were calling to talk about the possibility of us joining them for Thanksgiving that week. My mom answered and her eyes got very big as she handed the phone to Dad. "It's Brayden; he wants to talk to you." She said it in an almost whisper. My dad solemnly took the phone, said hello, and made his way upstairs.

Now Brayden was not the event planner in the family and neither was my dad, so chances were that they were not talking about Thanksgiving. Brayden was also not a big part of the communications department at the Waller house, so as my mom and I sat downstairs for the next half hour we had difficulty trying to remain calm. The struggle of my feelings for Brayden was not a big secret. However, as I had fought to not talk about him at all, my sweet mother had tried her hardest to catch any hint she could that Brayden was interested in me. She would say things like: "Brayden called on you quite a lot during that Hebrew class he gave," or, "He really liked that salad you made," or, "I noticed he went to see the goats exactly when you went down to milk." First of all, I can assure you that it took a lot for my mom to dream up these suspicions, because Brayden did not let on for a minute that he was interested in me. I also can't say that these comments helped me in my battle, but you couldn't blame her. Both my parents were more than impressed with Brayden's character, and of course they wanted to see the Father answer my prayers to be married.

So there we sat for what felt like forever. Could it be true? I don't remember saying a whole lot during those thirty minutes. As I sat trying to keep my mind from going wild, my dad came down the stairs with tears in his eyes and the phone in his hand. "Brayden Waller would like to know if you would be interested in marrying him."

I was speechless. My mom was now starting to get teary as she grabbed for my hand. I wish I could say that I took this moment to state some really profound things about God's goodness, but

I was in complete shock. My dad was very calm and collected, but my mom and I entered into a bit of a frenzy. I think the only words I could muster up were something like, "Are you serious!" and "What!?" We Skyped in my sisters to tell them the news and they were just as blown away as all of us. I finally calmed down enough to say something like, "Well, what do we do now?"

Tommy had taught a class at the Family Week camp the year before about the biblical concept of betrothal. That particular year they had put the teachings online so we decided it might be a good idea to get a little refresher on the subject. The teaching did not give the step by step instructions on the process that we were looking for, so I asked Dad, "So when are we going to call him back?!" My dad just smiled and said we were going to give it some time. I didn't understand it at first, but my dad is full of wisdom and I needed some time to process all of the emotions that were springing up in me.

During the next few days I had quite a spring in my step and I think my face was stuck in a smile, but soon the reality of what was happening started to sink in: This great man wants to marry me...but I feel far from great! Many things would need to be discussed before we could move on. Tommy and Sherri knew I came from a secular background, but they didn't know any of the details. If Brayden really was to be my husband, I had already sinned against him by not waiting for him. God had set Brayden aside for me all my life, but instead of waiting for God to bring him to me, I had taken things into my own hands and had entered into other relationships. Brayden had waited for me. There was no way I could even begin a relationship with him until he knew my past.

On the third day after the call, my mom decided that she really needed to talk to Sherri about Thanksgiving plans. When Sherri excitedly picked up my mom's phone call, my mom quickly said, "I'm just calling to talk about Thanksgiving!" I believe Sherri said something like, "Who cares about Thanksgiving! What does Tali say?!" Throughout the enthusiastic conversation my mom told Sherri that I was very interested in Brayden, but I needed to talk to him about things from my past before we went forward with things. The plan was that we would drive down to Tennessee for Thanksgiving that week and we would have the talk, face to face.

A few days later, the three of us loaded our big ol' diesel Mercedes and headed for Tennessee. At this point I hadn't told anyone besides my sisters that Brayden had called, because I knew that there was a definite chance that things wouldn't proceed. We picked up my sisters in Nashville on the way and the closer we got, the more my stomach knotted up. What would I say to him? How would I act? I had spent so long trying to keep a distance from him, but what now? What would he say about all the things in my past? We pulled into the driveway, and one by one the Wallers piled out of the house to say hello. Brayden walked up as I got out of the car and we gave a little nod and a smile to each other. I was not in charge of the schedule for the weekend, or I probably would have planned to have the big conversation right away. However, we arrived at the house just in time to have a five-minute sit down with Tommy, Sherri and Brayden before all of us would be heading to the Thanksgiving feast down the road. I was introduced as the girl that Brayden had called, although I had already met almost everyone who was there. Because Brayden was the first in the family to go through this whole betrothal process, no one knew what to expect. Should they welcome me into the family or pretend like I was just another person? I was one of those people who didn't know exactly how this was all supposed to go, so I just followed Brayden's lead. I can't say I ate too much there, because I was pretty nervous. That evening we had a meeting that included Brayden and me and all four of our parents. We both gave our testimonies in short and discussed our age difference (I am over two years older than Brayden). We also talked about what we felt like God had called us to and how our giftings would work together. Sherri asked if I was ready to take on the call in Brayden's life of fasting and prayer. I remember saying that this was one of the reasons I was so drawn to Brayden, and that I hoped the Father would grow me in those areas as a complement. To be honest, I felt a little inadequate.

The next day was spent in Shabbat preparations. We sat at the Shabbat table and everyone took turns saying what they were thankful for. I think most of the children said something like, "I'm thankful for everything that's going on." I don't think anyone was exactly sure of what was going on, but there was definitely something going on.

The big talk was scheduled for right after the Shabbat dinner. I decided to talk to Sherri and let her talk to Tommy and Brayden. I was so nervous as I sat on her bed with her and told her a fairly detailed description of the mistakes I had made in my past. She assured me that I was forgiven in Yeshua, and I assured her that I had walked away from these sins, never to return. I also told her I was fully ready to accept it if Brayden were to decide to discontinue any further thought of this proposed relationship.

Back at Mama Jo's house down the road, uneasiness started to sink in as I went to bed that night and awoke in the morning. The phone rang. It was Sherri: "Brayden has heard everything and he wants to deal with it right away. Come down to the house." We all loaded into the car and drove down to the Waller's house. I went with my mom to a room with Brayden and Sherri. Uneasy would be an understatement...nervous would be an understatement. My mom and I sat across from Brayden and Sherri. Brayden said he thought it would be good for me to tell him in person the things I had done, so he could forgive me and we could get past it. I told him a much less detailed summary of my past relationships and told him again that it was okay if he didn't want to go forward in the relationship. He looked at me right in the eyes and said, "I forgive you." He then reached down and grabbed his tallit, laid it over me and said, "Yeshua's banner over you is love and I want you to know that my banner over you is love. I will never look at you as that person. Yeshua has forgiven me much, and I want you to know that I will always look at you in forgiveness and love."

At that moment I was speechless, but I think I managed to squeak out a measly, "Thanks." Brayden's beautiful response and choice to forgive me were almost too much for me. While Brayden seemed to become more perfect, I felt more and more unworthy. Thoughts came to mind like, "What is he thinking?! Why would he forgive me? He deserves so much better!" I talked later with Tommy and Sherri and knew that Brayden did not take my past lightly. He was broken about the choices I had made, but he still chose to go forward and forgive. Brayden gave me his tallit to take with me, perhaps to remind me of his act of forgiveness. The tallit was very special and was one Sherri had made him when he was thirteen. He was ready to give himself to me. Now the decision was mine. I literally felt sick with confusion. We stayed with the Wallers for the rest of Shabbat, and on the following day both of our families went to Sherri's parents' house to celebrate Papa's birthday. During these two days, Brayden and I shared in lighthearted conversation and I don't think he knew me well enough at that point to pick up on my emotional turmoil inside. We left Papa's house for the twelve-hour ride back to our Pennsylvania house. For twelve hours I did not say a single word as we made our way north. My family could tell that something was not right. They tried talking to me, but I was really battling the onslaught of thoughts that were coming to mind, telling me I was not good enough and that this would never work out.

We had left Tennessee with a kind of unspoken understanding that things were going forward. I think we all knew that everyone needed a little time to process everything that had just taken place. Now I was back in Pennsylvania and was immediately flooded with nursing school assignments, including a ten-page paper and upcoming nursing finals. The fact that I was also working night shifts in the hospital put me in a sleep-deprived state, which didn't help in coping with the many emotions that were pulsing through me. It felt like there was an all-out war raging inside me, and I felt like I was drowning in the midst of it all. I remember sitting in the computer lab at school with tears in my eyes, in the midst of several hours of writing. Usually, when I was in the midst of a spiritual battle, I would sing or listen to Brayden's songs to encourage my spirit, but now I couldn't do even that.

The Wallers knew I was heading back to a very heavy work and school schedule, so communication for awhile was sparse after returning to Pennsylvania. Our parents stayed in touch and discussed how Brayden and I would begin communicating. My mom expressed to them that I was pretty overwhelmed, and that I was having a hard time finding my peace. I knew that Brayden had a great call on his life and that God was going to use him. I struggled because I did not want to marry him if there was someone else out there who would help him walk out that calling better than I could. I had a very hard time convincing myself that I would be the best one for the job. I knew I couldn't keep going on in this indecision for long. About four or five days after we returned to Pennsylvania, I found myself on our basement floor after everyone else had gone to sleep. I was crying out to God to help me. I needed a clear confirmation that I was the one. As I was praying, I experienced something I had never felt so tangibly before. I felt the redeeming power of God's love pour over me, and the only thing I could speak was, "I love you, Yeshua!" After a half hour on the floor in tears, I felt like I had my confirmation. Tommy also wrote me a very strong letter, basically encouraging me to embrace God's plan for me. He also assured me that Brayden was seriously excited about marrying me. I called

Tommy on the phone and let him know that I was ready to get excited about it too. At the end of the conversation he said, "I have someone here who wants to talk to you," and he handed the phone to Brayden.

So it was confirmed! We were going forward, with no holds barred. I wish I could say it was smooth sailing from there on out, but it seems that as soon as you get the victory in one area, the Father leads you to the next ground that needs to be won. But hallelujah! No matter how many battles we go through in life, we are assured victory every time if we cling to Yeshua!

Brayden and I began talking on the phone. I had very short time slots for phone conversations at this point. These last few weeks of nursing school were the most demanding, and I was trying to keep my brain focused enough to finish the semester. It was very difficult! If nursing school seemed trivial before, it certainly wasn't going up the ladder on my list of priorities. Brayden and I had a lot of ground to cover. I was very grateful that Brayden's calls were full of direction because I still felt overwhelmed at the magnitude of what was taking place. We started by having some "get to know each other" conversations. We talked about childhood stories, hobbies, and things that had made a big impact on our lives. Within the first week of these conversations we also began talking about betrothal and wedding plans. Usually the "get to know each other" talks and wedding plans do not take place within the same week, but both Brayden and I were accustomed to trailblazing. As firstborns, we had gotten used to plowing new ground, but this time we would be venturing into this whole new world together. Brayden was full of ideas. We had lots of decisions to make, and we weren't interested in wasting any time.

First things first: what is betrothal? The word was definitely more familiar to Brayden than to me. We both did lots of research and also talked with one of Brayden's best friends who had walked through a betrothal process.

Betrothal is impossible to walk out without a relationship with the Creator of the universe. The general concept of betrothal is that a covenant is established at the beginning of the relationship so that there is complete freedom for the couple to fall in love without fear of rejection. It's amazing how the Father gives us earthly pictures so that our excitement can build for the heavenly reality. This may be the greatest heavenly reality the Father wants us to grasp: the love that Yeshua, our Bridegroom, has for his people, the Bride. The enemy has worked hard to keep the betrothal picture hidden from God's people for hundreds of years, but the wedding is getting closer! We are so excited to see this picture come alive again for such a time as this.

After some discussion, Brayden and I both decided that we wanted to get legally married on the day of the betrothal. The betrothal date was set during winter break, just about a month and a half away. To be a more accurate picture of Yeshua and His Bride, Brayden presented the idea of not seeing each other after the betrothal until the wedding. Although I was a little hesitant about the idea at first, I prayed about it and felt a clear confirmation that this was what we were supposed to do. We decided that Brayden would travel up to Pennsylvania during Hanukkah with his brother, Zac, and his grandparents, Mama Jo and Pa Bill. The semester would be finished and we would be able to work on betrothal preparations—mainly writing the ketubah (marriage contract). My extended family would also be gathering for the winter holidays during this time, so we thought it would be a good idea to introduce my soon-to-be-husband to the family.

So now it was time for announcements. I began making calls to all our close friends telling them the news, and sent out an announcement to our family.

Hello Family!!!

So I have some news that some of you have heard and maybe some of you haven't heard.

I have been reading the 50+ family emails in my inbox and I have been trying to figure out what to write about this news but the short version is...

I am getting married!

Ok, so you know that the Ken Lupinacci family sometimes tends to be strange and peculiar, so some of you may not be at all shocked by this out-of-the-blue announcement, but I am going to try to explain further for everyone else. I'm sure there are lots of questions you may ask each other such as, "Was she even dating anyone?!" And the answer to that question is NO. And so now you may be asking yourselves, "So is this an arranged marriage!?" The answer is YES! But not in the scary sense of the word! This was only arranged by the Creator of the universe, and truthfully there is no better matchmaker.

I will give you a little of the story but this would get very long if I gave the full story so I will try to only tell the essentials. So his name is Brayden Waller and he is the oldest of 11 children. His family is from Franklin, TN and the whole family is involved in ministry to the people of Israel (Their website is www.hayovel.com for more info). So we met their family about 1 ½ years ago over Passover and since then our families have spent quite a bit of time together here and there. Over this time I have gotten to know Brayden's character and no man has ever matched it. So the whole family spent a week with us before they went to Israel in August. They were in Israel for 3 months and during that time Brayden prayed about me. When they got back from Israel they spent another three days with us and this time Brayden got a confirmation that I was the one! So Brayden called to talk to my dad about me three weeks ago and over Thanksgiving our whole family went to TN and we all talked together. So after much prayer and much conversation we both are sure that we are destined to walk out the rest of this life together. So these are exciting times for us!

So anyway, I probably just raised a lot more questions than answers but that's ok because we are happy to answer them! And the reason I am going through all this explaining and such is because Brayden is going to be coming up to PA with the next brother in line, Zac, to meet you all...

As far as a wedding date, it is going to be in the summer, probably in July sometime. It also looks like we will be having the wedding in TN so I hope that people will be able to make the trip! But I will keep you all posted on everything. Just be prepared for the unusual! And just to assure you all... I AM SO EXCITED!!!! I am blessed beyond imagination. I have prayed for my whole life about my husband and Brayden exceeds all of these prayers. Our God is good! I am also really excited to see you all, and Angela and Kendra are really excited to see you too!

And everyone BE NICE!! :)

Love,

Talitha and family

Brayden and I kept in communication as I finished out the semester of nursing school. We talked about a possible wedding in July because then I would be able to finish school, get my degree, and get certified before getting married. An RN license did not seem like it really was going to be useful in our life together, but it seemed silly to quit when I was only one semester away from a degree. So, as the stress of nursing school ended, I got excited for Brayden's visit.

As Mama Jo and Pa Bill's car pulled into the driveway, it was still rolling into its parking space when Brayden pushed the door open and came leaping up to the front door. As soon as my mom let him in, he bounded up the stairs and halted a few feet away from me with a big smile on his face. He nodded and said hello as he stuck his hands in his pockets. We decided to not touch each other until the betrothal, so it was always a little awkward trying to find a place for our hands as we greeted each other with smiles. On the next day, we would be heading to the gathering to see my dad's side of the family, so after some visiting we headed to bed.

The way most of my cousins introduced their spouses was by bringing their boyfriend/girlfriend to family parties for a couple years, and then the announcement would come out that they were engaged and the wedding invitations would follow. I warned

Brayden that we might be bombarded with questions. My family did not let me down. We made our way past cordial greetings, and before long, the firing began. Who could blame them? I was still trying to figure it all out myself. I don't think I understood how much they loved me and wanted to protect me until that day. It was very obvious that Brayden and I were still very early in the stages of getting to know each other and we were still working through the awkwardness of not touching each other. My one cousin in particular sat Brayden down across from her and fired one question after another: You've never dated anyone? How can you marry someone you've never kissed before? How are you going to provide money for her if you don't have a real job?

Brayden was not fazed one bit as he answered them all, one by one. Even though the answers Brayden gave to my cousins may have seemed peculiar, I think the questions they were asking seemed just as peculiar to him. To Brayden it all made perfect sense! I did have one uncle that sat with us and said, "I don't know why I would be too much surprised. I seem to remember that your parents did the same thing!" The evening wound down and my family piled into the car with Brayden and Zac.

Brayden had mentioned to my dad that he wanted to talk the next morning. I headed downstairs with my parents, and Brayden and Zac followed. I didn't know what was to be talked about during this meeting, but it seemed serious. Brayden began asking my parents questions about nursing school. It was a bit of a touchy subject because I had no desire of my own to continue; however, I wanted to do what my parents thought would be best. Brayden expressed his concerns that I would not be able to enter into the full joy of wedding preparations if I had the stress of nursing school. He said we should either postpone the betrothal and wedding plans until my schooling was over, or we should consider stopping the schooling. The thought of postponing plans was a bit emotional for me. Just as doubt began to make its way into my mind that this might be the end of our relationship, Brayden looked me right in the eyes and said, "Tali, you are the one." The tears started flowing and I told my parents that the decision was up to them. Brayden and Zac went upstairs while we talked it over. After my parents debated for about a half hour we walked upstairs. Brayden came out of the bedroom and my dad said, "We've decided that she doesn't need to go back to school." Brayden shouted "hallelujah" and began jumping so high we thought he was going to hit the ceiling! He then ran outside and began running up and down the street and then back into the house. As soon as he came in the house he motioned for me to follow him onto the porch. He said, "I've got an idea! Let's not say I l-o-v-e you until the betrothal. Let's say it in as many other ways that we can! For example, I think you're amazing!" His eyes were sparkling as he smiled, and I was so happy, I didn't know what to do with myself. I must say I did not come up with nearly the variety of ways to say it that he did. By the time of the betrothal, he had compiled quite a list.

In the midst of the excitement we got ready for family gathering part two. I am the first cousin on my mom's side of the family so it was my aunts and uncles who were in shock. When I had announced the news to them the week earlier, my aunt had said to me something like, "You're marrying someone you hardly know?!" Despite the original reaction, this family gathering seemed to be going well...until the question came: "So you're going to finish school first, right?" I think my dad answered the question that we had just decided that I wouldn't be going back. "Frank! Help!" my step-grandmother called out to my deceased grandfather. Brayden, realizing the effect this decision would have, made his way to stand by my side in support. The relatives then fired a whole new barrage of questions at us, but I think by the end of the night everything had calmed down and we peaceably made our way back home.

We now had three more days to start preparing for the betrothal. If you want a sure-fire way to fall in love, start writing a ketubah together. We sat at the table to start writing, and before long, everyone else in the world sort of disappeared. "I, Talitha Lupinacci, give myself to you Brayden Waller..." This was no small thing. We studied the Scriptures as we put together our marriage contract. In addition to our covenant with each other, we decided to write out the Ten Commandments, our marriage covenant with God, and to put to paper how we planned to walk out obedience as a couple. This time together was a major milestone in our relationship and, I believe, was the beginning of the "falling in love" process. Brayden was also writing me poems and notes during this time. One morning he had set up a trail of notes leading me outside where he had written a message in the snow. His joy over me was major ammunition against the thoughts of unworthiness the enemy was trying to tempt me with. Mama Jo and Pa Bill got a kick out of our lovey-dovey silliness. The time drew to an end and we parted ways.

A couple weeks later my family piled into the car again for another trip to Tennessee. This time I would come back with a new last name! Our car made the now-familiar trip down to the Waller house and we pulled into the driveway. The children all piled out of the house and Brayden came to meet me with a single pink rose. He led me in the house where all the lights were turned off. He pointed up. I looked and there was a glow-in-the-dark message that had the Hebrew letters on it that read "Ahavah." Ahavah is the Hebrew word for love. He looked at me and said, "My banner over you is love." It was a very sweet way to start the two-week preparation. I also gave Brayden back his tallit. When Sherri made it, she had embroidered a single sheaf of wheat on it. While I had it in Pennsylvania, I had embroidered a second sheaf to signify that I would stand with him.

We spent two weeks with the Waller family in preparations for the betrothal. My dad had released Brayden to work on building a house for us to live in that was located on my parents' Tennessee property. We discussed house plans. I began to better realize the influence the plain community had on Brayden when he suggested things like an outhouse and asked me if I preferred to have a refrigerator or to use the creek. Thankfully, my dad let him know that, as long as the house was on his property, he wanted to have proper sewage and electric. The question that really concerned me was when he asked if I thought it would be good for us to invest in good bicycles for transportation instead of owning a car. I politely stated my preferences, but in the back of my mind I wondered how our worlds were going to come together. The truth is, that with every new idea and strange quirk, I fell more in love with him.

There were a few other events scheduled in that two-week period. The Wallers hosted a pre-betrothal party where Brayden and I shared our story and encouraged the young people to continue to fight for purity as they waited for God to reveal their mate. The party was a lot of fun, and it was a chance to meet a lot of the Waller's old friends. There was also a dramatic reading of Revelation at a local church that we all attended. Brayden had studied the book of Revelation a lot so he was whispering insights to me throughout the night. On one very special day we headed to the Williamson County Clerk's office to get all we needed for our marriage license. It was funny because while we were signing papers, I discovered Brayden's middle name, Keith, and Brayden discovered that I didn't have a middle name. The days were also filled with singing Scripture songs (Brayden and I wrote our first Scripture song together to Psalm 145 during this time), practicing some Hebrew, and reading the Bible.

We made the drive to Mama Jo and Pa Bill's Lobelville house a few days before the betrothal would take place. The house was located right outside of Russell Creek, the plain community where the Wallers had lived, so Brayden told me lots of stories of their time there. We got settled into the Lobelville house, everybody helped to wrap up the final projects, and we all entered into Shabbat. The betrothal would take place at sundown the next day. Reality started to set in.

As evening drew near, the chuppah that Zac had made was placed in front of the room, and Brayden and I parted to separate rooms of the house to get dressed. Brayden wore a white linen tunic that I had made him with the help of Mama Jo, and I chose to wear my mom's wedding dress, which I had always admired. All the sisters got ready with me as I nervously figured out how to do my hair. The weight of what was taking place had been setting in all day. Earlier that morning Brayden and I decided we would each do a mikvah. It was a symbolic cleansing of all past unclean relational connections so we could enter into this marriage renewed. It was freeing for me to come up out of the water and leave behind all of that mess.

Once we were ready and everyone was in place, I made my way down to the main room. It was an intimate gathering with only our immediate families, Brayden's grandparents, and our congregational elders. The shofar sound began the ceremony and programs were given to everyone so they could follow the order of events. It was a beautiful night with worship and a song that Brayden wrote for me. We held hands for the first time and exchanged "I love you's," so it was a night bursting at the seams with emotion and joy. After the ketubah was read and we drank from the cup, it was time to rejoice. We all sat down to an excellent meal while dear friends of ours served us. The night was full of toasting, dancing, and music, but Brayden and I were content to just hold hands and smile at each other most of the night. As the evening drew to an end, Brayden stood up and looked at me. It was time for him to go, and we wouldn't see each other until the wedding. Before he let go of my hands, he said, "I'm going to prepare a place for you." We shared a last "I love you" before he headed out the door.

In the Song of Songs the bride talks about being "lovesick." This next chapter of our story would revolve around this word. My family maybe would have liked to call it "useless" because that's what I became after this betrothal night. This season was the time when the wooing got kicked up a notch, and I must say, Brayden was a pro. For the next two and a half months he wrote me poems, love letters, songs, etc., that were enough to send any young lady into the clouds, never to return. He sang songs on my voicemail almost everyday, and I would listen to them over and over. Here are some of my favorites: within a day or two of returning to Pennsylvania, Brayden left a voicemail, shouting, "I LOVE TALI WALLER!" It was fun to hear my new last name. Some of his songs he wrote for me were "Blowing Kisses Northward" and "My Love, My Dove, My Undefiled." There were many times in this season where I would literally be sick to my stomach because of our separation. I would get off the phone and just lay on the floor in tears as I longed to be with him. My sisters would see me, put their arms around me in comfort, and then kinda roll their eyes and go into the next room in bewilderment.

Brayden and I talked every morning before he started work on the house and we would sometimes talk again at night. We started off the day praying together and reading a Psalm in English and in Hebrew. There was a lot to be talked about. The day after the betrothal, our parents met together and decided that we would have the wedding at Family Week that year. It was two and a half months away—sooner than we expected, but we were not complaining! This wedding was going to be different than any wedding either one of us had been to. We invited people to come for three days at the campground, but no one would know the day or hour the wedding would actually take place. This was a hard decision to make because it made it hard for our close relatives to be a part. It was heavy on our hearts to be a picture of

Yeshua and the Bride, so to walk out the picture, it would involve a level of sacrifice.

Despite major brain fog, I was able to accomplish some things in this betrothal season. The white linen wedding dress was the most obvious preparation. The dress came together very nicely, and I also managed to get my sisters' dresses put together. My sisters had decided to move back to Pennsylvania to spend my last couple months at home together as a family. My very talented sister, Angela, had gone to school for audio recording, so she helped Brayden and me put seven original songs together that had a bride/bridegroom theme. It was an interesting feat because Brayden and I didn't see each other through this season. She recorded the song Brayden sang for me at the betrothal the day after the betrothal. Zac, who also had audio recording skills, recorded Brayden's vocals and some other instruments for five more songs and sent them to Pennsylvania. Once we received the tracks, Angela would record my harmony part and then put the finishing touches on it. One of my favorites was the song "Purple Robed Savior." I couldn't believe I was marrying my favorite songwriter! Lastly, I wrote a song to play for Brayden at the wedding. This was a fun project to work on with my sisters. I also ended up involving members from my former church's worship team. We gave this CD out to all the guests at our wedding, and have been sharing it with others ever since.

We made one trip to Tennessee during the betrothal time. Brayden went to spend time with his grandparents, Papa and Nana, while our family stayed with the Wallers. We reviewed wedding plans and took a trip up to the Kentucky campground where the wedding would be held. The invitation that went out invited one and all, so we were expecting a crowd. The practicalities were a little over the Lupinacci family's head so Sherri, who is well-versed in managing large groups of people, was taking up most of the practical organizing. Things were getting exciting! We headed back up to Pennsylvania and wouldn't return until it was time for the wedding!

The days got longer as the wedding got closer. Two and a half months was about all this bride's longing heart could handle. Our big green trailer was loaded up with all of my belongings, including all the gifts we got at the beautiful bridal shower my mom threw for me. This would be the adventure of a lifetime! There was a lot to ponder as we drove fourteen hours through the windy roads of West Virginia and Kentucky. We had quite a few aunts and uncles who were making the trip down, and some friends from Pennsylvania wanting to come and be a part of the excitement.

We pulled into the campground that was filled with close to seven hundred people. Most of them were children in big families. These children were about to become acquainted with a new wedding reality! My whole family was filled with excitement and anticipation, but no one knew what to expect. Brayden and I had invested a lot of prayer into the weekend. Many people were gathering to witness this parable, so we wanted the event to be full of an anointing to turn people's hearts toward Yeshua. There was a heavenly picture that we were about to experience in a very real way, and we hoped to cast the vision.

Our family had rented a cabin at the campground for the weekend, so we got settled in on Thursday. Brayden and I shared a last conversation that day. I vaguely remember him asking what I thought I would do while I was waiting for the shofar to sound. I think I said that I was probably going to be waiting in the cabin and hanging out with family (this conversation will have more relevance later in the story). We said our final "I love you's" as a betrothed couple. We wouldn't speak again until we were in each other's arms! LOVESICK! I had reached the epitome of the syndrome! The shofar could sound at any point from sundown Thursday night until sundown Sunday night. The whole place was buzzing with excitement and even the campground staff got into the emotion of everything. Tommy was the only person at this point who knew when the wedding would be. Everyone joined in the fun of exchanging their guesses on the time he would choose. This was the game plan: Tommy would tell Brayden and his brothers when the time was, the brothers would then run throughout the campground blowing their shofars, there would be one hour for last-minute preparations, then the whole group would gather together at the set place and we would all wait for the bridegroom! This was MY understanding of how things would play out.

There was a group of young men who knew the Wallers and who had received the invitation to our wedding and were intrigued. They had done some film projects so they asked if they could come to the wedding and make a documentary of the event. We thought it would be a good idea to have the wedding well documented, so they came from Colorado for the weekend. I was giddy with excitement, so I didn't notice their presence too much as they recorded the waiting period. They asked if they could do interviews with my family, so we all went down to the lake for the shoot. They explained to us afterward that they were looking forward to capturing what was about to take place.

We kept busy during our waiting time. We worked on a dance that all our sisters would do to the song I had recorded for Brayden. Some dear friends agreed to do my hair for the wedding, so they came for a little test run. The wedding dress being without spot or wrinkle was a big part of the whole picture, so I think that was the most serious time I had ever spent at the ironing board in my life. Everything was hanging and ready. The hours came and went. My family celebrated Shabbat together with my relatives. Would this be my last night with my family?

The next day we got up and hung out in our cabin with our relatives again. There were some friends from Pennsylvania in the main area of the campground, so I thought I should take a walk with my family to see them before the wedding. It was a beautiful day and I thought, at this point, the shofars probably won't blow until evening. We had asked everyone to bring lamps filled with oil so it seemed that Tommy might have in mind an evening wedding. There were a lot of people at the campground so I slowly made my way around, talking to everyone we ran into. Angela got a phone call and suggested that we should probably be heading back to the cabin. There were so many people I still hadn't talked to, so we didn't look too focused on getting back. She got another phone call and came over to us again. She said the film crew wanted to get an interview with the three of us sisters together. We agreed to start heading back, but we were still puttering along the way. Angela seemed very insistent and she said that the film crew only had a small time slot, so they needed us there right away. Finally she got us back to the cabin. The crew was there and they told us sisters to sit together on the couch for an interview. We all sat down and they started with their questions. The first one was directed to Angela, and I noticed her tripping on her words when all of a sudden the doors of the cabin flung open and all of Brayden's brothers came piling through at once, announcing that...

"THE BRIDEGROOM IS COMING!"

They handed me a note from Brayden, told me the projected arrival time, and ran back out. I would come to find out later that the brothers had banged on the door almost an hour earlier and (much to their surprise) I was not there. Brayden had assumed from our earlier conversation that I would be waiting in the cabin. I was never told that the bride was going to be given an extra hour before shofars went off in the rest of the campground. The interview with the film crew was the excuse to finally get me back. All the guys disappeared and left me and the rest of the cabin in an excited frenzy.

The next hour was a blur of excitement. First things first, I got my dress on! All the sisters began shuffling for their dresses and doing some last-minute choreographing for the dance. I received a phone call from the lodge receptionist, "Just wanted to let you know the shofars are blowing and the bridegroom is coming." I smiled and said thank you. It was fun to hear the resort staff joining in on the excitement. My friends scurried in to start working on my hair. I got out some essential oils of myrrh and frankincense, and another friend of mine generously anointed my head with them. These smells are still special to Brayden and me to this day. The sisters all got their hair done and were taking pictures and videos. Prayers were lifted up during all the preparations. I don't think there is anything more exhilarating than a bride's final hour of preparation. In reality, the hair, the dress, and the shoes didn't matter. It was now only a matter of minutes before I would be wrapped in Brayden's arms!

We all piled into the car and headed down the road where there was already a crowd of people waiting and singing. I walked into the center of the crowd, nervously clutching my sisters and parents. We all sang songs as my eyes fixed on the horizon where I knew Brayden would be coming from. I assumed he would come around the corner walking with his brothers. A car pulled up and Tommy got out. The time was so close! All of a sudden Sherri screamed and started pointing, "He's on a horse!" My eyes readjusted and sure enough Brayden came galloping up the path on a white horse! I grabbed the hands of my family members next to me and started down the grassy hill to meet him. My dad was holding me back so I wouldn't break into a full run. Brayden climbed off the horse and headed my way. The gap between us got smaller and smaller...ten feet...two feet...one foot...embrace!! To go into detail on the wave of emotions that went through us at this moment would be futile. It was the moment we had been dreaming of for two and a half months! Dreamy is definitely the way I would describe the following moments and even hours. I looked into Brayden's eyes, and he bent down to kiss me and we embraced once again. Even though there were seven hundred people gazing in a circle around us, neither of us knew there was anyone else out there in the world. Brayden finally pulled us out of our little dream world for a moment and shouted a greeting to everyone. Brayden and I began a mile-long walk with our seven hundred guests to the place where the wedding ceremony would take place. I think I floated on a cloud that whole mile. Brayden had hung the "Ahavah" banner he had made me above the pathway close to the gazebo where the wedding would take place. When we got right below the banner, he pulled me to him in another embrace and then bent down for another kiss. This was the first serious kiss. Everyone else started fading away again. Some would come to say that we maybe let them fade away a little too far. But we didn't notice for a second all the people awkwardly standing there observing our extended kiss of affection. Pictures would later show Olivia, Brayden's dear sister, standing behind us with mouth gaping wide in shock.

The wedding ceremony was very laid back. I found my place on Brayden's lap and we got lost into another embrace while our family members tried not to distract too much as they made runs to get all the things we had forgotten: a Bible to do the readings from, the CD to play my song, the ketubah, and the sheet music. I'm not sure that we actually remembered to have anything ready for this ceremony. But that's what happens when there is no wedding rehearsal! I don't think anyone noticed the small commotion as our family members one by one gathered the missing items. It was a holy atmosphere and I think it was felt by all. It is hard to go back to normal life after such a divine revelation is played out before your eyes. How can it be that our Heavenly Bridegroom is even more passionate about His people? Tommy spoke and encouraged the witnesses to get excited about the heavenly love story and the divine wedding that will one day take place. The ceremony came to an end and a glass cup was placed on the ground. We walked up to it and as soon as Brayden smashed it with his foot, Zac began playing the worship song "My God Reigns" by Darrell Evans that mentions rejoicing and dancing.

Brayden and I began jumping up and down in a circle, and soon all of our family members were dancing around us, basking in God's goodness. Brayden and I slipped to the side to be together while a crew of people headed to the pavilion to set up for the reception. We eventually made our way to the reception area and stood at the entrance to greet our guests. It was a blessing being able to talk to so many of the people who had come to be a part of the celebration. There were many people who attended that we had never met before. We headed to the main reception area for our first dance and afterwards a group of guys brought out chairs and hoisted us in the air. They jumped and ran around with us while the music played. They let us down after the excitement, and we stayed around just long enough for a toast to our first baby. It was a grand feast, and we later heard that the crowd danced late into the night. Brayden and I were happy to escape to our car and journey into the rest of our lives.

It has been five years since that day. We continually are blessed as we pursue God's will for our lives. Brayden took seriously the Scriptural command to stay home and make his wife happy during the first year of marriage. It was a year of investing. We could probably write another whole book on the lessons and experiences of our first year. Brayden and I had a lot to work through. The wedding was a dream, but within even the first week of marriage, we realized that becoming one is sometimes a challenging process. God uses marriage to sanctify us and the fire can get hot at times. Because of my past, Brayden and I had to work through quite a lot. The Scriptures call a husband to wash his wife in the Word. Brayden spoke the Word to me and my mind became more and more renewed. I still struggled with unworthiness. As Brayden spoke truth to me, I realized I was fully equipped to combat the attack of the enemy. I am so thankful that Yeshua strengthens us and will never lead us into a battle without the weapons to win the victory. God is good and I know that "all things work together for good to those who love God, to those who are the called according to His purpose" (Romans 8:28). He truly gives beauty for ashes.

About two months after the wedding we found out we were pregnant with our first baby! We were ecstatic! That first pregnancy was physically difficult, but it was also a sweet bonding time for Brayden and me. He went out of his way to pamper and care for me. It was during this pregnancy that we made our first trip to Israel together to join in the HaYovel harvest and celebrate Sukkot. I remember getting off the plane and telling Brayden that only a year ago I was crying out to God for three things: a husband, a child, and to be in Israel. A year ago it seemed so far away but here I stood in the Land with my amazing husband and our little baby kicking away inside me! Being blessed right away with a baby helped us to get focused. Brayden did an incredible job as he led us through that first birth. Yael was born at home in Tennessee into an atmosphere of prayer and praise. Both grandmothers, all her aunts, and some close friends surrounded us through it all. We could even hear the prayers of all her uncles and both grandfathers from outside the door. Since then we have been blessed with two more arrows: Keturah, who was born in our friends' Jerusalem apartment, and Zephaniah, who was born in our friends' farm home in Sweden.

Over the years we have been blessed to be a part of several of our siblings' and friends' betrothals and weddings. My spirit has been built up and encouraged every time I have witnessed this biblical picture. This is the time of wooing and we have an intense heavenly Bridegroom. Get ready to be lovesick!

Nate & Katie's
wedding,
very similar to
Brayden & Tali's

(See page 179)

84

Under the chuppah

Lovebirds

Colin (David) and Hannah Johnson

The topic of betrothal and marriage evokes many emotions and questions. One feels a sense of wonder at the thought of getting married someday—and maybe a bit of fear and anxiety about the unknown. Many questions also come up in a single person's heart when this topic arises. "When will I get married?" "What should I do before I get married?" "What are the steps that I should take towards marriage?" Both of us had many similar questions—both while growing up and when we reached marriageable ages. We want to share with you what we've experienced, what we've learned, and how God brought us together by His grace. As we begin telling you this story from our lives, we want to share our questions and convictions, our struggles and surrenders. This isn't a story of heroism or romance like the world would like to tell, but it's a story of our heroic God and how He brought redemption, purpose, and companionship into our lives.

A common question posed to a young married couple is, "So, how did you two meet?" For us it began long before we really remember meeting. When Hannah was just a baby in her mother's arms, Colin was a little boy peeking over the church pew in front of her to see the baby. When we were young, our families spent a lot of time together because we went to the same church. We saw each other a lot through the years because Colin was the youngest of four boys who were friends with Hannah's three brothers. But we were three years apart, and boys and girls didn't have too much reason to play together. For many years we didn't take much notice of each other, nor did we care to, and there were a number of years during which we didn't see each other at all. But around the time that we were in our adolescent years, both our families began an intense journey of seeking out the roots of our faith and beliefs and reassessing how God wanted us to walk out our lives. Because of this, our two families once again ended up in the same congregation. We are sure this was orchestrated by God for many reasons; one reason very special to us is that God was to bring us together in marriage.

We were in the same congregation for about eight years before we married each other. Early on in that time, unbeknownst to one another, we both began a hard struggle. We both had on our hearts a strong desire to marry each other, and for the next number of years we began learning how to surrender these desires completely to Yeshua. At different times each of us struggled with how to give those feelings to God. He preserved us from making the mistake of letting our feelings be known and bringing any heartbreak when we were too young for a relationship; He kept us from ruining what He wanted to make into a beautiful marriage. It was during this time that God began focusing our desires on Him and on His Kingdom in new ways. He began giving us many things to do in those early years that kept us from being consumed with questions and thoughts about relationships. It was much better to use our time serving God, family, and others, than to be consumed with worries about the future.

<u>Colin</u>

As I recall growing up, a number of things immediately come to mind: my parents instructing my brothers and me from God's Word around the table while we ate porridge, my oldest brother fasting and praying and encouraging us to walk in the ways of God, and all the fun times at our grandparents' farm with my brothers. I was homeschooled from grades one through twelve. I loved learning from my parents and studying every day with my best friends, my brothers. In 2000 there was a shift in my childhood when my dad left our home, and from that point on it was up to my mom and us four brothers to face more challenges of life alone. I was thirteen years old, and I distinctly remember the one question that raced through my mind when I heard the bad news that my dad was leaving: "Who's going to provide for us?" In some ways I've felt that question follow me through life, and even later it affected my trust in God for a mate.

Life continued on, and my dad did take care of us from a distance. Throughout the next number of years, I can remember my mom, and my oldest brother, Yisrael, spending much time in prayer and fasting. It was around this time that I also took on the challenge of following after God wholeheartedly. When I was fifteen years old, I remember sitting down to study the books of Proverbs, Jeremiah, and Isaiah and feeling so excited by what was written there. It often felt like God's Word was exploding with meaning as He drew me to His Scriptures and began to reveal Himself to me as my Father. During those years that He began revealing Himself to me as Father, He also began to awaken my desires to be a father myself.

It was also at this time that I started making choices about purity. There were so many things in the stores and in even household magazines that began to feel tempting to me at that age, but at the same time God was speaking to me through His Word and through my family, to make a covenant with my eyes not to look at anything unclean. My brother, Yisrael, would often tell us that we needed to keep ourselves totally pure for our wives. At that young age these words stuck with me, and I knew that every unrighteous and impure decision that I made was drawing me away from my future wife. One day, my brothers and I made a serious commitment that we would confess any impurity in our lives to each other immediately. We did this for many years. At a young age, I also started to wait and pray for the woman that God was choosing to be my wife. I believe that these decisions that I made early on have been invaluable and have helped prepare me for the woman that God had prepared for me. Some of those years felt so long and hard as I waited for the one that God had chosen for me; now as I look back at those long years of waiting, they seem like just a few days.

Hannah

I grew up having a very blessed childhood. I always knew my parents loved me and wanted what was best for me. I was homeschooled until I was twelve years old, and up until this time my only aspiration for adulthood was to be a wife and a mother. My example was my mom, an amazing homemaker, and I hardly knew that some women had careers, nor did that idea appeal to me. Under various circumstances, I ended up in a Christian school and eventually, for one year, in a public school from which I graduated. During that time, I lost my focus. I forgot about purity and holiness. I put my focus on the things of the world, and I started thinking about the different careers that I could have. I began thinking about the boys I knew in the context of relationships. Although I never had a "boyfriend," I still regret letting my emotions fix on anyone other than Colin. I also let my eyes see things they shouldn't have in movies and other media. I never thought twice about it, either. It was what "normal" was for me and everyone around me

After finishing school, I got a job at the local university. I didn't know what my future held: a career? marriage? I still hoped that I would marry someday. Though I struggled to not have feelings for Colin, I was also giving up hope that he was the one. I didn't feel good enough for him anymore. It was in that same year, 2008, that my brother, Joel, got betrothed, and in the spring of 2009 he married his wife, Noelle. Joel and Noelle are both very strong people in the areas of purity, modesty, and holiness. I started spending a lot of time around them, and before I knew it, without them ever telling me to change, I found that I was keeping my thoughts more pure, desiring holiness more than ever, and I was also dressing more modestly. God really used Joel and Noelle to turn me more to Him. I struggled for a time with feeling guilty for the years when I was walking in the world's ways, but I came to realize that I didn't need to walk in guilt for the past anymore, but that God had forgiven me, and I needed to walk in holiness from where I was. I started remembering my dreams from when I was a young girl. Once again I wanted to be a wife and a mother.

In the fall of 2009, when I was nineteen years old, I went on a trip to Israel to help with the grape harvest in Samaria. This was a life-changing trip for me. I learned so much about the Land of Israel, the importance of the Land according to Scripture, and what is being fulfilled according to prophecy in the Bible. I also learned a lot about prayer and God's Spirit, and I continued to learn about walking in holiness towards God in every area of my life. At the end of the trip, I was excited about all I had learned, seen, and done, but I also went back to Canada wondering what my future held. I had no plans, and I didn't want to go back to working at a job in a worldly setting, but instead, I wanted to stay at home more to serve my family. I had learned enough, though, to trust that God had a plan for me in which He would lead me.

Colin

When Hannah went to Israel, God began speaking to me in subtle ways about her. I was twenty-two years old and I had been thinking about marriage and starting a family. Years before this I had felt strong direction from God not to pursue Hannah in any way or to indicate my interest in her. After Hannah left on her trip, I started to miss seeing her with her family at our congregation on Shabbat, and I would find myself praying that God would bless her and her time serving in Israel. I talked with my mom and brothers about my thoughts and asked them to pray, and I asked an elder in our community what his counsel was. I began asking

God if I could pursue marriage with Hannah and if this would be the time of His choosing. I also remembered a conversation that I had had with my father a number of years before, and how he had asked if Hannah Paul might be a possible future mate for me.

I started thinking that if I felt direction from God, blessing from my parents and elders, and confidence about Hannah's beliefs and convictions, then the next step would be to talk to Hannah's father. Tom is a wise and approachable individual and a very caring person. Sometimes he shared teachings with our congregation, and he and I enjoyed talking. I knew that he would listen to my thoughts and hear me out. I decided that the best way to proceed would be to write a letter expressing my thoughts and my desire to get married. I didn't know exactly how to progress at this point, so I decided to ask Tom if I could "court" Hannah with the intention of marriage. (I realized later that it would have been better to ask to get betrothed from the very start.)

So, I called Tom and asked if he would be willing to meet me for coffee one day after work. He accepted my invitation, and we met at Tony Roma's for coffee on a cloudy day in November. I arrived early and found a booth in the almost empty restaurant. When Tom arrived, we visited for a few minutes, and then I told him my feelings, the leading that I was feeling, and the counsel that I had received from others. I also asked him what his thoughts were and if he would consider this matter in prayer with Hannah's mom, Laurie, and with Hannah. He told me that he would consider this and talk to Laurie about it. He also said that a relationship with Hannah could be a possibility.

Hannah

When I found out that Colin was interested in marrying me, I was shocked. You might wonder why, since I had been interested in him for so many years. Well, during the harvest trip that I had been on in Israel, I had come to a place where I felt I could put my focus on other things, such as what God had for me right then while I was single. I had come to a place in my heart where I wasn't battling feelings for Colin anymore. It was actually the night before my dad gave me Colin's letter that a small group of friends, which included Colin and me, were working on writing a musical for Hanukkah that was going to be performed. I remember looking at Colin while we were working and thinking to myself, "Wow, I am finally okay with just being friends with Colin; this is great!" I felt like I had victory in my struggle with infatuation for Colin! The next night my dad presented me with a letter from Colin about his interest and intentions. You might be able to see now why I was shocked. For a week I really struggled through all of this, wondering how it could be, wondering a lot of "why" questions about the past and present. However, I made the mistake of putting more time into my own thoughts and "logic" about why I couldn't marry Colin instead of praying hard about it. Much to my mom's chagrin, I told my parents I wasn't interested in Colin, and my dad, who was okay with whatever decision I made, relayed this on to him.

<u>Colin</u>

One day Tom called me and invited me out for coffee. He told me that after praying about this possibility they felt that the answer was no. I was stunned. We visited a bit. He spoke some affirmation into my life. Then we both drove away from the restaurant. The answer was no. This was a really hard answer for me because I thought that I had waited on God about a relationship with Hannah and that I had felt direction from Him. I spent a lot of time in prayer at home and also during some long walks in the bleak winter nights and evenings. It felt like I was going to be alone forever and that I had done everything wrong. I had to battle the feelings that were sent by the enemy to tear me down. In the middle of these feelings and this battle, God spoke to me.

He revealed that my attitude hadn't been right in this situation. He began showing me that I was trying to come to Hannah like a glorious knight in shining armor, ready to take her away. Instead, He wanted me to be a bondslave of Yeshua, joyfully coming to do the will of the Master. One freezing night in the middle of a snowstorm, with tears frozen to my cheeks, I submitted everything to God. I confessed that I had come to Tom with a wrong attitude, and I asked God to change my heart so that I could be the man that he wanted me to be. After this I was at peace. I finally accepted that the answer was no.

Hannah

About a week after my dad told Colin that the answer was no, my mom came to me and told me that she thought I had made a mistake. She told me frankly that she thought Colin was the one for me to marry and that I hadn't prayed about God's will like I should have. What could I say? I knew she was right; in fact I had started to have a few regrets about my decision. She said she wanted me to pray more about the matter, and I said I would. I struggled a lot over everything for maybe another week, praying a lot more than I previously had. I thought a lot about Colin, realizing that he was one of my favorite people to be around. I felt like God was going to take Colin great places in his life, and I began to realize that I didn't want any woman to go with him but me.

Even though I began to feel this way, I wanted more than a feeling; I needed real confirmation from God. I was still asking a lot of "why" questions about things that had happened in the past. It happened one night that I was awake late, and thinking hard, when I turned on the computer and there was a song that a friend had shared. The words were, "You know better than I, You know the way. I've let go the need to know why, for You know better than I." Well, there was the confirmation! I realized that I didn't need to be asking "why" questions, I just needed to trust

God that He knew why. I felt very peaceful and excited going to bed that night. I knew that God had spoken to me very clearly in a way that I understood. After this, I talked to my parents about what I felt from God. My mom was relieved, and my dad was happy as well. But I wondered if it was too late anyway; we had already told Colin no! But my dad said he would meet with Colin and talk to him. I felt closer to God than I ever had before and had some very blessed prayer times during this period while we continued to wait to see what would happen.

Colin

As I was working one day, my phone started to ring, and I saw that it was Tom. It was about two weeks after Hannah's answer, and Tom wanted to have a visit. We met at Tim Horton's, sat down with two coffees, and Tom got straight to the point. He told me that Hannah had been praying a lot since she had said no, and she felt that she had made a mistake. He explained more and told me that if I were to ask again the answer might be different. I sat and thought about it, and I realized that I had laid down the whole situation. I didn't feel like this was real; I really didn't know what to say. I told Tom that I had been brought to a place where I just wanted to serve God as a single for the next three months or more before I even thought about anything like this; however, I also told him that I would pray about it and see if God would give me some other direction. He thought that more prayer sounded wise. As I drove away from the coffee shop, I was confused but ready to wait on God.

For the next two weeks, I spent a lot of time in prayer and fasting. I really wanted to hear God's voice clearly. I didn't want any hurt that I had felt to influence what I would do from here on. I wanted to do what was right, and I didn't want to make mistakes in my next choices. During these weeks, I was shown that marrying Hannah was still a desire in my heart and that if I chose to ask again, God's blessing would be with me. After almost two weeks, I felt clearly that I needed to ask Hannah again. I wrote another letter, a bit more simple and down to earth than the first one, and I asked if Hannah and her parents would again consider us entering into a relationship with the intention of marriage. I gave it to Tom one day and waited to hear what the response would be.

Hannah

When we got another letter from Colin, naturally I was thrilled! I looked forward excitedly to what the future held as we contacted Colin. I thought back on the night before I was given the first letter from Colin, and how I felt good at that time about just having a friendship with him and nothing more. I realized that God had brought me to the point of laying down Colin and my feelings for him, and it was then that God gave me Colin. I had overcome the struggle, and God had blessed me for that.

Colin

Soon after Hannah said yes, I met together with Hannah and her parents and we discussed what our relationship would look like and what the parameters would be. After this, Hannah and I saw each other during meetings and at one another's homes for the next number of months, and it was a blessed time in our lives. But we began lacking direction. Honestly, I began lacking direction. I had told Tom that I wanted to marry Hannah, but I didn't have a plan regarding the timing of a wedding or how to work towards marriage. I started feeling that I didn't even know what marriage was because my parents were divorced, and I began feeling very discouraged about how to proceed. I could tell that Hannah was feeling hurt by my lack of direction. I realized that I needed to be a man and lead somehow, but I felt like the man inside me was just a little boy again. I didn't know what simple steps to take towards marriage or how to proceed.

One evening, after our Sabbath meeting, Tom pulled me aside and said that he wanted to visit with me. As we pulled up two of the little chairs in the nursery and sat down, Tom began sharing some thoughts with me. He asked what the earliest or latest dates were that Hannah and I could get betrothed and married. I thought for a second and told him a few ideas that came to my mind. We talked about timing for a betrothal and about different items that would have to be taken care of before our betrothal. He helped me start thinking through the details and making a plan that we could follow. It felt really right to be working with a father figure on the details, and I started feeling much more clarity about how to proceed.

One evening Hannah, her parents, and my mom and I got together at my mom's house. As we talked about the possible times to get betrothed and married I realized that I still hadn't officially asked Hannah to marry me. I knelt down on the floor, looked into Hannah's eyes, and asked, "Hannah, would you marry me?" She responded joyfully, "Yes, I will definitely marry you." At that moment we both had a feeling of relief. It felt so right to be asking this question in the presence of our parents and with their blessing. It felt so right to be able to make a plan with loving parents who wanted to see us betrothed, married, and thriving as a family.

Colin and Hannah

During the month of preparation for our betrothal, we had lots to do and many blessings to encounter. We needed to write a ketubah (the Hebrew word for written marriage vows), buy rings, schedule a legal marriage commissioner, and organize the ceremony. Our first project together was writing our ketubah. We prayed together, asked our parents for input, and pored over the

Word to understand what our roles should be in this covenant. We discovered so much, and formed a clear view of the roles to which God was calling each of us. We had an amazing time working on our ketubah project, and it felt so great to be working towards our betrothal. We felt God's blessing in so many ways during this time. One day when we went to buy our rings, we drove out from under a bleak stormy sky into the sun shining in its glory. As we looked up there was a huge rainbow over us. It felt wonderful to see a rainbow, the sign of God's covenant regarding the Flood, as we were going to buy our rings, the sign of our covenant. There were many similar blessings and confirmations that we received in the weeks leading up to our betrothal.

We got betrothed on a beautiful afternoon in August in the yard of Colin's grandparents' farm. The sun shone like God's favor upon us. Those in attendance were our immediate family: Colin's mom, Hannah's parents, our siblings and their spouses, our nieces and nephews, and Colin's grandparents. The betrothal began with Hannah coming out of the house, followed by Colin giving an introduction and presenting Hannah's dad with a gift, the bride price. After this our parents came up and blessed us and prayed for us. We entered the shade of the beautiful chuppah that Colin had made and that Hannah hadn't seen until the betrothal. Underneath the chuppah we read our vows from our ketubah, exchanged rings, and drank wine from a cup to seal our covenant. We then prayed for each other. Colin sang a song that he had written for Hannah, and everyone spent time worshiping together to praise the One who had brought us together! After this each of our family members shared a blessing, Scripture, or prayer for us. We signed the ketubah, and then we had a celebratory cookout. We also held hands for the first time that day. As it got to be evening, we all drove back to Saskatoon, where most of us were living. At Hannah's parents' house, we met with a marriage commissioner, who legally wed us. It felt like such a dream. We had entered into covenant with each other; we were completely committed to marrying one another. We were overflowing with joy, both with memory of the wonderful day and anticipation of what was to come!

Colin

We had three months until our wedding, so we started planning. We needed to prepare ourselves for marriage and plan how we wanted our wedding, and I needed to buy a vehicle and prepare a place for us to live. We had a lot of visits and planning meetings with our parents and started working out exciting details for the wedding. With our parents' blessing, we started meeting with a pastor friend of ours every week for some premarital counseling. One month before the wedding, God led me to the perfect suite for us. It was just what we had been asking God to provide. I found the perfect truck for us, two blocks from the location at which we later got married. I also began beautifying our ketubah with artwork. While I was preparing a place for Hannah and working toward the wedding, I felt God's blessing on me very strongly. It was so encouraging to feel the blessing of God on us as we prepared and worked towards our marriage. With the help of Hannah's detailed father, our families, and our community, we had almost everything ready for the wedding a week in advance.

Hannah

Getting ready for our wedding was a real season of joy for me. I felt such freedom in being myself with Colin and being emotionally attached. Since we were already in covenant together I knew I had no fear of heartbreak. I so enjoyed planning the ceremony with Colin, picking a location for the wedding, and shopping for decorations with my mom. With the help of my sister-in-law, I even made my wedding dress. It was also a miracle how I got the perfect handkerchief-weight white linen on sale, and there was the exact amount I needed left on the roll. I really felt God's face shining on me. I was also really blessed to have time to be able to prepare my heart for marriage, to ponder what it meant to be a wife, and to be blessed with counsel and mentoring from my sister-in-law, my mom, and our pastor friend. Most of all, I was blessed to look forward to becoming Colin's wife! God was granting me all the desires of my heart.

Colin and Hannah

There is a tradition in Hebrew culture for a bride and bridegroom not to see each other at all for the last week before their wedding. One of the biggest reasons for this is to build the excitement and anticipation for the wedding. We thought this would be an exciting thing to do as well. So, for the last week before our wedding we didn't see each other or talk to each other. Saying goodbye felt really surreal, knowing the next time we saw each other we would be getting married. It was hard not to see each other or talk for that week, but knowing it was just days until our wedding made it go by fast.

It is an amazing feeling to wake up and realize it is the day of your wedding! For both of us the morning was busy getting ready, but things were planned well in advance so that everything was quite relaxed too. We were very blessed to have many friends and family members help us with setting up and organizing different things that needed to be done. The anticipation and excitement continued to build!

We were married under the chuppah in a small-town Saskatchewan hall on November 14, 2010. It was a beautiful snowy and foggy day. We didn't see each other until after Colin had entered the hall and was waiting under the chuppah. When Hannah approached the stage with her family we broke out in huge smiles. It could be that neither of us had ever smiled so big before. We met each other, hugged, and then went under the chuppah together. There we read our ketubah to reaffirm our vows, exchanged rings again for the witnesses to see, and an elder gave a message on marriage. We then washed each other's feet as an act of showing how we wanted to serve each other in marriage. Our moms read Scriptures we had chosen, and seven traditional marriage blessings were prayed in Hebrew and English by two of Colin's brothers. We then once again drank from a cup together. Some friends and siblings then led everyone in a time of worship. Hannah's dad blessed us with the priestly blessing, followed by us kissing for the first time ever! After this Hannah's dad announced us as husband and wife, and Colin stomped on the glass we had drunk from to break it; no one else would ever drink from the same cup we had used! We left the hall to have our pictures taken outside (we were blessed that it wasn't too cold). We had a reception shortly after, which included delicious food, blessings from those in attendance, dancing, and even the bottle dance from Fiddler on the Roof performed by surprise by one of Colin's brothers and some friends! It was a joyous and celebratory time for all, but especially for us. We will never forget that day. Finally, while everyone sang and waved, we drove away to begin our life together as husband and wife!

The first week after our wedding, we spent at home in the suite that God had provided for us, and then we went off to the Rocky Mountains the following week where some friends had blessed us with a place to stay! It was such a wonderful time to grow in relationship together and to have fun being together all the time. The weeks and months that followed were equally joyous, learning about each other and how to work together.

About a month after our wedding, we found out that we were going to have a baby! Another blessing on top of our already overflowing cups! On August 25, 2011 we were blessed to welcome into our little family a baby boy named Yoav Serool Johnson.

Now we are enjoying life together so much, and God continues to bless us and lead us. We were fortunate to spend the remainder of that fall and winter in Israel, once again harvesting grapes and also learning Hebrew. We have seen God's faithfulness in giving us direction and leading in the past, and now we're still looking to God to direct our future. All praise and glory to the One who is the Author of our lives!

As a happily married couple with a baby in our arms, we look back on all that's happened, and we're simply relieved and full of praise to the Lord for His goodness, favor, and mercy to us. As we hear others talking about betrothal and marriage, we feel relieved as we think back to the journey on which God has led us. The topic doesn't bring with it all the same questions and concerns that it used to, but now we remember the lessons that we've been taught and the character that God has worked in our lives.

Here are some realizations that we've come to that we want to share with single young men and women and their parents. As we grew up we appreciated hearing the experiences and lessons of those who had gone before us, and we want to humbly share some ideas that have come from our experience.

So, why betrothal? As we look back on our story we see that betrothal can have better direction than courtship. Like dating, courtship tends to lack commitment and leaves room for heartbreak. Betrothal requires commitment and understanding of God's will, thus betrothal can provide greater security for everyone involved.

Colin

Young men, before you start thinking about a wife and a family, accept the task that God is giving you in regards to serving Him. If you want to get married and become the leader of a home one day, submit yourselves to your parents and honor them now. The greatest followers become the greatest leaders. If you want to begin leading a wife and family, become a great follower of your elders. In regards to purity, make a covenant with your eyes like Job when he said, "I made a covenant with my eyes; Why then should I look upon a young woman?" (Job 31:1). Join with mighty King David who decided not to look at anything unholy when he said, "I will set nothing wicked before my eyes" (Psalm 101:3).

If you're starting to plan for a betrothal, start leading in purity and in direction. Make a clear written list of physical boundaries to make sure that you agree to those standards. If you are in some kind of relationship right now, consider following God's leading to betrothal and marriage. If you have no leading towards marriage, consider discontinuing that type of relationship. The biggest encouragement that I want to give to any young man is that you have a Father in heaven who knows your need. Don't worry about this area of life like people in the world do. God gives gifts that are bigger and better than we can imagine. When we choose God before anything else, we realize that He gives His gifts to those who prioritize seeking His kingdom and His righteousness.

A few thoughts for fathers: be intentionally involved in your children's lives as they enter a marriageable age. If a young man approaches you for your daughter, make sure that he has a plan and is submitted to God, and that he's working with parents and elders. Your role as a father is hugely important in this process of betrothal and marriage, so seek God for his wisdom as you bless your children with your involvement.

Hannah

Young ladies, if you are waiting for the right man to come along, don't let that be your focus. Put your focus on other things, such as serving your family and serving others. When the time comes, pray as much as you can about any young man who is seeking to marry you. Take as much time as you need in prayer, and don't feel pressured by time because it's life changing and permanent to get married. Try not to let emotions make decisions for you. Also, I know that it's very easy for young ladies to fantasize about a young man coming for her, and about the future, etc. But this is not healthy, and it is a matter that should be taken to prayer and talked about with parents or a mentor. Most importantly of all, just enjoy your present situation. Be content with being single; for most people it's actually a very short stage of life. Also, enjoy the process of betrothal when it comes your way because that also happens only once!

We know that God takes care of those who trust in Him! We have seen this both in our own lives as well as in the lives of others. We hope that our story will be an encouragement to trust God to provide in every area of life. As we look back, we realize that being in a relationship to figure out if we were to marry was not God's way; it was us on our own strength trying to figure out God's plan. If we trust God, He gives confirmation and speaks to His children in a way that they understand at the right time. The romances that He writes are far more beautiful than those of the world, and they have happier endings. We look back on our story and praise God for helping us through by His grace. Now we look forward to what is to come. As we consider the future and wonder what God has for us, we remember the verse, "But you are the same, and Your years have no end" (Psalm 102:27). We know that God directed us in the past, and we know that He will direct us in the future. God hasn't changed, and He continues to lead those who trust in Him.

A Long Wait and a Quick Move

Lachlann and Shanna Thompson

Lachlann's story

I was thirty years old when I got married in 2010. Some have said, "Wow, you got a late start," but I am so thankful that I waited. I lived with my father until that year. I never dated a girl, but decided to wait for the one Yahweh had for me. Although the wait was long and at times I got very discouraged, I am glad I waited. Yahweh's will is best.

Below, I have shared the testimony of my search for a wife and the miracles Yahweh did for me in bringing Shanna and me together to be husband and wife. In retrospect, I have one word of caution for young single men preparing for marriage. Not only is it best to wait for Yahweh's will in choosing your life partner, but it is also best to wait for Yahweh's timing for when to marry the woman He has for you. Do not try to rush Yahweh's timing. Trust in Yahweh. He will bring about His will in His timing. Although I know beyond a shadow of a doubt that Shanna is the woman Yahweh had to be my wife, I realize now that I should have given both of our families more time. Because I did not wait for Yahweh to move, it caused unnecessary stress on both sides. I know now that it is important to allow the woman's family to have enough time to fully process, assess, and be at peace with the man and the situation they are releasing their daughter and sister into. Yahweh is good and faithful. We can trust that He will bring about His perfect will if we step out of the way and let Him work.

I have desired to give this testimony for some time. I actually desired to give this testimony before I asked Shanna if she wanted to be my wife and before Steve (her father) gave me permission to ask her. I cannot remember how far back—maybe it was shortly after I first called them. Although this may seem presumptuous, it is actually a demonstration of my faith—my faith that Yahweh was answering my fervent prayers by granting the request I had been making for about ten years. My request was that Yahweh would grant me a wife—not just any wife, but a wife who would fulfill the desires of my heart; a wife who loves Yahweh and desires to keep His law with all her heart, soul, and strength; a wife who loves her neighbor as herself; a wife who believes in modesty, sobriety, and submitting to her Elohim-given head, and adorns herself with good works and a gentle and quiet spirit; a wife who is virtuous; a wife who believes that long hair is a glory unto her and that she should wear a head covering; a wife who desires to have many children and be a keeper at home; a wife who believes that raising a family and growing your own food will produce the greatest physical riches this world has to offer, and that doing these things according to the good and perfect will of Yahweh will bring the greatest spiritual riches; a wife who desires to live a simple life so that the focus is on the people and not the possessions; a wife who had not been with a man before; a wife who would live up to the vow, "...till death do us part."

I know this list seems like a large set of lofty desires. I know this because people have told me so. They did not believe I could find such a girl. In the beginning of my ten-year search, I was confident I could find such a girl. As the years began to roll by, I remained hopeful, even though the families we knew were few and did not match my large set of lofty desires. By the seventh or eighth year, I was becoming discouraged and began to believe that the doubters might be right. "Maybe she does not exist." The time that had passed had large gaps with no prospects for a wife. The ninth year had one family shy of a handful, but none of them worked out. After all this searching and all these disappointing results, and wondering why I couldn't find her, I came to realize that it was not my searching that found these families—they were brought to my attention by someone else. I then realized that if I was going to find the wife of my dreams, Yahweh was going to bring it about. In spite of this revelation, I continued to be discouraged by what I considered to be the negative results of the past nine years, even though all of those circumstances were beneficial for learning. I told myself, "If I do find the woman I'm looking for, it will be a miracle."

In the tenth year, in about February of 2009, I called the Warren family, who had left Idaho and hit the road the year before. I was missing them and wondered what they were up to. They were traveling around, visiting families they had seen at the Feast of Tabernacles in 2008. One of the families they were visiting was the Fourniers. The Warrens knew I had been looking for a wife for many years, and they knew of the basics concerning my list, so Monty told me about the Fournier family. They kept Torah, were wanting to grow all their own food, and were planning to go without electricity . . . oh, and they had nine girls. So I asked for their phone number. I was still doubting that anything would come of it since the Fourniers lived over 2,000 miles away. I said to myself, "That's great for some guy who lives way over there. How could I spend enough time with them to get to know them?" I set their number aside and did not call them. After some weeks of feeling that I had found yet another dead end, I decided to give them a call. After the second phone call, each of them being hours long, I had heard enough to believe that Yahweh had answered my prayer. This was the family I had been waiting for.

My parents and I immediately began talking to Steve Fournier about visiting them for a couple of weeks. He was agreeable, so we planned to come down on June 8th. When I asked my boss for the time off, he said other workers were taking time off then, so I couldn't. After that, Mom had a family reunion, and then my parents' wedding anniversary, and it just kept getting pushed further and further out of reach. The Fourniers said that we might as well wait until the Feast of Tabernacles. Then Yahweh performed a miracle. He caused an inland hurricane to pass through Missouri, creating more work than Steve could handle, and He slowed down the building trade in northern Idaho to get me laid off. It was the perfect set-up. Then I got the bright idea, "I'll go work for Steve." I called him the very next morning. Steve asked, "How's it going?" I replied, "I got laid off." Steve responded, "How do you like roofing?" I was so surprised that he offered the job before I asked that I said, "Wow, that was too easy." Steve wanted me right away. I told him the soonest I could come was the second day of the following week, which happened to be June 8th, the very day we had originally planned to come down. Yahweh has impeccable timing.

Within the first week of being there, I could see Shanna's virtue and her gentle and quiet spirit. After about a month, I believed Shanna was the one, but I thought it was too soon to say, so I moved that thought to the back of my mind. Later, I saw a cross-stitch frame on the wall with all the Fourniers' names and meanings. I saw that *Shanna* meant "Yahweh's Gracious Gift." I thought to myself, "Perfect, she's got to be the one," but I still thought it was too soon.

Then Steve said that another young man was going to come and work with us. Without asking questions I supposed that he was after Shanna too. Knowing that jealousy and contempt are normal courses of human action, I determined that I would not go there. I decided to trust Yahweh, whatever the outcome. Instead, we became friends, and as it turned out, he was interested in one of the other girls.

By August, I made it known to Steve that I was interested in Shanna. Then began the more serious inquiries. In the meantime, I helped the Fournier family move to Tennessee. By September,

Shanna was told of my interest, and we were allowed to ask each other questions with company. In October, I went with Steve to Missouri to finish up some remodel work. On the way to our first day of work, Steve asked if I felt that Yahweh was bringing Shanna and me together, and I gave a summary of this testimony. He then said, "Did you know that two other men asked for Shanna this month?" In shock I said, "No." Steve said, "Well, she chose you." Still in shock, I said, "I'm honored." This was yet another sign to me that Yahweh was bringing us together. Steve gave me permission to ask Shanna to marry me, but I was away for three weeks; I asked her when I got back, and she said "yes."

So, in a way, those who doubted I would find the girl I was looking for were right. I did not find her; Yahweh gave her to me as a gracious gift. And even though I had a large set of lofty desires, Yahweh fulfilled every single one of them. Nothing is too difficult for Yahweh. So, trust in Yahweh and wait on Him. His gracious gifts are well worth the wait. As it says in Psalm 27:14, *"Wait on [Yahweh]: Be of good courage, And He shall strengthen your heart: Wait, I say, on [Yahweh]."*

From the first day of our marriage, I continued to discover time and time again that Yahweh had given me the desires of my heart as I continued to get to know my wife. This truly was a match made in heaven.

Shanna's story

I praise Yahweh for the miracle in bringing Lachlann and me together as husband and wife. Yahweh is so good! Lachlann and I have been married for almost two years now. We continually marvel at how perfectly Yahweh suited us for one another.

For as long as I can remember, I have always wanted to be a wife and mother. Growing up as the oldest of nine sisters and two brothers, I had the privilege and responsibility of helping my parents care for my younger brothers and sisters and run our large household. I am thankful for the practical training ground my father's house was for me, but more than that, I am very grateful for the desire my parents helped to instill in my heart at a young age to love and follow Yahweh. I am also very thankful for the strong convictions my parents helped to build in my life regarding emotional, moral, and spiritual purity.

I am sure that most young women can identify with similar desires in wanting to be cherished and loved by a husband. As a young single woman, I had to learn how to righteously deal with the desires I had for marriage. Yahweh, in His faithfulness, taught me so much about being content, trusting Him, and waiting on Him. I learned to guard my heart, my thoughts, and my eyes. My greatest desire was to save myself for the man Yahweh had for me. I knew this meant that I had to keep a tight rein on even my thought life.

Yahweh used many precious Scriptures to comfort and encourage my heart during those years of waiting: *"Whom have I in heaven but You? And there is none upon earth that I desire besides You. My flesh and my heart fail: But [Elohim] is the strength of my heart and my portion forever"* (Psalm 73:25-26). *"My soul, wait silently for [Elohim] alone; For my expectation is from Him. He only is my rock and my salvation: He is my defense; I shall not be moved"* (Psalm 62:5-6). *"...for I have learned, in whatever state I am, to be content ... I can do all things through*

[Messiah] *who strengthens me"* (Philippians 4:11,13). *"Trust in [Yahweh]* *with all your heart; and lean not on your own understanding"* (Proverbs 3:5). I knew that Yahweh's will was best—whether that meant single-ness or marriage. I recognized that singleness is a gift given by Yahweh, just as marriage is a gift. The Giver of every good and perfect gift had my best in mind, and I needed to trust Him. I learned that being content was a choice. I can walk joyously through life, giving thanks in all things, because my hope and trust are found in Yahweh. I knew that serving Yahweh in my father's house was Yahweh's will for me, and that even if Yahweh never blessed me with the gift of marriage, I could have joy and fulfillment in serving my family, submitting to my father's author-ity and covering over me, and working alongside my mother as a keeper at home.

When I was twenty-two years old, Yahweh led our family, through my father, to keep His Sabbaths and obey His Torah. I fully supported my dad in this new journey. I was very grate-ful and excited about all Yahweh was teaching and directing our family to do. However, if I thought the road was narrow before, I knew it was definitely narrow now! I honestly thought that I would never get married. Again and again, I had to give my desire to be married to Yahweh and put my trust in Him, knowing that He had my best in mind. Yahweh is an Elohim of miracles, and He delights in bringing about the things that we think are impos-sible! Another precious Scripture that Yahweh used over the years to encourage my heart is found in Ecclesiastes 3:11: *"He has made* *everything beautiful in His time . . ."* When one has to wait a long time to receive something he has longed for, he finds it worth so much more than if he got what he wanted as soon as he wanted it. I can testify that Yahweh does indeed make everything beauti-ful in His time!

There is a song based on Psalm 37:23 that had been on my heart for several days before Lachlann asked me to be his wife:

"The steps of a righteous man are ordered by Yahweh: and He delights in his way." I truly believe that Yahweh directed Lachlann's steps, bringing him all the way to Missouri from Idaho to work for my father. I believe that the two of us coming together in marriage for the purpose of honoring our Heavenly Father was also ordered of Yahweh. Lachlann had been living with our family for about four months before my parents came to me and told me that Lachlann had asked for my hand in marriage. Lachlann guarded his eyes very carefully during those several months of living with us. I did not know that he had his eye on me. He never paid special attention to me. I actually felt like he guarded himself even more when he was around me than when he was around my sisters. Besides necessary words of politeness and courtesy, Lachlann and I hardly spoke more than a few words to one another during those four months. During those months, Lachlann proved to me that he was a man of character and integrity. He was faithful, trustworthy, hardworking, and honest. These are character qualities that I knew I wanted in a man if Yahweh would see fit to give me a husband. I am grateful that Yahweh has blessed me with the desires of my heart!

After spending some time in prayer and sensing that it was Yahweh's will, I told my parents that I was willing to spend time getting to know Lachlann for the purpose of marriage. My parents had a few conversations with the two of us. We were given the freedom to talk a few times by ourselves, but in view of my family. However, we mostly talked around the meal table, asking each other questions and interacting with my whole family. After about a month of having some interaction with one another, Daddy and Mama needed to make a trip to Missouri to finish up the work commitments that my dad had there. Lachlann went with them to help finish up the work, but before leaving, my parents had individually asked both Lachlann and me to pray for confirmation from Yahweh that it was His will that we serve Him together. My parents and Lachlann were gone for three weeks. During that time, my theme Scripture was *"You will guide me with Your counsel..." (Psalm 73:24).* In those three weeks, I was praying and seeking Yahweh in a measure I never had before. I wanted Yahweh's will—whatever that meant. Yahweh gave me an unexplainable sense of peace. One morning, as I was by myself, just a couple days before Dad and Lachlann came back home, I felt the assurance and certainty of knowing that my answer for Lachlann was to be "yes."

The evening my dad and Lachlann got back from Missouri, my dad pulled me aside and told me that he had given Lachlann permission to talk with me on the front porch after supper. My whole family knew what was up—Lachlann was going to propose to me! The idea of him proposing to me at that point had not even crossed my mind. I was just excited to have the opportunity to talk alone with him, as it had been three weeks since I had seen or talked with him. My dad lit a lantern, put it on the porch, and told us to enjoy our visit. He then went inside. I knew my sisters and brothers were watching us from the windows, but I didn't mind! Lachlann started off by telling me a little bit about his recent trip. He then got to the point and told me that he wanted to live life with me. He then asked me if I would be his wife. I surprised even myself by responding without a moment's hesitation, "Yes, I would." Lachlann then gave me a beautiful bouquet of flowers. We sat and talked about the confirmation we both felt in knowing that Yahweh had us for each other. We then continued to talk about life and plans. I am not sure how long we sat and talked, but it must have been a while because my dad had to come out and ask us if we had any news to share with the family! We quickly went inside and shared the news. I felt like I was living in a dream. It didn't seem real—I was getting married! Of course, my family was very excited for me.

Lachlann and I were betrothed December 5, 2009. Betrothal is a covenant before marriage. Lachlann and I never dated each other or any other person. We both knew that when it came to the issue of marriage, we would wait until we knew in our hearts that Yahweh was the One bringing us together before ever interacting and getting to know one another. Before our betrothal, I hardly knew Lachlann at all. I did know that my father had gotten to know Lachlann very well and that I could trust my father's evaluation of his character. I also knew in my heart that Yahweh had given me a sense of peace and assurance that Lachlann was the man for me. Entering into a covenant with a man I didn't know very well was a huge step of faith, but because I knew it was Yahweh's will, I felt confident that I was doing the right thing.

At our betrothal ceremony, Lachlann and I shared our vows with one another before witnesses. We had the witnesses sign our ketubah. We also committed to not touch one another before our wedding. During the betrothal ceremony, my dad shared his important part in our story, and Lachlann's dad and my dad prayed over us and blessed us. My mother and my brothers and sisters also each shared a special blessing with Lachlann and me. The whole evening was very special and beautiful.

During the betrothal period, Lachlann and I spent more time talking with one another and getting to know each other, but in view of family members. We did this as a safety measure and to be above reproach. There were, of course, a lot of plans to make and things to do to prepare for the wedding, but I knew for myself that what was most important was that I would use the betrothal period to prepare my heart for Lachlann.

Lachlann and I had our wedding celebration on April 11, 2010. Lachlann was thirty years old and I was twenty-four. I am thankful that I can honestly say that I never gave my heart to another man and that I saved myself for Lachlann. The years of waiting were well worth it. Our heavenly Father does indeed make everything beautiful in His time.

Lachlann and I love each other more and more as time passes. Without a doubt, we know that it was Yahweh who made us for each other. It was Yahweh who orchestrated the multitude of miracles that brought about our union, giving us the confirmation that we were to spend our lives honoring and serving Him together. We praise Yahweh for His goodness and faithfulness in our lives, and we thank Him for the love and life we share together as husband and wife.

[Note: We now have been married four years and are so blessed in each other's love as we serve Yahweh together. We have been blessed with three precious children— Eliysheva, Chizkiyah and Chaya whom we are endeavoring to raise for the furthering of His Kingdom.]

The Proposal Story

Fournier Sisters

The day when Lachlann proposed to Shanna is a day that we shall always remember. It was preparation day, which is always very busy. We were cleaning the house and also awaiting the arrival of Daddy, Mama, Charis, Hannah, and Lachlann. It was a very exciting reunion; we hadn't been together as a family for three weeks! As soon as they pulled up, everyone ran outside to greet them, as we always do. Something was different though; our younger sister, Shava, was going crazy with excitement and there was lots of whispering! It wasn't long before the secret was exposed. Lachlann was going to ask for Shanna's hand in marriage that very night. After we had eaten Shabbat dinner, Lachlann asked Daddy if he could speak with Shanna alone. Of course, everyone knew why, with the exception of Shanna. It was very comical observing the younger children peering out the windows at the young couple as they conversed together on the porch. Every so often, they would run into the living room and inform us of what they thought was happening. "I see them both looking in front of them into the darkness!" "Lachlann has asked Shanna by now, I am sure!" "I think I heard something about the Coovers." "He gave her the flowers, finally!" "She is smiling so big!" On and on they updated us on the exciting event.

Kirsten had the privilege of serenading Lachlann and Shanna for nearly half of it, but then she ran out of songs to play. "My!" She exclaimed as she stood up from her long performance, "I never knew it would take this long to ask such a simple question! They only must exchange six words! Lachlann can ask, "Will you be my wife?" and Shanna can agree with an, "Uha." Everyone laughed in agreement. Proposing shouldn't take that long! Maybe this is how he said it – Will… (15 minutes) you… (another 15 minutes) be… (5 minutes) my… (15 minutes) W…I…F…E…?

One detail that will never be forgotten about the night Lachlann proposed to Shanna is the presence of an unwanted guest. We had an extra pair of ears trying to listen in on Lachlann and Shanna's conversation. This obtrusive visitor was no friend! The only way we could tell his presence—for he was very secretive—was by the putrid odor that wafted through the air! Yes, this nighttime visitor was a skunk! It was quite surprising that the couple didn't speed up their time together, for the smell was quite overpowering! Christopher said they were probably oblivious to it. Well, maybe not. After all, Shanna did put her nose into her bouquet for several long sniffs, the children said!

Waiting 'til She's Old Enough

Barrett and Devin Warren

Barrett—Spring 2009

It all started for me in the spring of 2009. We were invited to a week-long camping trip in Kentucky called "Family Week," a week of fellowship and fun with like-minded believers. I was excited about going and seeing some of my good friends, never knowing that this trip would be the start of something amazing.

I first noticed Devin Schaefer during a Hebraic dance class where I saw that she picked up on the dance steps quickly and I found myself following her when I couldn't see the leader. I didn't think anything more than, "Wow, she is a great dancer!" A few days later, after seeing her beat some guys in a foot race, I thought to myself, "Not only is she a great dancer, she can beat my friends in a race." There were other things I noticed about her, like the fact that wherever she was, everyone always seemed to be having fun. She was always smiling and laughing, and she could play guitar and sing really well. I approached my Dad about the possibility of pursuing Devin and was told that she was only sixteen years old and to pursue her would not be an option because of her age. I was disappointed, but I understood. I tried to put her out of my mind but there were different times throughout the next year when I would see a picture of her and think, "Man, it's too bad she is only sixteen . . ."

The following year, my family made the trip to Kentucky for Family Week again, after so enjoying our time the previous year. Devin was also there with her family. When I saw her, I realized that I still admired a lot of things about her and I once again approached my dad about pursuing a relationship with her. Dad felt that she was still too young, but said he would pray about it. He encouraged me to maybe think about pursuing someone closer to my age. He had nothing against Devin or her family, but felt that her age, as well as the seven-year age difference between us would be a concern to her and her parents. So, once again, I tried to push that idea from my mind, but because of my age and my desire to get married and the fact that I liked Devin, it was a thought that remained in the back of my mind.

That summer, plans came together for my family to go to Israel for two and a half months in the fall. When I found out that Devin would also be in Israel with some of her family, I got an anxious, excited feeling. I was hoping that during this trip, my parents and I would get to spend some time with Devin and her family to get to know her better. My mom really liked Devin, so she kept that idea in my dad's mind.

During the grape harvest, I saw Devin a lot in the vineyards and on tours. Whenever I was around her, I got really nervous. After spending time with Devin and her family in groups, I got to know more about her. I discovered that she would turn eighteen in March of the following year. My family really enjoyed spending time with their family, so before they left Israel we planned an afternoon together, touring around Jerusalem. I had a blast that day. The Schaefers had supper with us at our apartment that evening, and we spent our time talking and laughing. We took them to the airport the next morning and through conversation I found out that Devin's mom and dad were six years apart. That reassured me somewhat about the issue of our age difference. That evening, I talked to my dad and he gave me a couple of options: I could consider pursuing someone else, or I could wait until Devin turned eighteen. He also mentioned that he wasn't sure Devin's dad would say yes, for a few reasons: one, he had two older daughters who were not married yet (she was the youngest and was not yet eighteen), and also the age difference could be a possible concern. I didn't hesitate with my answer: "I will wait till she turns eighteen and then ask her dad." I was willing to wait—even if there was the possibility he would say no. A few days later, my dad came to me and asked me again if I was sure I was willing to wait. He wanted to make sure I was committed to this. When once again, my answer was "yes," he said, "Okay, then that's what we'll do." Thus, it was decided that we would wait until Devin turned eighteen to approach her dad. Once the decision was made, I felt so much more at peace about the situation. I no longer felt stressed or anxious.

The following January, it was a pleasant surprise for me to see Devin and her family in Tennessee at a gathering. We happened to be passing through, and didn't expect to see them there from Virginia. But once again, we had a great time with them. As usual, our time was spent in much fun and laughter.

The next time I saw Devin was in April 2011 at Family Week in Kentucky, the place where this all began. But it was different this year. Devin had turned eighteen the month before. Now she was old enough that I could ask her dad. I talked to my dad about it and asked him how we were going to do "this thing." Was I supposed to ask Devin's dad, was he going to ask him, or would we both go together and talk to him? Dad told me he would pray about it and left it at that. I was fine with his answer. Our family spent time with Devin's family that week as we shared meals together and enjoyed visiting at each other's campsites. I was waiting for Dad to tell me it was time to talk to Gene (Devin's dad). When the days started going by and my dad hadn't said anything yet, I started to kind of get upset. What was he waiting for? But Family Week wasn't over yet and I knew that before they left, we would talk to Gene. You can imagine how I felt when the last day of Family Week came and the Schaefers left and Dad hadn't said anything more about talking to Devin's dad. I was quite upset. I had waited all this time to ask, and now they were gone and so was my opportunity to talk to Gene about Devin. I was off by myself when Dad came to me and said, "Well, I talked to Gene…" What! He had talked to him? Suddenly my anger left and all I felt was nervous excitement. "So, what did you say? What did he say?" Dad then proceeded to tell me that he had talked to Devin's dad about my intentions and after Gene got over the initial shock that someone had asked about his "baby girl," he said that he would pray about it and talk to Devin's mom, Lorrie. He also told my dad that he wanted to get to know me, personally, a little better.

Over the next couple of weeks, Dad and I emailed Gene, sharing about our family, our beliefs, and some of my personal convictions. He replied with some questions for me, and shared with us some things about his family and their beliefs. We had a few phone conversations, as well. That was definitely a stressful time of wondering and waiting for me—wondering what kinds of questions Gene would ask, what he wanted to know about me, and if there was at all a possibility that he would say "yes."

<u>Devin—May 2011</u>

I will never forget the day I was out in the garden with my mom and she turned to me and said, "Devin, I need to talk to you about something." My first thought was, "Uh oh, what did I do now?" Mom quickly assured me that I had done nothing wrong, but there was something she needed to tell me. I don't know why—maybe it was how she said it or the look on her face, but I started to get kind of nervous. She then proceeded to tell me that someone had asked about me. I was shocked! With two older sisters, it had never occurred to me that I could get married before they did. I always knew that someday I would want to get married and have a family, but for some reason, I always thought I would be older when that happened. Now I know that our lives don't always go the way we think they will or should. The Father has a plan that is much bigger and definitely much better than we could ever imagine or hope for.

So after I got over the initial shock (well, actually, I'm not sure I did get over being shocked), Mom asked me if I wanted to know who it was who had asked about me. My first thought was, "Yes, I want to know!" But just as soon as that thought entered my head, another one followed. I voiced this next thought aloud to Mom. I told her that after thinking about it I wanted to wait and pray before knowing who it was. I had never made a decision like this before, and I wanted to be able to pray for peace as well as the ability to hear the Father's voice when making a decision about this. I felt for myself that to know who it was might prevent me from truly hearing. I spent about three days praying, and felt a peace about the situation, confident that I would be able to give an answer based on what I heard from the Father and not just from what I felt was right. So, a few days later, when Mom asked me if I was ready to know who had asked, I told her I was. In the few seconds between when she asked me and when she told me I think every emotion possible went through my head. I was nervous, excited, and anxious. I held my breath as she turned to me and said, "It is Barrett Warren." She was smiling and I was crying. If I thought I was shocked before, I was really shocked now. But the shock didn't last long. Almost as soon as that feeling hit me it was quickly exchanged for an amazing sense of peace. I couldn't stop crying—but they were happy tears. I was still trying to wrap my mind around the fact that someone wanted to marry me. And it wasn't just anybody, it was Barrett Warren. Soon after meeting the Warrens at Family Week, I had begun to admire Barrett and his family a lot. The thought of pursuing a relationship with him was exciting, but it was also very new for me.

The next couple of months were the hardest for me, though. Our family had never experienced anything like this before. I think it was hard for my dad to grasp that not only his youngest daughter but his youngest child would possibly be getting married. We talked about it several times, and I think he wanted to make sure I was ready to get married. He stayed in contact with Barrett through emails and got to know more about him and his family throughout the summer. Both of our families were planning on being in Israel that fall and Dad told Barrett that he wanted to talk to him in person. So I knew that an answer would be given in Israel. I already knew my answer was "yes," but Dad had not yet made a final decision. It was not because he had anything against Barrett or his family; he was just not sure if I was old enough yet, and he wanted to talk in person with Barrett because he finds it easier to talk to a person face to face instead of by email or phone. I did a lot of praying that summer. I prayed for patience for myself as I waited, and I prayed for peace and understanding for my dad. I knew this was not an easy decision for him to make. This was his daughter's future he was looking at. The waiting was hard and sometimes stressful, but looking back, I see that it was a time of growing for me and I am thankful for the time and thought Dad put into making his decision.

Barrett—Summer 2011

I spent my summer waiting and praying, praying and waiting. In one of my conversations with Gene, he told me that since both our families would be in Israel, he wanted to talk with me there so we could talk in person. There were many times during those months when I felt impatient and anxious, wondering what we would talk about and what his answer might be if indeed I got an answer in Israel. When those times came, I tried to occupy myself to get my mind off the impatient feelings. I prayed often during the weeks and months before leaving for Israel that his answer would be "yes." But I had no way of knowing what he would say.

Devin—Fall 2011

I was nervous about seeing Barrett in Israel, and wouldn't you know it, the very first day we got there, we were on our way from the airport and had to stop by the Warren's apartment. I was planning on just staying in the van, but Barrett's mom and his sister Sarah came down to say "hi," so I figured I should get out and say "hello." Barrett had also come down, but I didn't even look at him. I just gave his mom and his sister hugs, said "hi," and got back into the van.

Barrett—Fall 2011

My family had been in Israel a month before Devin got there with her mom and her sister. Her dad came two weeks later to join them for his three-week stay. I was excited about seeing Devin, but also a bit nervous, so that day when they showed up at our apartment unexpectedly, I didn't know what to think. I wanted to see her, but I was so nervous that I decided to just stay inside. My mom had other ideas. She never said a word. She just pointed at me, then pointed outside. I knew exactly what that meant. She wanted me to go outside and say "hi" to Devin and her family. But when I got out there Devin wouldn't even look at me, much less say hello. She talked to my mom and my sister, then got right back into the van. That made me really nervous. That she didn't say "hi" to me or anything was out of character for her, and that made me think that she must have known something, and that her answer would probably be "no." I tried not to worry about it, but I couldn't help it. I worried.

Devin—In the Vineyards

I saw Barrett and his family a lot while we were working in the vineyards, on tours, and at gatherings. I was anxious for my dad to get there so they could talk. But before he got there, I talked a lot with my sister who was in Israel with me. She really encouraged me to be patient, and when I started feeling anxious or worried, to pray about it. That really helped me, but I was still wishing for the time to go by faster so Dad would arrive soon.

Barrett—In the Vineyards

The original nervous and awkward feelings of our first meeting were quickly replaced with an ease and comfort of being around each other. It really helped that I enjoyed being around Devin, listening to her talking and laughing with me as well as other friends she was with. I was still very anxious for Gene to arrive in Israel, so we could talk.

The day finally came when Gene was in Israel. Because we were staying in two different locations, it was several days before I saw him and got a chance to talk with him. I remember the day well. We were in a vineyard spreading fertilizer, and I asked Gene if we could talk. He said that was fine, so we grabbed our buckets and headed for an empty row, hoping to find some privacy to talk. However, with so many other people working in the field that day, that was not the case. Nonetheless, we were able to exchange a few questions and answers every once in a while. In those few private moments I learned that Gene had tried to talk to Devin but was facing the same problem we were facing that day. There were so many people around that he was having a hard time finding a time when he could talk to her alone. He did share with me that Lorrie was all for it, and that she was very excited about the possibility. He told me he still had some questions for me and would like to try to find a time when we could talk. So, I left that day with no definite answer but I did have the assurance that we would talk again—so that helped.

Devin

It was very frustrating at times—finally having my dad there in Israel, but not having an opportunity to talk with him and have the long conversation that we needed to have. We did get a few words in here and there, but there was still more that needed to be discussed. We rarely got the chance to talk, so our conversations were spread out throughout the first week he was there.

Barrett—The Talk

The time finally came when I got an opportunity to talk to Gene alone. Two days after our talk in the field, their family came to our apartment for Shabbat. After we had eaten, I asked Gene if he would go on a walk with me so we could talk. He agreed, and I found myself walking the streets of Jerusalem with Devin's dad. It was on that walk that Gene turned to me and said, "Barrett, I give you my blessing to pursue a relationship with my daughter." I was very happy to hear those words, and enjoyed the rest of my walk as we talked about family and other things.

Since I now had Gene and Lorrie's blessing, I wanted to move forward with things, but I didn't know what the next step should be. Several days later, during a tour in Jerusalem, I approached Gene and asked him if he had had a chance to talk more with Devin, and if so, what was the next step. He replied that since we had last talked, he had not been able to speak with Devin alone. I then asked him what he thought about the possibility of me talking to Devin. He gave me his permission to approach Devin and talk to her about pursuing a relationship.

Devin—The Talk

It is funny how a person's timing for things works out, sometimes. On the same day that I later found out Barrett had talked to my dad, Mom came to me and said that I really needed to find a time when Dad and I could talk, because Barrett was going to want an answer, and we still hadn't really had much time to talk. I decided that I was going to talk with Dad that evening, when we got back to our house. Little did I know what was in store for me that very day!

Barrett—No Pizza Today

I now had Gene's blessing, as well as his permission to ask Devin to marry me, and I wasn't about to let another day go by without talking to her, after having waited so long for this day. I was excited, yes, but I was also more nervous than I had ever been before. I was waiting for the right time to talk to Devin, but with so many people around that day, it was proving to be quite difficult. The wait wasn't helping my nerves one bit. We continued our tour of Jerusalem, stopping at various points of interest where the whole group would gather for a bit of discussion about the particular place we happened to be. I sat there at every group gathering, watching Devin and waiting for the opportunity to talk to present itself. The longer I had to wait, the more nervous I became, but I knew the time wasn't right yet. Waiting was my only option, at this point.

Lunchtime came and I, usually a big eater, was not at all hungry, due to the multitude of butterflies dancing in my stomach. A friend of ours who was eating with us kept handing me slices of pizza, saying that I needed more, that I hadn't eaten very much yet. Of course, he knew nothing of my nervous excitement, nor could I tell him yet, so I just quietly slipped the many offered slices of pizza to my dad, who understood completely why I could not eat. After lunch, the group was told that we would all be meeting at a shop in the Old City of Jerusalem owned by a Jewish man who would be speaking to our group. I had been wondering all day how I was going to go about approaching Devin with people around all the time. When Mom heard about the meeting at the shop she came to me with an idea. Why not talk to Devin while everyone was in the shop talking? That way, there would be no one around, and we could have the privacy we would need for our conversation. I thought it was a perfect idea, so I asked Gene if he was okay with that, and he said that was fine. A plan was made for us to get Devin away from the group, so we could talk. I thought I was nervous before. Well, I was even more nervous now than I had been at lunch. But mixed with those nervous feelings were also feelings of excitement. The time had finally come, and I could hardly wait.

Devin—In the Old City

We continued our touring that day by making our way to the Mount of Olives, and from there, we walked down into the streets of the Old City. I was enjoying the time spent in Jerusalem, and several times during the day, I found myself with the Warrens, talking and laughing and just having a great time. Later on, the groups split up for lunch and were told to meet at a particular shop when we had finished eating. After we had eaten, we made our way to the small shop where I began to help set up chairs for the meeting. I had just reached for another stack of chairs when Barrett's mom, Nancy, entered the shop and asked, "Devin, could you come here a minute?"

I set down the chairs and went over to the door where she was standing, wondering to myself, "What could she want?" We stepped out of the shop and she told me that Sarah (Barrett's sister) wanted to know if I would go on a walk with her because she wanted to talk to me about something. My first thought was, "Oh no! What did I do?" My next thought was, "Oh, great, she probably wants to know why I am taking so long to give her brother an answer." I'm not sure where those thoughts came from, and they made me kind of nervous, but I didn't want Sarah to know that, so I agreed to walk with her. We started walking down a small side street and I was waiting for Sarah to start talking—but she wasn't saying anything. I really started to get nervous then. She had asked me to go on a walk with her so we could talk, and she wasn't talking. Not only was she not talking, she was glancing around nervously as though she was looking for someone.

Just when I thought I could take the awkward silence no longer, we came around a corner and there, a little ways away, stood Barrett and his dad, Monty. I stopped suddenly and then the realization hit me. I had not come out here to talk with Sarah; I was here to talk with Barrett. We walked over to where the guys were standing, and then Sarah left my side and went to stand beside her dad. I was standing there awkwardly by myself when Barrett stepped toward me and asked if I wanted to go on a walk with him. I could tell he was nervous by the look on his face and also by the fact that he would not make eye contact with me. I was nervous as well, but decided to just act calm, cool, and collected so Barrett wouldn't know just how nervous I really was. We started walking, never getting out of sight of Barrett's dad and his sister. What made me most nervous was the fact that I thought my parents did not know Barrett was going to talk to me and that we were doing this in secret. But the first words out of Barrett's mouth reassured me that my parents were aware of what was going on. He said, "I talked to your dad and he gave me his blessing and permission to talk to you."

Barrett—In the Old City

As my dad and I went to wait for Sarah to bring Devin to us, my nerves were working overtime. This was the moment that I had been waiting for and it was finally here. I had it all planned out: what I was going to say, how I was going to ask her, and all that good stuff. And then she walked around the corner with

Sarah and all those well-thought-out words went right out of my head. Sarah went over to stand by our dad and I knew that was my cue. I went over and asked Devin if she would go on a walk with me. She said "sure" in such a way that she didn't appear to be nervous at all. We started walking and after telling her that her dad had given me permission to talk to her, I said, "So, I guess you know that I asked your dad if I could marry you?" She said she did and then about the time when I would have given my "speech" that I had planned and rehearsed in my mind, she started telling me about the past few months from her side, about her family and different things that had been going on that had caused the long wait for an answer. By this time, I had already forgotten all my preplanned words, so before any more time could go by, I just said the first thing that came to my mind: "So, does that mean your answer is 'yes'?" She stopped talking and looked at me, and then without hesitating any longer she said, "Well, yeah, I guess it is." When I heard her answer, I let out my breath that I hadn't even realized I had been holding. She said "yes!" She really said "yes!" We were both just standing there looking at each other and I realized how awkward it was. I voiced that: "Uh, this is kind of awkward." She agreed with me. I asked her what we were supposed to do now. "Do we hug, shake hands . . . ?" Devin laughed, and we just decided to walk back over to where my dad and Sarah were standing.

Devin—The Plan

I can't even describe the way I was feeling as we walked back to tell Barrett's dad. All I could think was, "I am going to get married!" When Barrett told his dad that I had said "yes," Sarah came over and gave me a big hug. Monty had tears in his eyes as he also gave me a hug. The three of us waited there, while Monty went to get Nancy and tell her the happy news. When they came back to where we were waiting, I saw that Barrett's mom also had tears in her eyes—and a huge smile on her face. There was not much said—just lots of smiles, hugs and happy tears. We talked about it and decided that we would wait to tell the group, but that we would tell a few friends. We went to join the group and I was sure that Barrett was going to give our "secret" away because he kept looking at me with this big goofy grin on his face the whole rest of the day.

That evening, we went to the Warren's apartment so we could start making plans. First, we had to come up with a way to tell everyone. Different ideas were suggested, but the one we all agreed on was given by a friend who had thrown out an idea, not really being serious. The more we thought about it, the more we liked it.

This was the plan. We decided to announce our betrothal using the story from Judges 21 about the Benjamites who stole their brides while the women were dancing in the vineyard. So the day of the "announcement" came and we told only a handful of people what was going to take place so they could help it all work out. We got a group of people to play music and picked a handful of girls to dance, including my sister, Leah, and Barrett's sister, Sarah. They were the only dancers who knew what we were planning. The rest of the group was told that they were going to be a part of a promotional video that was being filmed. So everyone gathered in the vineyard and "picked" grapes while the musicians played and the girls danced. I was in one of the dance circles, and as the music started, I danced as I waited for our plan to unfold. I had this nervous, excited feeling, and I kept looking around for Barrett. Leah told me to stop looking around, or people were going to start wondering if more was going on here than what they were told. After the music had been playing for a few minutes, I heard someone shout something through the vineyard and thought, "Here we go. This is it!"

Barrett—Back in the Vineyard

I was told that I would know when to go "steal" my bride, so I waited and listened for what would be my signal to go. Then I heard a voice saying this: "Look at all those beautiful young ladies up there dancing. Someone should go get himself a wife. Barrett, you should go pick one of those girls for a wife!" I knew that was my cue to go, so I took off running through the vineyard and up to the hill, where the girls were dancing. I grabbed Devin's hand and brought her with me as I kept running further up the hill and to the other side, where my dad was waiting with the "getaway car." The three of us drove around the vineyard, and then came back—to help explain to the mostly surprised and confused group, who were standing there in shock over what they had just seen. We gave them the short version of how all this had come together, and let them know that they were all invited to the betrothal ceremony that would be taking place there in Israel. Everyone was excited to hear our news, and we got many hugs and congratulations that day.

The next few days were spent planning our betrothal. We both wanted to have it in Israel, but Devin's dad was leaving in a week, so we had to have it before he left. We spent long hours with our parents, planning the ceremony, what we would say, what Scriptures we wanted to read, and planning all the fine details.

Devin—The Betrothal

Things went really smoothly as we made plans for our betrothal. Since it was such a short amount of time that we had to get ready for it, we were quite busy, but everything got done. We were able to get a ketubah in Jerusalem that we both really liked, as did our parents.

The day of the betrothal came and the ceremony was perfect. Our dads read Scriptures and Barrett's dad shared about different things in our ceremony that paralleled with Scripture. Barrett washed my feet, as Yeshua had washed His disciples' feet, and then he gave me a ring. We read a Scripture, and then our parents took turns blessing us and praying for us. We read our ketubah together, then we had some of the elders in our group come up and have a time of blessing and prayer for us as well. After the ceremony, we had a time of fellowship with celebration and dancing.

Our Story

We give all thanks to the Father for bringing us together and orchestrating our story. At the time of this writing, we are looking forward to the day of our wedding feast, where we will be joined as bride and bridegroom. But even more so, we are looking forward to the day when we as the Bride of Yeshua will be joined with our Bridegroom at the great Wedding Feast!

[Note: Barrett and Devin were happily married on April 1, 2012, at the yearly Family Week event, where it all began. They are now the proud parents of a little boy named Sar Kolel, and they have another baby on the way!]

From Impossible to Swift and Glorious

Zac and Becca Waller

Zac's Story

As we hung a sharp right into the park, I wondered if there was more to this outing than Dad had let on. He had asked me to come with him into town to run a few errands. That's all I knew about. My curiosity began to build as we wound down the narrow park road, through the tall pines, and pulled off beside an old wooden picnic table. It was a cool spring morning; the birds were chirping and the trees were swaying in the brisk spring breeze, but as I stepped out of the car, the only thing I noticed was the white envelope in Dad's hand. He walked over and sat down at the table. As I followed, I began to realize that this expedition to the park was to ease the blow from the information contained in that envelope. Dad handed me the envelope. Yes, my assumption was correct. Her decision was "NO."

I guess my story really starts when I was about thirteen years old. I remember Dad sitting my brothers and me down on several occasions and telling us about what he referred to as "the game plan." He would explain, "Your mom and I made a lot of mistakes. We have a lot of regrets about the way we interacted with the opposite gender, and we don't want you to make those same mistakes." Starting with, "Here's the game plan," he would teach us, "When you feel like the Father is showing you that a certain young lady is 'the one,' don't try to get her attention in any way, and don't try to see if she likes you. Pray and ask the Father to confirm to you that she is actually "the one." Give it a little time and then come talk to me about it. You see, when you're in a situation where there's a little electricity going on between you and a young lady, you may become blind to very obvious reasons why there's absolutely no way she could be "the one." Things that would normally be clear may become a little blurry. I want to be here to help you work those things out. I will pray with you, and together we'll seek the Father's confirmation. Once we have that, we'll go to her father and see if he's willing to pray about it and seek confirmation that it is the Father's will. If he gets the green light, then he will talk to his daughter and give her some time to pray about it. If her answer is yes, then we're ready to make a commitment through betrothal and prepare for a wedding."

At that point, we didn't know anyone who had done anything like this before. Dad just knew that he wanted to do whatever it took to keep his children from adding to the devastating number of divorces and broken homes in our world today.

Nothing overly "electric" transpired until I turned seventeen. I prayed and felt like I got confirmation, and talked to Dad about it. Dad felt good about it, Mom was really excited, she talked to the young lady's mom, and eventually word got to the young lady. I guess we were thinking in a more "conservative courtship" type of mindset. By that, I mean that we were very serious about physical purity, but we weren't aware that we should also be concerned about emotional purity. I went into the relationship knowing that I wouldn't hold hands, hug, kiss, etc.—at least until there was a commitment (betrothal/binding agreement to marry), but I figured it would be a good idea to get to know each other (spend a lot of time talking and doing things together), if we were seriously thinking about getting married. I began fasting one day every week and asking the Father to direct my steps. We only saw each other once a week at fellowship, so that was pretty much our only chance to get to know each other. Things didn't quite go like I had imagined, though. Even though I knew that getting to know her was the next step, I just couldn't do it. I would show up at fellowship and leave without saying more than "hello" and "goodbye." All my natural instincts were saying, "Well . . . go talk to her!" But it was like the Father was supernaturally holding me back. I still, to this day, don't know how she felt about that. I'm sure it had to be pretty strange, bless her heart. I had ideas about why I couldn't feel a release to pursue her. I thought maybe it was just a timing thing. After all, we were both pretty young. Obviously, now we know why; the Father was supernaturally saving us for the spouses He had in store for each of us. But at that time it was—well—AWKWARD.

Several months went by, and then a few more. Around that same time, the Father was directing my family to take some big steps in getting HaYovel ministry up and running. My family and I were definitely being called to go to Israel. I guess a combination of the awkwardness, the call to Israel, and direction from the Father compelled the young lady to write the letter that Dad handed me at the park, where we were sitting at the picnic table.

I have to admit that I was a little gun shy after that. I was so sure that I had heard the Father, but I hadn't. What had I done wrong? How could I avoid all that next time? It took me a while to process the questions and consider pursuing anyone.

Several years later, I had an experience where a very unsuspecting young lady was being a little bit forward. To make a short story shorter, I realized that I had defrauded my sister in Yeshua through eye contact. I'm not talking about long stares or goog-eyed gazes. I realized that when that "electricity" started with this young lady, I had started catching her eyes. Every time either of us said or did something funny or walked into the same room, we immediately made eye contact. It may seem somewhat trivial at first. You could say, "Well, you just looked at her; come on." But what I realized is that I was unconsciously feeling her out, seeing if she "liked" me and enjoyed my attention, and seeing whether she would return that attention. I was offering something that was not available, and I was therefore defrauding her.

Though these experiences are difficult to write about, I have decided to write it for you. I want you to learn from my mistakes. PLEASE take this for real and be serious about your personal purity—for His Name's sake.

My regrets:

1. I should have been more careful in conversation with the young lady. I subsequently realized that emotional purity, not just physical purity, IS a big deal.

2. Because I was not 100% committed to marrying the young lady, I should have treated her the way I would feel comfortable with another man treating my future wife.

3. I should have minimized interaction with the young lady. There's a reason why secretaries have "affairs" and high divorce rates. They have very high interaction with persons of the opposite gender. I realized that high interaction equals higher battle intensity. Any good soldier would not intentionally put him/herself in a place of unnecessary, very intense battle.

4. It was wrong to have had eye contact with the intent of giving/receiving attention from a person of the opposite gender.

To put it bluntly, I consider all the above sin and have repented of them to my wife.

The year of 2009 was a big year. HaYovel, as an organization, had taken off and was growing at a rapid pace. We had tripled the number of our volunteers that year. One of those new harvesters was Becca Jackson. She had come with her friend, and was staying for three weeks. It was decided that she would be on the team that I was leading. We had pretty minimal interaction. To be honest, the thought of marriage never crossed my mind.

A year went by, and the ministry was continuing to grow. More harvesters than ever showed up and yep—you guessed it—Becca

Jackson was again among the harvesters. I guess that was the first sign that she was really into what was going on in Israel. Not only had she returned . . . but she had brought a couple of her friends.

About halfway through the harvest, Becca was becoming famous for her hard work and her really good cooking. She was always working in the kitchen and volunteering for whatever there was to be done. I noticed that she had changed a lot from the year before. Somehow, she seemed a lot more mature and focused. Sometime around then, the "electricity" set in, and I went straight to Dad. I wanted to be really careful this time not to give ANY hint of an idea away to anybody. I was surprised to find that Mom and Dad had also "noticed" Becca and were already praying about her for me. Also, I confess I can be a bit of a romantic, and I have memories of Becca dancing on a boat out in the sea of Galilee with a full moon shining down brightly behind her.

After harvest, Dad, Mom, and I continued to pray. I wondered how this long-distance deal was going to work. Becca lived in Kansas, and who could know what might happen between then and the next harvest—if she even came to the next harvest at all. For all I knew, she might already be in a relationship with someone else back home.

One day that December, we received a pruning application request from Rick Jackson, Becca's dad. I was excited to get to meet Mr. Rick, and could see a glimpse of the Father working on details behind the scenes. I remember the day he arrived in Israel. Dad picked him up from the airport and brought him right out to the fields. He walked up, carrying his little medic bag (he's a paramedic), and introduced himself. I remember having some small talk at lunch. We threw a couple jokes around and I could tell he really enjoyed having fun.

Over the next couple of weeks, I took all the non-obvious chances I could to get to know Mr. Rick. We would just happen to end up on the same row, and I would ask him things like, "So, what's your testimony, Mr. Rick?" and "Have you always lived in Kansas?" My question to myself was, "Now what?" Was this trip just supposed to be a get-to-know-each-other trip, or was I actually supposed to pop the question? I prayed so hard and talked it over with Dad. He suggested that maybe we should begin email correspondence with the intention of getting to know each other better and to see if indeed Becca and I are for each other. With the long-distance factor and a slim possibility of seeing Mr. Rick for a long time afterward, if ever, I thought it was a good idea. However, as I prayed about it, I felt strongly that I wasn't supposed to ask Mr. Rick until I was 100% sure that this was the Father's will. One night, just a few days before Mr. Rick left, I was really crying out to God. He showed me very clearly that He hadn't brought me this far for nothing, and it was His will for me to move forward. That was my confirmation; now I just needed a plan. I thought it would be really awesome to ask Mr. Rick in Shiloh, at the Tabernacle site. As it turned out, we were planning a tour for him and a few other fellows the next day.

The next morning, Dad took a van load of guys on a tour up north. Dad had a meeting in Jerusalem that evening, so it made perfect sense for me to take the rest of the group over to Tel Shiloh. It was a beautiful day for a tour, with clear blue skies, great visibility, and perfect temperature. The spring rains had encouraged little sprigs of green grass that now coated the valleys and flowed up the hillsides. From the Byzantine church to the Canaanite ruins, and all the way to the Tabernacle site, I gave the whole grand tour. As is our custom, I finished the tour there at the Tabernacle site and told the men that they were free to have some individual prayer time. The men dispersed, and Mr. Rick went right over to the spot where the Holy of Holies would have been—and the exact spot where I wanted to ask him. I figured I would give him about ten minutes, and then would walk over. I was a little concerned when one of the other guys sat down close by him. Now what?! At nine minutes and thirty seconds, the other guy got up and walked away.

I was surprised at how calm and collected I felt. I had always thought I'd be a nervous wreck when this moment finally came. It was as if the Father gave me a supernatural peace and confidence. I was very thankful for another confirmation that I was in the center of His will. I made my way to the spot and sat down.

"It's amazing to be sitting right here where the Holy of Holies was. Such a special place," I said. "Well," I continued, "I've been wanting to talk to you about something. I've been praying since the harvest about your daughter, Becca. Since then, Mom, Dad, and I have been praying, and we feel that the Father has confirmed to us that she is "the one" for me. Now, I would like to ask if you would be willing to pray and see if the Father would confirm that to you."

"Well, as far as I'm concerned, you're qualified!" Mr. Rick replied. "I've been watching you, and the way you work with your brothers. I knew from the first day I met you that you were the one for Becca. Like I said, as far as I'm concerned, you're qualified."

I was blown away. I had imagined tons of fifty-page emails, long theological essays and handwritten letters that I would have to submit to a young lady's father before he would even consider me.

Mr. Rick said he would call his wife and let her know and he would talk to Becca as soon as he got back. We decided that we would get back together the next day with Dad, and discuss more of the details. Right about then, the rest of the guys started coming back around, so we saddled up and headed back to the ponderosa.

The next morning, I hopped out of bed and headed down to the kitchen for breakfast. I happened to run into Mr. Rick on the way, and noticed he had an almost mischievous little twinkle in his eye. "I couldn't sleep last night, so I went ahead and called Becca," he said.

"Really?!"

"Yep, she's really excited!"

I went into Dad's room and told him. He fell back on the bed saying, "Oh my goodness. I guess we'll talk to him later on today and make a plan." Both of us were really excited. We just weren't expecting it to move along quite so fast!

It was decided that we would make a trip out to Kansas as soon as we got back to the States. I didn't want to talk to Becca for the first time over the phone or through Skype. I wanted our first conversation to be face to face. In the meantime, I began writing emails to Mr. Rick with basic things about what I felt the Father has gifted me in and/or called me to do. In one of the emails, I asked Mr. Rick to let Becca know that my decision was made. I wasn't coming out to Kansas to see if she passed a test or was good enough. From here on, the decision was hers.

It was a long drive from Franklin, Tennessee to Kansas City, but the old HaYovel bus got the whole family there safe and sound. As the bus rolled down the gravel driveway and the red tin house got closer, I could see a couple of people standing out on the porch to greet us. There she was! We all piled out of the bus and started the hugs and handshakes. I greeted Becca, and handed her a flower. It was awkward, but it was a beautiful awkward. We were both in a situation that neither of us had ever been in before. It felt right. There was a purity to the awkwardness that made it almost feel good.

After a delicious supper, I asked if it was possible to have a little meeting with just the four parents, and Becca and me. We made our way over to her Grandpa's house next door, and found our seats. I didn't want to pursue Becca emotionally in any way until she was 100% sure that this was the Father's will for us. So I said, "Becca, I've been praying since harvest and felt that the

Father confirmed to me that you are 'the one.' I talked to Mom, Dad and your dad, and they also feel a confirmation, so now I would like to know how you're feeling about all this. If you need more time to pray, that's perfectly fine. I want you to be 100% sure that this is the Father's will."

Right on cue, her grandpa entered the room. He didn't know exactly what was going on, so he started talking about which day he thought the Feast of Passover really should be kept. After about an hour, Ms. Julie finally said, "Dad, Zac just asked Becca a really important question."

"Oh—well, I thought all that was already taken care of," Grandpa replied.

"Well," Becca said, "after Dad told me, I took three days to fast and pray. Since then, I've really felt a peace about everything. So, my answer is . . . 'yes.'"

The next morning, we went for a walk—with my sister Victoria as our chaperone. Becca knew quite a bit about my past because of the videos, the HaYovel website, and different things, so most of the first walk was Becca filling me in on her life story. The awkwardness really started melting away as we talked and got to know a little bit more about each other. Mr. Rick had a chicken house he wanted to get built, so my brothers and I were able to help out with that, while Becca and my sisters cooked and worked together inside the house. We went for another walk the next morning. This time, my sister, Olivia, was our chaperone. Towards the end of our walk, I asked Becca, "So, what are we thinking time frame-wise?"

She said, "I don't know. What do you think?"

I responded, "I think maybe the really fast option would be to have the betrothal in a month or so and have the wedding at Family Week Texas, a month after that. A more long-term plan would be to have the betrothal after all the Family Weeks, and do the wedding in Israel with Caleb and Kendra this fall. Having the wedding in Israel would be really cool, but I think I like the faster time frame better. Maybe we can have another meeting with our parents tonight and discuss dates all together."

"Sounds good," she said.

That evening, we went back over to her grandpa's house and Mom pulled out her calendar. *This* date wouldn't work because so and so couldn't be there, and *that* date wouldn't work because of the other event. Finally, Dad said, "Wait! There is a perfect day for this to happen; we just need to pray."

After we prayed, Mom said, "If we're sure that this is the Father's will, why should we wait around? Why don't we have the betrothal *next* weekend . . . and the wedding the weekend after that?" All the parents seemed to think it was a great idea.

I was a little too shocked to respond right away. Once I regained my composure, I said, "Becca, do you think that's possible? We don't have a ketubah, chuppah, rings, or anything!"

"I think so," she answered. The decision was made. I was getting married in two weeks! What in the world was happening? This was too good to be true. Better than any of my wildest dreams! I don't really remember what happened after that. At some point, I just took off running down the dirt road, praising God for His goodness!

Once we got back to the house and told everyone there, it dawned on us. We were getting married in two weeks and none of our family or friends knew anything about it! We'd better get on the phone! The rest of the night was spent calling everyone and getting lots of interesting responses to our big news.

From then on, we were busy, busy, busy with betrothal and wedding preparations. We laid out everything that we needed to get done each day and every day we were able to get all of it and even more done. In one week, we wrote our ketubah (marriage contract), got rings, built a chuppah, laid out the betrothal program, and even went horseback riding. The betrothal was beautiful. We had a cedar log chuppah and straw bale seating right out in the middle of a wide open green Kansas field.

We started the program with some praise and worship, and then had the parents say a blessing, releasing their children into marriage. Mr. Rick gave me a key that Becca had given him symbolizing the key to her heart. We read our ketubah, performed a salt covenant, washed each other's feet and exchanged rings. During the betrothal we touched each other for the first time. It was truly amazing! Talk about electricity—WOW! We had a big dinner, stayed up as late as we could, and then Becca and I separated until the wedding.

I went back to Tennessee to butcher a calf and make other preparations, while Becca and her sister made her wedding dress and did prep work on their end. We crammed a lot into that week!

By Friday, about five hundred people had gathered at the campground. Dad, my brothers and I were staying in a cabin close to the campground, while my bride-to-be and her family were in another cabin about a mile away. The intensity was building. At any moment, Dad could give the word (only the Father knows the day and the hour!) and the celebration would begin! Everything was set up, ready, and waiting expectantly for the time to come.

The weather wasn't exactly the best for a wedding that day, so I don't blame Dad for not giving the word then. To be honest, at that moment, I would have been fine having the wedding in the freezing cold and pouring rain! But I guess Dad was considering everyone else's needs. Friday came and went. The excitement and anticipation became more intense as everyone watched and waited all day Saturday. That night, I asked all the young men to come over for a "friends of the bridegroom party." We had goodies to eat and I shared my testimony with all the fellows. After everyone left, Dad called all of us bro's into the cabin living room. My heart started beating a little bit faster. Was this it? "I'm thinking that we'll have a sunrise wedding in the morning," he said. "If we can shoot for having Becca there at five-thirty, then you could come in around six, just as the sun is coming up. What do ya'll think?" Of course, we were all very excited and thought it was a great idea. We threw around time frames and ideas for a bit, set our alarms for 3:00 a.m., and went to bed.

I jumped out of bed more full of energy than I had ever had at three in the morning. The bro's got dressed, got the camera guys ready, and lit off for Becca's cabin. The plan was for them to blast the shofar, bang on her cabin door, yell, "THE BRIDEGROOM IS COMING," let her know that she needed to be at the campground waiting spot at five-thirty, hand her a note I had written, and head over to the campground. "THE BRIDEGROOM IS COMING!" Their voices boomed, and the shofars blasted throughout the campground. Folks began streaming out of their tents and campers. The campground was alive and moving at four in the morning!

Meanwhile, I was pacing the floor, waiting for the time to arrive. I brushed my teeth a couple times, then I realized that I had left my beard trimmer back at the campground, so I pulled out "me rusty, trusty Gerber multi-tool and carved me beard with me scissors." Dad and I drove over to the Tennis Center where all the young men of the camp were waiting. I wanted to ride in with a troop! We did several practice rounds of what I wanted the guys to do when we got to the meeting place.

After mounting my slick Arabian steed, my entourage of about thirty warriors and I set out. Through the darkness we went. All you could hear was the sound of many footsteps and the horse's hooves rhythmically thumping the ground—clip, clop, clip, clop. As we rounded the bend, I could see the lanterns lighting up the meeting place. There she was! I prodded the horse on a little faster. As I came to the edge of the field, I quickly dismounted. For a split second, I stood and let my romantic mind wonder. The incredible thing was that this wasn't some figment of my imagination—some far off, distant dream. The reality of a wedding day, a horse, a gorgeous bride dressed in the most beautiful pure white linen dress waiting for me to ride in at sunrise and sweep her off her feet was *reality*, right in front of me. The years of waiting, the daily battle to stay pure, the fasting and tears, was worth it! The sacrifices were a small price to pay for the picture that my eyes beheld. As my mind caught back up to the present, Becca and I couldn't hold ourselves back any longer. As the distance closed between us, I was overwhelmed. My beautiful bride was running into my arms! I held her tightly for a bit, and then lifted her veil and we gave each other what we had both fought so hard to keep for this special day: our first kiss.

Becca's Story

I was driving a white fifteen-passenger van on the way to take thirteen-year-old Natalee to orchestra lessons. Just two days before, I had received a call from my dad (who was in Israel at the time), saying that Zac Waller had asked him for my hand in marriage! I had spent the last two days fasting and praying about the turn of events. I wasn't good enough for Zac. That I was sure of. He didn't know anything about me. The months I had spent in Israel for the harvest hadn't shown him who I was, right?

Who was I? I wasn't perfect by any means. I hadn't grown up in an Amish community, nor had it even appealed to me. I wasn't like his sisters, and hadn't held convictions as strong as his family. There was only one chord that struck in my heart. I was striving to dress modestly and to stay pure, and more than anything else, I wanted to be a wife and a mother.

When I was growing up, my parents had taught me and my siblings that dating was wrong. The problem was, we really didn't know what to do instead. The homeschool movement, at the time, taught the courtship model. I had read many books on the subject and listened to teachings, trying to see my way through the myriad of options.

When I was little, I was the ultimate tomboy. My favorite attire was overalls and rubber boots. As I grew older, my mom was desperate to get me to see my feminine side. I remember a picture in a devotional we went through that impacted me a lot. It had a picture of a girl with short boy-cropped hair, jeans, and a T-shirt looking in a mirror. In her reflection, she was wearing a long, prairie-looking dress. The words on the picture were, "Am I a maiden, after all?" It struck something inside me, and I went searching to find "me," as a daughter of my heavenly Father. I knew I didn't want to wear prairie dresses, so what should it look like now, in our culture? I started looking in all the wrong places.

Beauty websites became my source of information. It took me awhile to find my own fashion style.

I entered my first rodeo beauty pageant when I was fourteen. It was a huge learning curve for me in the fashion world. I felt like I had found my spot competing in style revue and rodeo pageants. I believed I had captured it all. I was modest and fashionable—or so I thought. I was going to be a light in that world. It was true, I didn't really fit in completely. I didn't have boyfriends, hang out late at the parties, watch the latest movies, or go to public school. But yet I could compete in front of the judges.

When I was eleven, my family had started getting into the Hebrew Roots/Messianic movement and looking into the Jewish roots of our faith. At this time, we started growing a love for Israel. One day, when our *Above Rubies* magazine came in the mail, there was an article in it about a family working in Israel. My sister and I got on their website, watched *A Journey Home,* and started following this unique family. In some ways, we related to the Wallers. We were home schooled and loved Israel. We loved to watch all of the videos that Zac posted on the children's page on the website, and together, we dreamed of someday helping in Israel. I remember that we got a family picture of the Wallers in the mail, and my sister and I tried to guess how old everyone was. To my sister, these men were like what she wanted her husband to be, someday. I looked at it and thought, "No way!" They didn't look like they fit my fashion world. When the interview came out about Brayden and Tali's betrothal, my sister thought it sounded so neat and beautiful. That was the last thing on my mind, when I read it. "No way," I thought. "I am never going to do my wedding like that!"

At sixteen, I watched my older sister, Brandi, at age twenty, go through a wonderful courtship, which, a few months later, ended in a beautiful July wedding. My sister and her new groom flew away to spend their honeymoon in Israel. It turned out to be perfectly beautiful. Before her wedding that year, I had written a poem to my dad, telling him that I wanted him to protect me. I gave him a key that read "A Key to My Heart." I asked him to save it for my future husband. He gave me back a purity ring that said "Love Waits." I knew there were things I wanted to save for my husband. I knew beyond a shadow of doubt that I wanted to save my first kiss for my wedding day. Later, I watched my brother date a young lady and hold no convictions about touching before their marriage, and it, too, ended in a wedding on Lake Michigan.

I had grown up from the girl who was trying to find herself into a confident young woman who thought she had it all together. I thought I knew who I was, covered in makeup and fashion styles. Everyone else told me all the time, "You are so modest," "You are so beautiful," etc.

At Sukkot the following fall, after my sister had gotten married, we attended the same gathering we had joined for the last few years. I hung out with a friend that I had met and connected with before. We had a common love for the land of Israel, and her family knew the Wallers. At this Sukkot, I had a guy that just started following me around. He all the sudden "just happened" to be in the same dance class as me, or he would "just happen" to hang back after youth meeting, while I was talking to someone else. I just brushed it off. I didn't realize how serious he was until a youth game time. Every time he threw the ball, it headed in my direction, and he would never get me out. His attentions were obvious; everyone knew that this guy liked me. We were paired up before I knew what hit me. Now what? I knew I didn't want to date him, so what next? How do I mark him off the list as a possibility or not? My dad talked to him and made it clear that we didn't do casual romantic relationships. This young man was ready for the next step, whatever that was. I wasn't even sure. We started corresponding. My goal was to see if he was a possible choice. I started with giving him ten detailed questions. Some were about what he believed, where he saw himself in ten years, etc. We continued corresponding for awhile, and he came to visit me for my birthday. It was a surprise visit that my parents had planned. I felt unstable and not sure how to handle all of it, but at the same time, it felt good to impress a guy. It didn't take long for me to realize that it wasn't going to work, so I sent him an email letting him know that I didn't think we should continue corresponding, and that was it. I deleted every email, every picture, and tried to erase every memory. He wasn't the one for me. All the books I read said that was okay, because courtships don't all end in marriage. I was happy to be free of the relationship, and knew I had made the right decision.

That spring, when I was seventeen, a friend called me and said she and her dad were going to volunteer to help with the harvest on the mountains of Israel that fall with the Wallers, and asked whether I would like to come with them. I was so excited, and yes, I totally took them up on their offer. My friend said that the Wallers were going to a conference, and maybe we could talk to them there and work out the details. All the lights were green. I started quizzing their daughters, Victoria and Olivia, about what I would need and asked if everyone wore skirts all the time. One day during the conference, my family was sitting right behind the Wallers, and my sister and I were trying to figure out who everyone was. I went home and started the process of preparing to participate in the harvest. I listened to every conference call, took notes, printed off each email, highlighted the important information, and had a binder ready for my trip. I went and stayed for three weeks. That was just enough time to fall in love—with the Land.

I was on Zac's team that year, but we didn't really talk at all. I was just a giggly little girl to him. I went home impacted and set on going back the next year, whatever that would require. We arrived back in the States just in time for another Sukkot gathering. My friend and I hung out together the whole week, working on a presentation about our trip to Israel. I was shocked when, at the end of the week, another young man asked my dad for permission to correspond with me. So again, I started the process, to see if he was the right one. This time, it was different, I had let my guard down more. We not only emailed, but called some on the phone, and started building an emotional relationship. He came and visited me, showering me with gifts and attention. There were times we found ourselves alone and he would push me toward compromising. I started questioning that maybe it wasn't that bad to hold hands, or to sit close . . . but he wanted to push me further than I was willing, and I felt trapped. One time, as he was leaving, he whispered, "I guess you can't say you've never hugged a guy before anymore." It stuck like a haunting whisper in my mind. After he had left, I poured my heart out to God, begging Him to show me the way. I felt like I somehow had to make it work, even though I saw red flags blaring in my face. My parents planned a visit to his family's house. I knew I could not keep this up, so I prayerfully wrote a letter and read it to him in person. I explained to him that I didn't think our relationship was God's will and that I felt like we should end it. However, it wasn't really that simple. I had spent hours trying to see if he was the right one, and in the process had spent time on someone who wasn't. It ended in hurt and disappointment.

I had had this preconceived, fairy tale dream that the first man who asked would be the right one. But instead, I had gone through two bad experiences. Most people would say that this was very harmless, but now, having gone through it, I would strongly disagree. I spent hours in prayer, hoping to discover God's will. I found that the longer the whole process lasted, the more complicated it became. Afterwards, I erased every picture and tore out every journal entry. I wish I could look back and say I handled it all with wisdom, and nothing happened. Instead, I have regrets from the whole experience. I didn't make it through without tears and pain. No matter how hard I try, I can't erase all the memories or forget that it ever happened. I made so many mistakes, while waiting. I was far from perfect, but in my heart I was still trying to follow God's will wholeheartedly. In the world's eyes, nothing did happen. We followed the plan of courtship to a T. We found out that we weren't for each other, it ended, and we went our separate ways. I could brush it off. It wasn't dating, but I knew that I had stolen from my future husband. I didn't stay as emotionally or physically pure as I should have. I spent hours on my knees, asking for forgiveness. It took even longer for me to forgive myself. I was done with guys; I wanted nothing to do with them. I chopped off my hair and wanted to erase it all.

Meanwhile, I had graduated from high school and had to start figuring out what I was going to do with my life. If you asked me what I was going to be, I would have told you a wife and a mother. My mom felt, though, that I needed to do something until then. So I decided to do an online photography course, since it was a hobby of mine. That winter, I got the devastating news that the little girl of family friends had been diagnosed with cancer. I felt the calling to go help their family, and volunteered to be a nanny for them. It was one of the most maturing experiences I had ever had, as I helped fix meals, cleaned house and was there for the children when their mom had to go to treatments with her daughter. I turned from a girl to a quiet woman.

In the back of my mind (or maybe it was in the front), I was thinking about going to Israel again that fall, for the harvest. The family I nannied for helped pay my way, and I applied to go again. I carefully picked through my wardrobe to try to follow the guidelines set for the harvest. That year, I stayed two months on the harvest team. It was an amazing and refreshing time; I didn't have to worry about guys chasing me, and I learned about the beauty of biblical betrothal. This time, I was much more in the background. I was actively involved, working in the kitchen, helping cook and preparing meals for everyone. The conversations Zac and I had were pretty brief—things like, "We need pitas for lunch," or, "Here is a receipt." Overall, it was a very fulfilling time. Though there were challenges, I knew this was where I was supposed to be, serving in Israel. I didn't know how I would do it each year, but this was my calling.

When I arrived back from Israel, Mr. and Mrs. Kenny and Diane Lupinacci stopped by our house on their way back to Tennessee. Before they left, they gave my family the *Betrothed* DVD. I was so excited to watch it and show my parents. I wanted them to catch the vision. I was resolved not go through what I had in the past. Soon after that, I set off to nanny again. I was becoming really close to that family. My dad had decided to go on the HaYovel pruning trip in the spring of 2011. I was really excited for what God had in store for him there. I was glad that he would get to experience it all for himself, and not just through hearing my stories.

It was 8 p.m., and I was lying on Natalee's bed, scanning through one of her books, when her dad came in with the phone, saying that my dad was on the line. I got up, took the phone, and headed to my room. He started off with just the normal news of what the pruning men had been doing, and telling me of their recent tour to Shiloh. As he finished telling me about the tour, he said that someone had talked to him at the Tabernacle site that day. He paused. I wondered why he was telling me that, and waited for him to continue. He went on to say that Zac Waller had asked for my hand in marriage. What did I think?

I was shocked and blown away. That was the last thing on my mind. I hadn't even dreamed of marrying Zac. He was a *Waller*. I didn't even think he knew I existed. After I got off the phone, I called my mom and my sister and talked to them (they already knew). I spent the next few days praying and seeking the will of the Father. Zac was everything I wanted in a husband—everything I felt I needed—but I felt I wasn't good enough for him. Why didn't he pick some girl in his circle? I was sure many more would have qualified better. However, on that Saturday, driving the van and pondering, a peace from above flowed over me and I felt God saying, "Becca, you are a daughter of the Kings of Kings, and this is what I have for you. I created you for a special purpose. I'm a loving Elohim who will give you the desires of your heart." I wish I could say that this was the end of all such doubts, but I can say it was the first breakthrough—the first freedom for me to dream and smile.

Zac and my dad emailed back and forth, discussing how things would go from there. Zac decided that he wanted the first time we talked to be in person, not over the phone or by email. Therefore, they planned a trip to my family's house a week after Zac got back from Israel. I came home the week before, and started to prepare for a visit from the whole Waller clan. I kept myself very busy doing one of my favorite things—baking. My dad and Zac were still corresponding through email, and Dad had started letting me read the emails. In one email, Zac sent a song he had written three years earlier, called "Somewhere Out There." In the song, Zac was saying how he prayed that God would keep his future wife safe and in purity. I listened to the song quietly, and went to find a place by myself to cry. I cried because it was overwhelming to think that Zac had been praying for me.

It was Wednesday, and they were to arrive at any time. My dad left to help lead them to our place. I was making guacamole for the supper that evening, when my little sister, Chaeli, yelled, "I see it! I see the big red bus!" I had been proud of myself, up to this point. I had kept myself completely together, and wasn't nervous. However, when Chaeli saw them, it hit me all at once. Suddenly, I was so nervous! What was I going to say, and how should I act? The only thing I had ever talked to Zac about was food at the Harvest, and maybe a few other things. My mom pulled me to the door, which was against everything I was feeling at that moment. When I walked outside, everyone started piling out of the bus. Caleb was videoing everything. Smiles and laughter, hugs and greetings warmed the air. Zac approached me, handing me a rose, saying, "I got this for you."

Zac and I didn't say much that evening during supper, but afterward we headed over to my grandpa's house. There, with both of our parents, Zac told me his side of the story for the first time. To my amazement, he told me how he had noticed me at the harvest, how he had told his parents (who had noticed me as well), and how they had all prayed about it. He described the clear confirmation he had received at the winter pruning, just before he had talked to my dad. He said he felt it was God's will, and now he was just waiting on my response. If I needed more time to pray about it, that was fine. Just then, my grandpa walked in and gave a speech about when he thought everyone should be keeping Passover. Grandpa's speech gave me time to let what Zac had said sink in, and to let the weight of my reply become a reality. When I gave my reply, even with all the extra time, I knew there was certainly nothing poetic about it. I simply told him, "yes," that I accepted, and that I, too, felt it was God's will.

That was the beginning of some of the most special weeks of my life. The next day, we went on a walk together, chaperoned by Zac's sister, Victoria. I was still a little nervous, and not sure what to say. Zac broke the ice, easily opening up conversation between us. He asked me to share about myself. By the end of our walk that day, all the tension and nervousness had disappeared. During the remainder of the day, we enjoyed good family time, cooking over a campfire with our families. The next day began much the same; we went on a walk again, before beginning preparations for the start of Shabbat that evening. We started the walk taking the same path we had taken the day before, out in my grandpa's pasture. This was the first moment I realized how much of a romantic Zac really is. It started with a hidden blanket in the grass to pray together on, then the discovery of his sweet handwritten letters on fence posts along the way. While we were talking about favorite memories of Israel, we came to a tree that was distinguished by a necklace that Zac had brought me from the Sea of Galilee. Toward the end of the walk, we discussed when we wanted to do the betrothal and wedding. Zac said, "Well, tonight before Shabbat, we'll sit down with our parents and discuss it with them."

We all sat down at Grandpa's table. Zac's mom, Sherri, had her calendar out, ready to discuss dates. We all sat there for an hour, tossing around one date after another. Nothing seemed to be working out. Every idea seemed to hit a rock wall. Tommy, Zac's dad, decided that we should pray about it. Later, before I knew it, everyone was discussing the possibilities of having the betrothal the next weekend and the wedding the weekend after that—at the Family Week event in Kentucky. I must say, I was shocked at first; was this all really happening to me?! Zac turned to me and asked if I thought it was really possible to be ready in two weeks. I'm not sure what crossed my mind when I answered him, but I don't regret a word I said. I looked at him and said "Yeah, I think we can do it." That evening was a whirlwind of events, announcing the news to family and friends. It was fun to hear everyone's shocked reactions and their excited responses.

Thankfully, the next day was Shabbat, which slowed everyone down and slowly let everything start to sink in. When I woke up that morning, I crawled into bed with my parents. It had been a long time since I had done that, and it was a very special time together. Later that day, Zac and I went for another walk. This time, Zac decided to keep it casual, and we just discussed our likes and dislikes. That evening, after the sunset, when Shabbat ended, Sherri sat down with my mom, Zac, and me, to discuss details. All of the Wallers except Zac and his brother, Joshua, were leaving the next day, and Sherri wanted to have food, decorations, and clothing plans set for the wedding before they left. We had already decided that we didn't want to know the day or the hour, but instead have a three-day waiting period. Tommy would announce when the bridegroom was coming, right before Family Week Kentucky. While Mrs. Waller ran through what they did for Brayden and Tali's wedding that was done very similarly, I sat suddenly overwhelmed. Could I really get my wedding all together in two weeks? This is it—the day I had always dreamed about. I had no ideas popping in my mind. At that point, whatever Sherri said sounded great. Zac definitely shared more input that night than I did. Zac tossed around lighting details and his wish to butcher a calf for the wedding feast. After the whirlwind discussion, Zac ended it with a prayer that spoke right to my heart. He said just what I needed to hear, and we all headed to bed.

It is amazing what sleep, a few calls to friends, and talking with your older sister can really do. By the next night, I had brainstormed and compiled a menu for the wedding feast to go with Zac's calf, found a pattern for my wedding dress, and decided colors for the family to wear. The next week flew by so fast, planning for both the betrothal and the wedding. My older sister Brandi had agreed to sew my 100% linen wedding dress for me, and to come stay at my family's house until the wedding.

Zac and I started working on our ketubah (marriage contract) right away. It seemed a little overwhelming at first. I wasn't sure where to start. Zac and I read all the Scriptures together, discussed our roles as husband and wife, talked a little about how we wanted to write it, and then, sitting across the table from one another and looking at our pads of paper, we each began to write. I stared at my paper for a while, not sure how to start or even what to say. I had really no idea what this was supposed to look like, and writing a formal document isn't quite my style of writing.

So, looking up at Zac, I asked what he thought of writing it more personally instead of formally. He liked the idea. Deep breath . . . *now* how do I start? I found I just had to begin writing, and was amazed at how quickly the words came. The hardest thing I had ever done was to hand Zac my paper to read. Worry crossed my mind as I wondered whether he would like what I had written or not. I read his, and again felt overwhelmed by what he was promising to me and how much he was giving me. We looked up from what each of us had written and gazed at each other. The reality of what had happened over the last few days, and what was about to happen in the next few days sank in. At the same time, a complete peace fell over the whole thing. The days were filled with shopping for decorations, baking, making the ketubah and many other things. My mom and sister kept asking, what about this or that? I'd smile and say, "I'm not worried; everything will get done." They shook their heads and said they would worry for me. The Friday morning before the betrothal, Zac and I went horseback riding. It didn't matter about the whole list we had to do that day; we wanted to set a precedent that no matter how busy life got, we would always take time for each other.

The betrothal day was beautiful. All the little last-minute details worked themselves out perfectly, and the Kansas wind blew one last time for me. The chuppah Zac made was set out in my grandpa's hay pasture, surrounded by hay bales for the guests to sit on. The ceremony went well and was beautiful. It was all over too soon, and Zac had to leave. We had decided not to see each other or talk to each other until the wedding day, to show a picture of Messiah coming for His Bride. The separation was really hard, but held much anticipation for the wedding celebration to come.

The next few days of preparation went by very quickly, as the last pieces for the wedding fell together perfectly. I had the cake made and ready to be assembled when we reached Kentucky.

Brandi had my dress finished and pressed, and decorations were all laid out. Everything was ready, and now we just had to get there. We were planning on taking two cars—my dad's truck and my "adopted" sister Rebecca's van. Right before we left, the transmission went out on her van and we found it couldn't be fixed in time. That left us one car short. The first thing that popped into my sister's head and mine was that we could take the train! I had done this with a friend before, and she would be coming with us, so it would be perfect. We looked up all the details, and the train went to a town forty-five minutes away from where the wedding was going to be. Perfect; now we would just have to find someone to pick us up at 3:15 in the morning, and we were set. I texted Zac to see what he thought, and to see if someone could pick us up. His first response was, "A train?" and he expressed his concerns about the idea. He thought it wasn't a good idea for us to be traveling through St. Louis in the middle of the night, unescorted. My dad was sure that it would be fine and that it was safe, so he called Zac, and they booked our tickets. It was the Wednesday before the wedding, and that Friday was the start of the waiting period. I quickly packed what I thought I would need, keeping in mind that I would probably be back soon to get the rest. At three o'clock in the afternoon, Dad dropped Brandi, my little niece Aliyah, my good friend Annaka, and me at the train station. We were soon on our way; everything was going as planned.

We all enjoyed the moments of relaxing and fellowshipping as the train chugged across the countryside. Unexpectedly, the train came to a stop in the middle of a small town in Missouri. Many hours later, we learned that the train had broken down, and that we would have to take a bus to St. Louis, our next connection spot. By then, we had already missed our connection there, so Brandi had to call Zac at midnight to let him know. When she called him, Zac said to stay in St. Louis and Nate, one of Zac's brothers, would come pick us up. We were really glad to see him when he got there, since the bus station in downtown St. Louis didn't appear to be the friendliest place.

On the way to Kenlake State Park, where the wedding was going to be, I asked Nate if we could stop at Wal-Mart. He pulled into the next one, and we went in and bought them out of flowers at five o'clock in the morning. We finally made it in, safe and sound, and spent the day setting up everything and prepping the food. I finished assembling our wedding cake, and made the flower bouquets with the help of Annaka. Everything was set; all the details were laid out. Everyone knew what their job would be when the shofar sounded.

Now it was time to wait—and wait. It was one of the hardest things in my life to wait for that blast of the shofar. I was on the edge of my seat! I couldn't wait to see my bridegroom face to face. It made me ponder my relationship with Messiah. I'm waiting for Him, as my Bridegroom, to return. How anxious am I? I wouldn't trade my waiting period for anything.

It was Saturday night, and we all knew there was only one more day left. My cabin that night was a mess. Everyone was jumping at the slightest noise. Is it them? Is it time? Finally, we all drifted off to sleep, but were awakened at 4 a.m. by all of Zac's brothers pounding on the door and shouting, "The bridegroom is coming!!" I was so excited, to say the least. The time had finally come; what now? I had an hour and a half to get ready before we would meet all the guests at the campground area and wait together for my bridegroom to come. Before I knew it, the time had passed. I was dressed in my white linen dress and bare feet, waiting and watching for Zac. I wanted to be the first to see him. In the distance, I could see the whole group of friends of the bridegroom surrounding my beloved—my bridegroom. He was in the middle of the group, riding in on a horse. I did the first natural thing that came to mind, and took off running toward my man. Zac and I ran into each other's arms, embracing and kissing for the first time. The day turned out perfect. It was my dream-come-true. My Prince Charming had ridden in and saved the day. I'm the most blessed girl ever—to get to have such a beautiful wedding, and such a loving, caring husband. Many people stand amazed, and wonder how we could marry each other without really talking ahead of time or "knowing each other." The world makes us believe that we have to make sure our personalities match up first, and many other misconceptions. The beauty of biblical betrothal is the foundation of waiting and following God's leading through parental authority, commitment to protect the girl, and most importantly, the commitment to stay emotionally and physically pure before God.

As girls, especially as we get older, people are always telling us to stop having faith and believing in a fairy tale—that we can't just wait on our Prince Charming to come. We even let thoughts creep in that maybe dressing conservatively isn't beautiful enough. Doubts come to try to convince us that we won't get married unless we do something to initiate it ourselves. Soon, it becomes difficult to hold steadfast and to keep our thoughts and emotions pure. I want to encourage every girl who is still waiting on that fairy tale to come true: hold fast! Your Prince Charming will come. Don't compromise anything! Don't give up, don't be afraid, and don't settle for anything less than the best.

"Enter Into the Joy I Have Prepared For You"

Joel and Noelle Paul

Joel and Noelle first met in Israel, in a picturesque town called Zichron Ya'akov, high on a mountain overlooking the sparkling Mediterranean Sea. Joel is Canadian, born and raised on the vast prairies of western Canada. Noelle is American, and grew up surrounded by the Rocky Mountains of Colorado. They lived over a thousand miles from each other, each unaware of the other's existence. But each of them was called by God to go to the land of Israel in 2006, and since then their lives have become connected.

Joel – Growing Up

Joel Paul, the oldest of four children, grew up in Saskatchewan, Canada. He and his siblings grew up in a Christian home, lovingly taught by parents who honored God and genuinely wanted to grow in their faith and walk with Yeshua (Jesus). Joel accepted Christ as his Savior when he was three years old. His parents made a decision early on to homeschool their children, and Joel remained homeschooled until he finished high school.

As a part of his parents' instruction, Joel was taught that casual dating was not an option because it is a path with great potential for hardship and hurt for all parties involved. He understood this in principle, but in his high school years he eventually found himself in a friendship that made it hard for him to practice the principle.

He was good friends with a young lady who attended his church, and this friendship became something more serious. They were always very careful to avoid physical contact, but emotionally they became very close. Joel's father approached him with the counsel that he needed to put the "brakes" on his relationship with this young lady. So they set up some strong boundaries and basically broke off communication. It was very hard, of course. The relationship was over, but the feelings he had built up towards her took several years to subside. Joel learned first-hand the great hurt that comes from "awakening love before it is time."

Noelle – Growing Up

Noelle Miller also grew up in a Christian home and was raised to know and love the Bible. She was homeschooled and was best friends with her three older siblings. The Miller family moved a few times over the years, and finally settled in the Grand Valley of western Colorado when Noelle was nine. Noelle's life revolved around homeschool activities, music, animals on the small family farm, 4-H, and lots of time centered on God's Word and family life. She made her personal commitment to Yeshua as a twelve-year-old.

Noelle's girlhood dream was to get married someday, have children, and together with her husband raise a strong family for the Father's Kingdom. Her parents taught her the importance of guarding her heart and living a set-apart life. Even before she was a teen, she knew that she would never date and would save herself completely for one man that God would bring into her life at the right time. Even when the courtship model was becoming popular, her family still felt that there was a better way to establish relationships. Betrothal was a term that was used and talked about often in her home, from the time she was about ten years old. Though at times young men would catch her attention, she would quickly realize that their beliefs and standards didn't match hers and so she was always able to rule them out and not let her day-dreamy emotions go anywhere. She knew that temporary emotional interests only cause trouble and pain. She wanted to bring her husband "good and not harm all the days of her life," and she sought to live as though she was already spoken for, being saved for her future husband.

Going to Israel

Noelle's and Joel's families were Christian, but they both eventually came to a more complete understanding of their faith. Noelle's family had this revelation when she was quite young; Joel's family had it when he was a young adult. They learned that as believers in Yeshua (Jesus) they were made a part of the family and nation of Israel. Therefore, the covenants that God made with Israel were relevant in their lives. They started learning to keep the commands of God as written in Scripture, and the welfare of both the Land and people of Israel started to become a burning passion for both families.

Noelle's family had long dreamed of going to the Land of Israel. They always said, "We'll go when Noelle is seven years old, so she'll be old enough to remember the trip!" That didn't happen, but in God's perfect timing and through miracles that He did, Noelle, her mom, and her sister were finally able to travel to Israel for the first time in 2006. Noelle was twenty-two.

When Joel traveled to Israel in the winter of 2005-2006, at age twenty-one, it was already his second trip there. He had been to the Land in 2003 for several months, and his love for that country was growing. Now, on this second trip, he was going to be there for an entire six months. His goals were to grow in his faith in God, to gain valuable wisdom and knowledge, and to be of service to the land and people of Israel. He wanted to get married, but finding a wife was not one of the goals that he had for that trip. Immediately before the trip, God spoke to him clearly and gave him a peace about finding his mate. He went to Israel trusting his Heavenly Father, not worried about the future but learning to depend on Him to lead each day.

The Meeting

Joel met Noelle, along with her sister, Megan, and mother, Joan, in February of 2006. As part of a group of eighteen people from North America, they spent five weeks traveling around Israel together, doing volunteer work (mostly working in fruit orchards belonging to the kibbutz where they stayed), and participating in Bible studies.

Noelle remembers very clearly the moment that she met Joel Paul:

> Part of our group had arrived early in the day and at supper time we were waiting in the cafeteria for the next part of our group to arrive, which they soon did. We ate at separate tables that night—those who came first at one table and the newcomers at another. After supper, we were all standing around listening to our leader as he tried to talk with the kibbutz folks and figure out details for the next day. Things were dragging out and we were still just standing there.
>
> Finally, one of the newcomers stepped out towards us and said, "Well, we may as well introduce ourselves."
>
> He stuck his hand out to me and I shook it and said, "I'm Noelle."
>
> He smiled and said, 'Oh—well, I'm Yo'el' (the Hebrew way of pronouncing the name Joel).
>
> I said, "Oh, that could be a bit confusing." And indeed, during our time together our names caused confusion more than once.

The group became a team in the five weeks they were together. They all felt a deep bond with each other, and yet there wasn't any flirting or trying to get attention or coupling among the young people at all, in any way. It was a very pure and focused time for each one.

Joel remembers: "During this time, I grew to appreciate the Millers, and we became good friends. However, I had no feelings at all towards Noelle during our time together in Israel. God really guarded me and kept me focused on everything that I was experiencing and learning there."

The group had some fabulous and special times together, and they all felt that God had called them together for a purpose even beyond their time together in the Land, but none of them knew what that meant. They wanted to stay in touch, so once they all made it back home to North America, they started what they called "bulk email." If Noelle wrote to her friends from the Israel trip, she sent it to all of them and if someone else wrote, they sent it to everyone. Noelle's parents also read most of these emails, and because everyone knew that everyone else was reading them, they were always very appropriate and pure. These emails were an encouragement to many of the participants, and for some, they became one of their main sources of fellowship and friendship with other godly young people. They were full of Scriptures, of things each one had been learning, things the Lord was showing or teaching, and words of encouragement and edification. They served as a way for many of them to get to know each other better and grow in their friendships.

Back From Israel and "Fond Thoughts of Noelle"

A few months after Noelle returned home from Israel, a friend asked her if she had met anyone she could marry. She was thoughtful and replied, "Not that I know of right now." She recounts, "I truly had no indication that I had met my future husband, and yet I also realized that I had finally met a couple of young men who had enough of the same beliefs and lifestyles to actually be possibilities. That, in itself, was very encouraging! There was hope that there was someone out there for me!"

Once Joel had returned to Canada, he had a lot of time for reflection. "It was now that I began to have fond thoughts of Noelle. I kept these thoughts to myself, only bringing them before the Lord in prayer. The more I pondered, the more I became quite convinced that Noelle would be a good wife for me. Many of the young people that had been in our group in Israel kept in contact after our trip through our group emails, so I kept learning more about Noelle as we both participated in these emails. But even as I became convinced that I should marry Noelle, I had to struggle with trusting God—trusting that I would know when it would be the right time to pursue marriage with her and trusting that, if God wanted me to marry Noelle, she would still be available when that time came." Joel knew that it would be unwise to initiate a relationship with Noelle until he felt able to commit to marriage.

Trips to the U.S. and Canada

Joel worked hard doing construction work for much of that following year. In the summer of 2007, he went on a road trip to the U.S. with his friend Paul Daniel. During this trip, they spent several days staying with Noelle's family in Colorado. Joel was thinking strongly about the possibility of marrying Noelle at this time, but he had not spoken about it to anyone. He was able to meet Noelle's father, one of her brothers and his family, and many of her friends. It was helpful to be able to observe what Noelle's family life was like. From Noelle's perspective, she and her family were thrilled to have Joel and Paul Daniel come for a visit! Megan and Noelle considered them dear brothers, and their mom loved them. They were happy that their dad could meet some of their "Israel trip friends." Noelle had no idea of Joel's interest in her. His patience and discretion served to protect her heart.

Shortly after that visit, Noelle, her sister, their mother, and another friend all traveled up to Joel's hometown of Saskatoon, in the fall of 2007, to attend the wedding of two of their mutual friends. Joel's family was blessed to have the Millers stay in their home. This was a marvelous reunion of many friends from the 2006 Israel trip. The fellowship was joyous and fulfilling. Joel was secretly pleased to have Noelle and some of her family meet his family. He remembers: "Throughout all these times, I kept silent about my feelings toward and growing convictions about Noelle. God had shown me the value of patience in this area."

Soon, But Not Yet

Right after their trip to Saskatoon that fall, Noelle and her sister, Megan, flew to Israel to spend three months working on the same Christian kibbutz where Joel and Noelle had originally met.

On September 10, 2007, Joel wrote in his journal, "It feels like the time may be close when I can pursue a wife. I have my mind set on Noelle Miller. She's so special. I'm very interested. Maybe when she gets back from Israel in a few months, I should make a move. But I need to get working in the meantime."

Joel intended to start university classes that fall, but after attending several days of classes, he felt a clear leading from the Holy Spirit that he needed to drop out, and so he did. Joel mentioned this decision in a group email, and when Noelle read it, she felt happy and it brought a peace to her, although she didn't understand why it mattered. It seemed to Joel that it would be prudent to start learning a trade that would enable him to provide for his family in the future. He started working with a plumbing and heating company, and soon began an apprenticeship with them. It was good to have a goal in this area.

Waiting

When Megan and Noelle returned to Colorado from Israel at the end of 2007, they felt the Lord directing them into a season of waiting. Instead of returning to her regular life of teaching music lessons and leading 4-H activities, Noelle focused on strengthening her relationship with the Lord and being faithful in little things at home. The months passed, and Noelle alternated between feelings of discouragement and wondering what the point of this season was, and being content to learn patience and trust, learning that waiting on the Lord was just as important as being busy.

From Joel's journal, Dec. 25, 2007: "Megan and Noelle are back in Colorado with their parents, waiting to know what they should do next. I'm still thinking a lot of Noelle."

Winter slowly passed. Joel continued to pray and seek his Heavenly Father's voice regarding Noelle. He was growing in confidence that he should seek to make Noelle his wife. At the same time, it was a dark, hard winter for him, personally, in some ways. It felt as though his hopes for the future were hibernating.

Taking Action

Joel continued working at his job, biding his time. Then spring arrived, and with it some news that in June there was to be a Shavuot (Pentecost) conference for believers in Yeshua in Salt Lake City, Utah. Of special interest to Joel was the news that the Miller family was planning to attend! He thought that this would be a great opportunity to see Noelle and her family again, and perhaps give him an inconspicuous opportunity to speak to Kenton, Noelle's dad, about the possibility of marrying Noelle. When a man is interested in marrying a woman, it is important that he have the blessing and counsel of the authorities in her life, usually, her parents. Joel knew that he had to speak to Kenton first.

Before Joel went to Salt Lake City, he sought the counsel of his parents, and they gave him their blessing to pursue marriage with Noelle. He also spoke to his siblings and some of his close friends to let them know what he was doing. They were all very positive. All this time, Noelle still didn't even know that he was interested in her!

Joel flew down to Utah in June 2008. It was great to see the Millers again. He felt quite nervous inside, trying to figure out when he could speak with Noelle's dad. Finally, on the last afternoon of the conference, he asked Kenton if they could talk. They found a quiet place, and Joel told him of his desire to pursue marriage with Noelle. Kenton responded graciously, and said that he would have to get to know Joel better. They agreed to correspond after they had both returned to their homes. He also asked Joel to say nothing to Noelle until he gave permission, and Joel agreed.

"Not 'Not Interested'"

For the next two months, Joel and his parents, Tom and Laurie, secretly corresponded with Kenton and Joan by email and sometimes by telephone. They were all able to ask questions and become better acquainted with one another's core beliefs and the principles by which they lived.

During these two months, Noelle had a few suspicions that something was going on. She knew that Joel had asked to talk to her dad during the conference, but occasionally young men asked to talk to her dad, and she and her sister knew it didn't necessarily mean it was about them. But there were several questions from her mom and dad over those weeks; questions like, "You've always wanted to grow up and get married, but we haven't talked about it in a while. Do you still want that?" Noelle told a friend that she thought maybe Joel had talked to her dad about her. The friend asked her if she would be interested in Joel. Noelle said, "I don't know . . . I know I'm not *not* interested!" Because she had been raised with the mindset of guarding her heart, she hadn't considered him before—and she had no prompting or direction from the Father about Joel or anyone else.

On July 4, 2008, Noelle wrote in her journal about her suspicion:

> I'm not sure what to think. I always kind of dismissed the possibility to some extent. He's a little younger than I am, though I know that doesn't matter, and I guess I just didn't think he'd be in a position to pursue marriage yet. I admire him immensely. I like him and am fond of him, but I also feel very sisterly toward him. If Joel is interested in me, he is absolutely masterful at hiding it! But he is very much what I look for in a husband, in so many ways. He actually matches beliefs enough to be a possibility! Now, *that* is a rare find!! But I don't know if anything is going on, and I'd better be careful.

Noelle knew that if something was going on, eventually she would hear about it, and if not, then it would be wise to guard her heart and not dwell on mere suspicion.

Finally, Noelle's parents gave Joel their blessing to marry Noelle. Now it was time to present the idea to Noelle and see what she thought about it! There were five "green lights"—from Joel, his parents, and Noelle's parents. Now, they would find out if the sixth (and most important) light was green!

"So they said, "We will call the young woman and ask her personally."
(Genesis 24:57)

The Next Step

On August 25, 2008, Kenton and Joan told Noelle of Joel's desire to marry her, and all that had been happening over the past two months. They told her that they had a great peace about Joel marrying her, and that they had given their blessing, should Noelle decide that she wanted to marry Joel. Kenton told her it was now up to her to pray and decide if she wanted to go to the next step, which would be Joel communicating with Noelle directly.

Noelle's suspicions were confirmed, and yet she still felt surprise, in a way. Her reaction was rather dull at the time. She sat quietly and said, "Wow. Very interesting." Her dad asked her if that was all she was going to say. Noelle told her parents that she knew Joel had a real security in the Lord and vision and purpose in life, and she valued that very highly.

When the three of them finished talking, they prayed together, and then Kenton wrapped his wife and daughter in a hug and said, "Well, this is exciting, and it could get *more* exciting!" Noelle thanked him for leading, directing and protecting through the whole process so far. He said, "That's my job, ma'am." He gave her all the emails he and Joel had written to each other. Noelle went to bed and read the emails, and they left her with a sense of awe for how much unity of belief and purpose she and Joel had. She cried a bit, prayed, wrote in her journal, and then lay awake until after 3:00 a.m. She didn't know that night if she would marry Joel or not, but two things she did know. She knew she trusted Joel's relationship with the Lord, and she knew Joel was praying for her that night.

Her journal from August 27, 2008 says

> "Even though I had my suspicions, when it's reality and something you actually have to consider, it's totally different. I think I'm more

surprised now than when Dad first told me. It sinks in at different times and gets me either crying, seeking and praying, daydreaming about any myriad of related things, or sets my tummy's butterflies to dancing. Deep down, I do have a peace and confidence that this is from God; I'm just not *sure* yet. But I know that I do want to talk to Joel, to take the next step."

A few days later, Mr. Miller let Joel know that he finally had permission to talk to Noelle! With a nervous joy, he called her that night. It was great! In a way, they just chatted like the good friends they had become. But there was an underlying awkward excitement about the potential future that they might have together. Noelle remembers telling her mom later, "After a little while, we just chatted, and it felt like I was just talking with good-old-brother-Joel."

Joan responded, "There's a lot of good in it feeling just like good-old-brother-Joel."

Seeking

As Noelle prayed and sought the Lord and talked to her family about all that was happening, she began to feel frustrated that she wasn't hearing from the Lord in a clear way. Every time she prayed for the Lord to clearly show her His will, all she seemed to hear was, "What's not clear? How can I make it any clearer?" Still, not having any negatives wasn't enough for her. She wanted to receive a positive leading from Him.

Noelle and Joel talked often, and discussed many things. Joel was sure that he was supposed to marry Noelle, but in order to give her the freedom to decide, he hadn't shared this confidence with her. Therefore, in their initial phone call, he had asked Noelle if she would enter into a time of seeking the Lord's will to know if they should marry. About two weeks after they first talked, Noelle felt she really needed to know where Joel stood. Noelle wasn't yet sure of the Lord's will, but she wondered, *"What if I feel we should marry and what if the Lord is showing him we shouldn't . . . I don't feel like I can say how I'm being led without knowing where he stands."* So Noelle asked him: "I'm assuming from the steps you've taken that you are fairly certain that this is God's will for you?" He responded that he was indeed very confident, and that he had no doubts.

Noelle wrote in her journal: "This was a big thing to take in, but it made a huge difference for me. I needed so much to hear from him his complete confidence that this was right; that it was God's will for him." Noelle felt a real freedom and security after hearing Joel express his confidence.

About a month after Joel and Noelle first started talking, God spoke clearly to her through verses from the Bible, to let her know that it was in His will for her to marry Joel. Her family had gone to a mountain cabin for the weekend, and Noelle spent some quiet time with the Lord.

> One rainy, cloudy, beautiful morning, I walked to the top of a hill. I was feeling stressed, doubting and seeking. I just stood praying, saying, "God, I need to know! I need to hear Your voice. Please show me!!"

> And on that mountain, He showed me. He spoke three verses to my heart. The first one was from Matthew 7:11, the second part. *". . . how much more will your Father who is in heaven give good things to those who ask Him!"* I felt that God was telling me to trust Him. I was asking, and how much more would He give good gifts to me?

> Immediately after that verse came another, from James 1:6-8: *"But let him ask in faith, with no doubting, for he who doubts is like a wave of the sea*

driven and tossed by the wind. For let not that man suppose that he will receive anything from the Lord; he is a double-minded man, unstable in all his ways." I'm not a man, of course, but still, those verses were clearly spoken to me as if God was saying, "I'm your Heavenly Father, longing to give good gifts when you ask . . . but you need to believe Me and stop doubting." Both the verse from Matthew and those from James were, I felt, spoken to me by my Heavenly Father, for me.

Then, a third verse came to my mind as I walked down the hill, also from James, verse 1:17: *"Every good gift and every perfect gift is from above, and comes down from the Father of the lights, with whom there is no variation or shadow of turning."* That verse was spoken to me as what Joel is to me: my good and perfect gift from my Heavenly Father. Incredible. It's more real to me now than it was when it was spoken to me, and I am in awe.

The next morning, I awoke very early. Even after all those verses, after God speaking to my heart in confirmation, as I lay there still half asleep, I was praying again, "Lord, if there is any caution, any reason that this isn't of You, please just show us!" And again, part of a verse came to my heart. *". . . Enter into the joy I have prepared for you."* And here, words fail me.

Betrothal

Noelle told Joel what God had shown her, and there was much rejoicing! Kenton said they could now start planning a betrothal. Since they had committed to getting married, they wanted to be betrothed as soon as possible. Betrothal is when a man and a woman make a covenant in the presence of witnesses to be set apart for each other in marriage for life. This was a bit difficult, logistically, since they were separated physically by many miles. But about a month later, they managed to get all of their parents and siblings, as well as many dear friends, gathered together in Saskatoon for a betrothal ceremony on November 15, 2008.

As a part of the betrothal ceremony, Joel actually made his official marriage proposal to Noelle, and she accepted. To demonstrate the joining of their lives together, they both drank from a single cup of wine. In the days before the betrothal, Joel and Noelle had written a "ketubah" (a document containing their vows to one another), and now they read their vows to each other, and they and their parents signed it. Joel gave Noelle a ring as a sign of their covenant.

On the same day as their betrothal, Joel and Noelle were also legally married. However, they did not start living together as husband and wife at this time. Rather, their legal marriage was an act of commitment made in the pattern of a traditional Jewish betrothal, in which the promise to marry was considered legally binding. (Also, in their case, being legally married meant that they could get started right away on the process of Noelle's immigration to Canada.)

Falling in Love

Noelle stayed with Joel's family for two weeks following their betrothal, before returning to the U.S. to prepare for the coming wedding. This time was especially helpful for Noelle. It was a time for her love for Joel to grow. When she agreed to marry him, she wasn't in love with him, as our world thinks of love—yet, she was confident and joy-filled in her decision. Spending time together in the security of the betrothal commitment made it easy for her to release her heart, which had been guarded for so long; falling in love was easy. They both really appreciated this time to get better acquainted with the one they were growing to love. Noelle also enjoyed getting to know her new family better.

The decision was made to have the wedding in Colorado, six months after the betrothal, on May 17, 2009. During those six months, Joel and Noelle spoke on the phone almost every day. They discussed wedding plans, immigration issues, and the important principles and beliefs that they both held that would guide their lives together. Sometimes, they couldn't think of anything to talk about, and they would simply sit holding their phones in silence, reluctant to say "good-bye" and hang up.

Joel was able to make one week-long trip to Colorado in February 2009. It was good to spend some time with Noelle and her family and work on plans together. Other than this visit, they did not see each other until the time of the wedding. During their time apart, each constantly longed for the other, and through this, the longing that Yeshua has for His Bride became more real to them. For Noelle: "It also brought new meaning to how we, as the Bride of Messiah, need to be focused on our Bridegroom and on preparing ourselves for Him. A bride waiting for her bridegroom has such focus and singularity of purpose, and that is how we should be toward our Messiah." This time of separation was special, as Joel and Noelle grew in their love and friendship and looked forward to being together forever.

One of the greatest blessings throughout Joel and Noelle's relationship was the support and love of their families. To be in unity with all of their parents brought great peace during their betrothal time, and this unity serves as one of the foundations of their marriage today.

Wedding

At last, May came, and Joel and his family drove down to Colorado for the wedding! They also had many friends in attendance from all over North America. Their wedding was in a lovely park on a sunshine-filled, spring morning. Joel was commissioned and blessed by his father, the shofar sounded, and Joel led the guests across the park, with singing and rejoicing, to where Noelle was waiting!

Joel brought his bride to the "chuppah" (traditional Jewish wedding canopy) and there, surrounded by their parents and siblings, they reiterated their vows, exchanged rings, washed each other's feet, and shared their first kiss. Then there was a feast and great rejoicing!

<u>Entering Into the Joy</u>

After the wedding, Joel brought Noelle back to Canada with him, and they made their home in Saskatoon. In the fall of 2010, Joel and Noelle returned to Israel for a short trip, revisiting the place where they met.

God has blessed them with four children so far: Kerenor, Joseph, Miriam and a new baby, Ruhamah. They give thanks to God for bringing them together, and are joyously looking forward to all the years to come.

Here is an excerpt from a letter Noelle wrote to Joel on their first anniversary:

> Joel, my husband,
>
> So one year has gone by already. It seems fast and yet I also feel like I can't really remember what life was like without you. I love you so much, Joel. I love seeing you being an Abba to our Kerenor. You are doing an incredible job being a daddy. It is hard to write much or put into words my feelings for you . . . the way I feel when I'm with you—the contentment, the security, the peace, the love. Being with you is my favourite thing in life, my greatest joy. I am a very blessed girl and I am honoured to be the one you love.

You are handsome. You are patient with me. You are kind. You are diligent. You said when we were betrothed that you really looked forward to being a picture of Yeshua to me. So, after one year together, 365 days without any arguing or cross words, 365 days of joy in being with you, I want to say, "Well done, my Beloved."

With all my love, Noelle.

"In that day, you will ask Me nothing. Most assuredly, I say to you, whatever you ask the Father in My name He will give you. Until now you have asked nothing in My name. Ask, and you will receive, that your joy may be full." (John 16:23-24)

The Biggest Surprise of Her Life

Nate and Katie Waller

Nate

It all started in January 2011. I was mixing sound for the worship team at our fellowship, and Katie was playing cello, when I felt that the Spirit had told me that she was to be my wife. It took me by surprise, because I was only eighteen years old at the time and not even really thinking of marriage. I hadn't paid much attention to Katie in the past, and didn't really know that much about her. I didn't even know how old she was. All I knew was that she was a few years younger than I was. In the next few weeks, I tried not to think about her too much. After all, what if it was just me making this up? Plus, we were both fairly young. A month or two went by before I decided I would start praying about the possibility of Katie being the one. As time passed, I realized that there wasn't really anything about Katie that I didn't want in a wife. I observed that she was submitted to her parents, she loved children, was very compassionate, and was strong in her convictions. So I continued to pray, pray, pray, saying, "Father, is this Your will, or is this just me?"

In July, I decided to go to Mom and Dad, to be able to have some accountability and to get their thoughts. I told them that I thought Katie might be my future wife. They weren't really expecting that, although they were very supportive and agreed to pray about it with me. We went to Israel soon after that for the harvest, and stayed very busy, but I still prayed for the Father to show me His will. During the harvest, Katie's brother, Luke, was working with us, and Mom took the opportunity to ask him some "inconspicuous" questions about his family, including Katie.

Through this line of questioning, we found out that Katie was sixteen, and her birthday was in April.

December rolled around, and with it, another Zion's Sake road trip: my brother Josh and I, with a team of guys, went on a speaking tour around the U.S. On one of our long driving stretches from Alabama to Texas, I went to the back of the van to pray, as I had often done. In that time of prayer, I felt a definite "yes" from God that Katie was to be my wife. I was thrilled because, for the past year, as I had been praying, I had never gotten a "no," but at the same time I had never felt a "go-ahead" from the Father, until now.

When I returned to Israel, I told my parents; they were excited and thought that when we got back to the States before Passover, I could talk to Katie's father, Mr. Randy Hilton, about my feelings for his daughter.

A few days after Katie's seventeenth birthday, when we were still camping for our annual Family Week/Passover gathering, I woke up early and saw Mr. Randy sitting at his campfire alone. I approached him and asked if we could take a walk. We walked down to the lake and I told him, "I believe Katie is the one."

He was totally shocked. He said, "Can you say that again?" He had no idea that was coming. Katie was only seventeen, and he definitely wasn't expecting anybody to ask for her anytime soon. I summarized the last year for him, filling him in on the story up to that point. Mr. Randy was very supportive, and he said he'd pray about it and tell Ms. Lynne, Katie's mom. I thought maybe they would talk to Katie about it in the next several days, or at the most, in a few weeks.

One month went by, then two, then three months without Katie knowing anything of my feelings for her. Meanwhile, I was around her family quite a bit, and I had to hide my feelings and emotions for her and just content myself to wait. Whenever we would see them, I'd think maybe she knew. Several times, when

I'd walk up to a circle of people including Katie, she would leave, which made me wonder if she knew. Mr. Randy was always encouraging whenever I saw or talked to him. About a month after I had asked, he told me that he was reading some rabbinic teachings; one of them said a good marrying age is from age sixteen to age twenty-four, and another recommended eighteen to twenty-four, and that he liked the first one. Comments like these kept me excited. Each time I would get a call on my cell phone from one of the Hilton numbers, my heart would skip a beat, thinking this could be "the call."

A Zion's Sake conference was coming up on the weekend before I would leave for Israel, so I thought something would happen then. My family arrived at the conference site first, to start setting up. Soon, Katie and her younger brother, Josiah, came and got their cabin key from me, and from that moment on, I had a knot in my stomach. I was nervous, excited, and not sure what was going to happen.

On Shabbat morning, Ms. Lynne came to me and asked if she, Mr. Randy, and I could get together and talk sometime. I could not think straight for the rest of the day. That night, we ended up getting together, trying not to be too suspicious as we sneaked out the back door of the meeting center at about 9:15 p.m. We talked until nearly midnight. We discussed everything from how it started for me, to what I saw in Katie, to what I felt my life's calling was. It was just a really good discussion, getting to know each other better. I was a little disappointed, but realized how difficult it would be for me to leave for Israel if she knew. It was hard enough already. As the Hiltons were leaving to go home from the conference, I was trying to get a last glimpse of Katie to take a snapshot in my mind. She didn't know anything; how soon would she? I didn't know—but my emotions were running pretty high, and I was trying to act normal and carry on a conversation with her older brother, Luke (I don't know if he noticed).

In Nashville a few days later, I said goodbye to Mom and Dad and headed into the airport terminal. It was the hardest flight I believe I ever flew. All by myself, I felt that part of me was being left behind.

Katie

On a Shabbat morning in July 2012, a few short words changed my life forever. My parents came into my room when I was up early by myself, and sat on my bed. Suddenly, Dad was saying, "We have something to tell you." My first thought was that one of my older siblings was getting married. Little did I dream that it was actually me that they were talking about! Dad went on to tell me that someone had asked for me. "He has been praying about you for a year and a half, and six months ago he received confirmation that you are the one."

In that moment, my life was forever changed. I had a mixture of feelings at first. "I'm not old enough . . . not yet! I'm not ready for this!" And right away I wondered, naturally, of course, who this person was. I was a bit anxious, you could say, because this was so much of a shock to me. Mom wanted to make sure I was ready for this before she told me who it was. She wanted to give me the choice that if I wasn't ready to hear any more—if I felt I should wait—then she wouldn't tell me who it was who had asked. Once she told me, my childhood would be over, and I would look at life a lot differently.

I felt like I couldn't stop there. If I didn't know, then I would be guessing who it was. I sat there with mixed emotions. One minute, I wanted to know; the next minute I didn't. Finally I said, "Yes, tell me!"

At the very moment when Mom said, "Nate Waller," all my anxiety went away, and a great peace flooded my heart.

All I could respond was, "Really," and then I was speechless. I don't remember a lot of the conversation after that, but I knew that my life had changed forever, and I would never be the same.

I never had any checks or reservations about Nate being the one, but I knew I needed to pray about it. This was one of the most important decisions of my life, and I wanted to seek the Father about this man who had asked to become my husband.

All that day, I prayed and prayed and prayed. I had to know for sure, from God, that this was His will—not just what I wanted. That night, as I got in bed and prayed again, I felt the Father say, "Why are you asking me again? I've already given you an answer (yes!)." The next morning, I heard the same thing, and I excitedly told Mom and Dad my answer. After Mom told Nate that I had said "yes," he asked to talk to me, and he and I had our first conversation. He and I had never talked to each other before. I think he might have said two words to me when he was setting up a mic for my cello and once when his mom asked him to show me how to use his phone. This was amazing—to start a relationship completely from scratch with the person I knew I was going to marry! At this time, Nate was in Sweden, headed to Israel, so it was six long weeks before we would see each other when I would reach Israel for the fall Harvest. We talked on the phone once a week with a chaperone, and we emailed every day, with all of our emails going to our parents as well. One of the purposes of this accountability was to keep us from getting too emotional with each other too fast, because we hadn't yet set a date for the betrothal or the wedding.

<u>Nate</u>

Three months had passed since I had asked for Katie, and still, I had no idea when her parents would tell her, or if they had already told her. So when I got an email from Ms. Lynne late one night, it was a little unexpected: "Nate, we thought you'd like to know that Randy and I told Katie this morning that you have asked for her. She was very shocked, then excited, but definitely wants to take some time to pray about it." I couldn't sleep the rest of the night, so I started group-texting my brothers and Luke, Katie's brother. I think it was the first time I had seen the sun rise in Sweden (understandably, because it rose at three o'clock in the morning).

That day, as I was helping Doron (whom I was staying with) fix his camper, I kept losing the screws I was working with. I was so excited that I couldn't think straight. That night, I got an email from Dad. "We're having a going away party at Puckett's Boathouse to make the announcement. Oh, by the way, did you hear her answer was yes!?" He emailed again a little while later, saying he wasn't supposed to tell me. The Hiltons were going to call the next morning. I hardly slept again that night, and when the next afternoon rolled around (morning for Tennessee, with the time change), I talked to Ms. Lynne, and she told me that Katie's answer was "yes." A little while later, I got permission to talk to Katie. My heart was beating quicker now, as this would be the first time we'd ever talked. I calmed myself down, took a deep breath, and called. She answered, and it was so amazing to hear her voice for the first time since she knew. At first, I was a little nervous, but after we had chatted for about fifteen minutes, I think we were both a little more confident. It was a little more reassuring for me to hear the answer from her directly, as well.

Katie

In order to make the announcement to the rest of the family, we planned a going away party for the Wallers, who were about to leave for Sweden. All the family gathered, that were in town, including grandparents, and the rest were on Skype. Mr. Waller began by saying, "We have some big news . . . Nate, do you want to tell everyone?" At that point, Mama Jo shouted, "You're getting married!" Nate played off of her comment and said, "Well, I don't know if I should tell you, or if Katie should tell you that we're getting married." After some of the excitement had died down, Nate told the story. Then he sang to me the first verse of "Pour My Love on You" by Phillips, Craig and Dean. It was only the first hint of how romantic a man I was getting.

> I don't know how to say exactly how I feel
> And I can't begin to tell you what your love
> has meant
> I'm lost for words…

A few weeks later, Nate's mom and his brother, Joshua, flew back to the U.S. from Sweden to be at the birth of Joshua's twin brother Caleb's first child. Josh was staying with us one night, and when I went into my room to go to bed, I found a small jewelry box on my pillow. My heart beat with excitement as I immediately knew it was from Nate. I opened it and found a note and a beautiful necklace. It was so special, knowing it had come all the way from Sweden from my beloved, by the hand of his brother. The necklace, it turned out, actually came from Israel. Nate had bought it about six months before, with the help of his brother Caleb and his wife Kendra, so none of the other guys would get suspicious. This was before he had even asked my dad, so nobody knew, other than Nate's married siblings.

Nate

At this point, the Hiltons still weren't sure if they were going to be able to come to the Harvest or not. A few weeks later, as I was booking a flight, I found a flight to Tel Aviv for a very good price and immediately told the Hiltons about it. To my relief, they bought the tickets and began getting ready.

Throughout this time, we were all tossing around different ideas as to when the betrothal and the wedding should be. I wanted to be betrothed in a vineyard on the mountains of Israel, but that wasn't really possible because all the family wouldn't be there. Our parents finally decided that we should wait until we were all together in person to plan it.

My family and I flew from Sweden to Israel; the Hiltons were due to arrive a few days later. When the day came, Dad and I went to pick them up. We arrived a little early, and I waited nervously for them to appear, trying to think of something to say to Katie. I brought her a large, colored fabric flower, because the roses I had brought from Psagot had already wilted. Then I saw them coming. Katie waved to me and I waved back. I was still nervous, but more excited. I noticed that she was wearing the necklace I had sent her, and she was so beautiful. I was holding the flower behind my back until she walked up, then I said, "Hi, Katie, I got you a flower." She laughed; I think the flower helped break the ice. After that, we didn't really know what to say.

On the way to our base at Har Bracha, Katie's mom sat between us in the van. It was still pretty awkward being around each other. It was strange after having guarded ourselves for so long, and being almost strangers to each other, to now be starting a relationship together. I think it was more awkward for Katie. After all, I had been praying about her for a year and a half, so I had gotten used to the idea. She had only known about it for a few weeks. I tried to make her feel as comfortable as possible.

Katie

It took both of us a little while to get used to being around each other, but we were blessed to be able to spend time together every day in Israel, so we quickly grew more comfortable with each other in our new roles. A few weeks after we arrived, the whole group of harvesters went up to Elon Moreh for a sunrise breakfast. Elon Moreh is the place where God spoke to Abraham, telling him that all the land he could see was God's gift to him and his descendants forever. It is a special place. After a short teaching, we were all allowed some time to go off by ourselves and pray. Caroline (my younger sister) and I sat facing the sunrise. After a few minutes, Nate came up and sat beside me. It was an overwhelming moment. We didn't say much, but the few words we did exchange were special. We sang "Pour My Love on You" together, and then we prayed together. That was one of the highlights of the whole trip for me.

Nate

I was very busy with all the logistics of the harvest and we weren't yet exactly sure when the betrothal and wedding were going to be, so we were taking it pretty slow with our relationship. I think we were both pretty comfortable with that. Having never had a relationship with a girl before, it took me a little time to switch from not showing any attention to Katie to pursuing a relationship with her. It was a little awkward at times, but it was good; that's the way it's supposed to be. For the first few months, we were in that stage of just getting used to being around each other. It became less and less awkward as the days went by and we spent more time together. At this point I was still very busy, so we mostly spent meal times and evenings together. Also, when we went on tours we would spend a lot of time together.

Finally, Mr. Randy arrived in early October. We could now set the dates! He got there right before the Festival of Sukkot. It was party time, feast time! One day during Sukkot, there was an event in Jerusalem and several families, including the Hiltons, were supposed to go. We had a big harvest work day scheduled for that day as well. We were picking about ten tons of grapes, so it didn't look like I was going to be able to go, but in the back of my mind I was trying to figure out some way I could make it work. I could tell Katie was a little down that I was not going. At the last minute before they were due to leave, we were about done harvesting, so I put some other guys in charge to finish it up. I dashed off to get a shower and get ready without Katie knowing I was coming. I told Luke to tell me once she was on the bus (I knew that she always sat at the front), so I could slip through the back door unseen and ride down there to surprise her upon our arrival. When we stopped at Rami Levi (a grocery store) to get pizza, Luke and I decided that he should take Katie with him so she wouldn't get restless and stand up and see me in the back. While they were in the store, I spotted some flowers on the side of the parking lot and sent Katie's brother, Ben, to fetch them for me. When I spotted the group returning to the bus I slid down in my seat as far as possible. Everything was fine and we were back on the road. Katie still had not noticed me, although by now everyone else on the bus knew I was there. I decided I would be the first one off the back door and meet her at the front as she stepped off. Before the bus stopped I was already at the door and as soon as it opened I was out and waiting with my bouquet of flowers. As she stepped off the bus I said, "Hey, Katie, I got you some flowers." She was so shocked to see me standing there, she didn't know what to say. I had been watching her from the back of the bus and knew she had been disappointed that I was not going to be there. It was a fun evening together.

A couple days after Sukkot, we still had not made any plans. I was trying to be patient and wait. We had wanted Mr. Randy to be around so that all of us could sit down and talk about times and dates. But he had already been there for over a week and he was only going to be there for two. So finally, I went to Mom and said, "Mom, this is getting really stressful for me." I guess it was so stressful because we had all said yes and it seemed like we were at the point of going deeper in our relationship, but I didn't feel like we had the blessing to go further. I told Mom all this, and a few hours later she came to me and told me that Katie and I and all the parents were going to have a meeting that afternoon to discuss everything.

That afternoon, we went to an amazing place called Kiryat Hayovel, a beautiful overlook just above the Tabernacle site in Shiloh. The sun was setting, giving it a very romantic atmosphere. We all sat down, Dad prayed, and then we discussed all our options. We came to the conclusion that Katie and I would get betrothed on December 21st and married sometime on the weekend of March 21st. We then had toasts. After that, the rest of our siblings showed up with food, and we had a party! That night was a really big step in our relationship going deeper. I really felt things change; we had the blessing to go deeper.

Starting the next week or so, Katie and I started reading the Bible together every day, with a goal of reading through all of the Torah and the Gospels. I would read the Torah; she read me the Gospels. Soon after that, I asked to resign from my job as Logistics Manager of the Harvest. This made sense, because Erez was getting a new vineyard manager who would be working with my brother, Joshua, for the wintertime pruning. I was not going to be at the pruning, but the main reason was that I was falling in love.

The day I resigned, the Hilton family and I went to Jerusalem to have fun, and for Katie and me to look at rings. And fun it was! First we went through Hezekiah's Tunnel and got soaked splashing each other. Then we went to Ben Yehuda Street and began to look at rings. We looked at so many rings that by the end of the day we didn't know what we liked and what we didn't like.

We ended the day on the Mount of Olives, overlooking Jerusalem. It was so romantic; it was dark with an almost full moon over the city, and we were sitting on a Jerusalem-stone bench under a street light. It was just the two of us (the rest of the family was within sight, not far away) reading our Bible portion together and praying together. At that moment, I felt more emotionally attached to Katie than I ever had before. I felt very connected that night. I was so lost for words, I couldn't say anything. Before too long, Katie suggested we join the rest of the family, as they were waiting on us. Off we went, back to Har Bracha.

Our relationship really began to go deeper after that. We started looking into each other's eyes longer, falling more in love with one another as the days went by, but we both knew we still had a long wait till the betrothal and wedding, so we didn't want to go too fast.

One day, we had picked grapes all morning and ended up having to go to Shiloh to pick a little bit more that afternoon. Katie's foot had been hurting her when she was on it a lot, so I told her I didn't think she should come. I could tell she really wanted to—and I wanted her to come, as well—but knew she needed to stay off her foot. She was in the yurt (round, tent-like strcture) taking care of Asaph (my nephew), and I really felt the need to confirm to her that I loved her. I was getting something out of the yurt, and just before I walked out I remember looking into her beautiful eyes and saying "Ani ohev otkha" (which means "I love you" in Hebrew). I held her gaze for a second longer before saying goodbye.

We knew of a lady in the nearby settlement of Yitzhar who hand made jewelry, so we decided to ask her to make our rings. We had just watched a short video about the significance of wine at a wedding. When you buy something like oranges and make them into orange juice, it doesn't really increase the value. But when you take grapes and make them into wine, the result is exponential. The idea is that the bride and the groom are two clusters of grapes. They can choose to remain separate clusters, even in marriage, and not increase in value at all, or they can choose to become completely one and be so much more useful for God's Kingdom. My sister Havah drew this idea into a design for our rings. It was two grape clusters with a wine glass in between them. A ruby filled the glass with wine. When the rings were ready, we kept each other's without seeing our own until the betrothal.

Katie

Nate and I flew back from Israel together and had a good time talking on the long flight, with Caroline as our chaperone. From then on, we saw each other about once a week until the start of Hebrew classes taught by Nate's oldest brother, Brayden. My family was attending these classes, so this gave Nate and me an opportunity to work on our ketubah. This was a serious time—a time to sit down and think about how we wanted to live out our lives together and care for one another, and how we wanted to show each other our love. When we had finished after several days, we exchanged papers. It was incredible to read Nate's vows to me. To see his feelings that he couldn't say aloud expressed on paper, was truly amazing. I felt safe and secure in his love. After that we wrote out the Ten Commandments and how we wanted to live them out in our family.

Nate

I was able to go down to the Hilton's for our last Shabbat before the betrothal. It was really a special Shabbat. While Katie was making dinner, I washed the dishes. It had been amazing to be able to bless Katie almost every Shabbat before the betrothal. We ate dinner and it was really good; I think it was so delicious because Katie made it. After dinner, we played some kind of spelling game. We were all on teams, so of course, Katie and I were teamed up. I never have been that great of a speller, so she did most of the spelling and I chipped in every now and again. After a while, Katie and I moved to the living room to do our reading and praying together. This was really a special time, staring into each other's eyes and sharing our hearts with each other. It was late before we finally decided to go to bed. We only went to bed because everyone else was, and there wouldn't be anyone to stay up with us. The next morning we read the Torah together, and then we were off to fellowship, Katie riding with me. It was a wonderful feeling to have my bride-to-be sitting in the passenger's seat. I was just wishing I could hold her hand. It was a wonderful Shabbat.

Katie

On December 18th, my family arrived at Cedars of Lebanon State Park, where the betrothal was to be held on Thursday the 20th. Nate got there a few hours after we did, and as I went to meet him, he remarked, "We're finally here; it's exciting!" Oh, it was exciting. To be there at last, with not much more to do to prepare, to just spend two days with Nate, and then to be betrothed to him!

Wednesday was a fun day; we played softball almost all day and then took a walk, and Mr. Tommy took some pictures of Nate and me on a wooden bridge. He got some good pictures, and we made some fun memories. That night, we sat around as families and everyone started telling stories about Nate and me when we were little. Then we played games, and while everyone was still playing, Nate and I decided we wanted to read. It was really loud in the cabin, and there was a bench on the front porch, so we got permission to go out there, left the cabin door open, and settled down to read our Scripture portion. We especially wanted to get our reading time in because we only had one more chance (the next day) to read when we were together before we would separate. That was a special night, reading and praying together, then talking and gazing into each other's eyes. Oh, it was so amazing to look into Nate's eyes. It was so hard saying "goodnight" when it was time to go to bed, but exciting at the same time, because the betrothal was the next day.

Thursday was rainy, and very cold. We had Scripture reading in the morning, together as families, and then my oldest brother, Alex, and his wife, Katie, arrived. Everyone was busy getting

ready, ironing, decorating, setting up, and writing out their blessings. Nate and I sat out on the porch again on the couch in front
of the window, so everyone could see us. It was windy and cold
out there, but we were just happy to be together, knowing that
we didn't have very long before we wouldn't see each other again
for three months. We read our Scripture portion for the last time
together before the betrothal, and prayed and shared with each
other.

Later, we went over to our cabin where the betrothal was
going to be and added some last minute things to our ketubah,
and I ironed Nate's shirt and pants. Then I needed to go iron my
dress and get ready, because it was getting close to the time and
Nate needed to get ready as well, so we separated about an hour
before it was supposed to begin. I still had very mixed feelings. I
was so looking forward to being able to feel Nate's touch and to
hold his hand, and for us to fully commit ourselves to each other,
but I knew that afterwards he would be leaving, and I wouldn't
see him for three months.

Nate

I was soon ready, and as everyone was gathering I sat at a small
table in the front of the room. Dad opened in prayer, and with
that Mr. Randy walked Katie downstairs. She was so beautiful, so
lovely, and her dress was gorgeous. Her hair was down—it was
beautiful. She sat across the table from me as I stood and read my
vows and poured a glass of wine. I held it up, said the blessing,
and drank from it. As I handed the cup to Katie, my hand began
to shake. Even though she had already said "yes," her drinking
the cup was the final yes; after that, we would be completely committed. She took it and drank it! I then took Katie's hand in mine
and slid on her ring to seal the covenant. Oh, the first touch was
exhilarating, and my heart was fluttering—to hold my beloved's
hand for the first time—it was beautiful, so amazing. Katie then

read her vows and slipped a ring onto my finger. The covenant was made and we were betrothed. We moved the table and sat right beside each other. It was the most awesome feeling to hold her hand and to feel her tight grip on mine. After she slipped the ring onto my finger, she said "I love you" for the first time. It was so incredible to hear her say that. Next, we washed each other's feet. It was amazing to wash my beloved's feet—just to feel them, to rub my hands over them—oh, they were beautiful—and to look up into her loving eyes as the song "Pour My Love on You" played. Then I felt my beloved washing my feet with her gentle, loving hands. It was an awesome feeling to look down into her longing eyes and to feel her love so strong. Our parents blessed us, we did a salt covenant, and then all of our siblings and the elders blessed us. It was a memorable time.

After the ceremony, we, along with our parents, signed our ketubah. After we got some pictures, everyone else went over to the other cabin, where we would be eating. Katie had to run upstairs to get her shoes, which gave me a brief moment to take in everything that had just happened. She was back and out we went on our first walk, holding each other's hands. Even though it was short, it was special. As we walked I looked down into her eyes and said, "Ani ohev otach," and she looked up at me and said, "I love you." It was a special moment. We went in and our plates were served. I ate with my left hand so that I could hold Katie's hand as we ate. After eating, we just sat there and leaned against each other, inching closer and closer. Soon our fingers were intertwined and we were resting our heads on each other's while I caressed Katie's beautiful arms of love. Others cleared up from the meal while we stood in the corner and then moved to the stairs, but we soon realized that this was not going to work, as there was too much traffic. A couple of the guys carried one of the couches back in for us. We were going to sit on the couch, but before we reached it we decided to dance. Dad turned on some slower music, and Katie and I began to waltz around the room.

There is something romantic about dancing with your bride. Oh, the romance at that moment was so overwhelming: my first dance with a girl who was not one of my sisters, and to look into her eyes as we moved in step. We moved to the couch after our first dance. Sitting so close, rubbing her arms, I was longing for the day when I could put my arms around her and kiss her beautiful face. When Katie laid her head on my shoulder, it almost took my breath away. It felt so incredible for a beautiful girl to rest against me.

Before long, Dad said the time had come for us to separate for a time. As Dad prayed over us, Katie snuggled her face into my shoulder and I rested my head on hers. When he said "amen," I turned and took her hands that I had held so close from the moment we had first touched, looked into her beautiful, longing eyes, and said, "I'm going to prepare a place for you." We slowly slipped our hands away from each other. I walked over and grabbed my backpack and stopped at the door to gaze into her eyes one last time. She walked over and took my hand once again. We said our final "goodbyes" and "I love you," and I was off. I wouldn't see her again for thirteen long weeks.

Katie

The morning after the betrothal, I woke up a different person. I had a ring on my finger signifying that I belonged to Nate, and I began to wear a head covering. Nate and I had talked about this beforehand, and we decided that I would begin to wear a head covering after the betrothal. I wear one to show that I am submitted to Nate and that he covers me. Another reason I believe a head covering is important for me to wear is to save my hair only for my husband.

I found an email from Nate that morning—a most romantic email, I might add—and we had a very special phone conversation that afternoon.

The weeks that followed were very difficult. We had given our hearts away to each other, so being separated was very hard. Nate was busy building our house (a yurt), and I was trying to graduate from high school, so we talked on the phone after dinner every night. We would talk for several hours, read our Scripture portions, and pray together. This went on for three months. This season was a time for us to learn to trust and draw closer to our Father, and it was also a time of drawing close to each other long- (or short-) distance. It was definitely a difficult season, but it was well worth it.

My sisters, Nate's sisters, and I got together several times to sew clothes for all the siblings to wear at the wedding. They made most of my wedding dress, since I don't do much sewing. I embroidered my sash and also made Nate's shirt, with supervision.

One special memory I have happened a couple of weeks before the wedding. It was preparation day, getting ready for Shabbat, and that afternoon, I offered to mail a package at the post office for Mom. I knew it would help her, and also, I didn't mind getting out of the house for a few minutes. I stopped by Dollar General as well, and was probably gone for about twenty minutes. When I returned, I walked into my room, and there were two dozen roses on my bed! Immediately, I guessed that they were from Nate, but I was confused as to how they had gotten there! There was a romantic note next to the flowers. It turns out Nate and my sister Abby had been plotting all day how to surprise me. Mom was going to send me to the post office if I hadn't asked. Nate was waiting behind the gas station down the street, and as soon as I left he drove into the driveway and left the flowers on my bed. When he came through the door, my younger siblings looked at him and exclaimed, "What are you doing here? Wait, where's Katie?" They thought there must be some terrible mistake.

The closest we ever got to each other was when we were both in Franklin, Tennessee, shopping at the same time. We were about five minutes away from each other, texting each other to make sure we weren't at the same store.

The week before the wedding, Nate and I decided to discontinue our nightly phone calls. It was becoming too difficult to even talk to each other without seeing one another, because of how close we had gotten in our relationship. There were a few more reasons as well. First, we wanted to be able to spend more time with our families, and second, we thought it would make the wedding even more special if we hadn't even talked in a while. We continued to text each other until the Wednesday night before the wedding weekend. The "weekend" officially started on Thursday evening, and went through Sunday morning.

On Thursday, my sisters and Mom and I moved into a cabin to wait for the announcement that the bridegroom was coming. Later that afternoon, Nate's sisters also came to be with me, and they decided to spend the night. After all, they didn't want to miss the announcement! We spent a fun girls' night, but I don't think I was all there in my mind. My heart was beating faster than normal, and I had a false alarm once when my dad knocked on the door! It sounded like pounding to me :-). The next morning I went out to look for something in the car, when I looked up and saw our green fifteen-passenger van approaching! It must be "time"! I quickly exited the car and turned to go inside so we could all hear the announcement together, but I was stopped as the van pulled to a halt in front of me and Brayden jumped out and shouted, "We have an announcement!" Then most of my brothers and all of Nate's brothers yelled, "The bridegroom is coming!" Luke (my older brother) ran forward and handed me a note from Nate, and told me that the bridegroom would arrive at the campground at ten o'clock. I ran inside and they all followed, making their announcement again at the door for everyone else.

From there, they went to the campground, letting everyone there know that "the bridegroom is coming!"

All the sisters and I started getting ready in a hurry. We only had one curling iron, and seven girls' hair to be curled. This was about 8:30 a.m., and we had to be ready at ten. Nobody had eaten breakfast yet, and no one wanted to stop to eat, so Mom made us smoothies. The problem was, we were all already in our white and cream dresses, so how could we drink blueberry smoothies without any spills? This was the funniest memory of the morning. We ended up bending over, trying to drink without spilling. It was pretty hilarious.

We had a grand time getting ready. Excitement was mounting. After all, I hadn't seen Nate in three long months, and now I was getting ready to run into his arms, never to be separated from him in that way again. Finally, we got all seven girls and our moms ready and off we drove to the campground to wait for Nate's arrival. It was about forty degrees outside, so we were shivering a bit as we stood there waiting. A crowd had gathered, and the atmosphere grew more intense as time ticked away. I was surrounded by my parents and sisters and new family, and we waited and waited, straining to look for the coming bridegroom. Finally, I caught a glimpse of a horse through the trees, and everyone started shouting, "He's coming, he's coming!" My beloved was galloping closer and closer on a majestic horse, followed by a truck and trailer filled with our brothers playing instruments and singing. As he came around the corner of the woods I waved high in the air. He was actually coming! I began to walk to meet him, and as I drew close he dismounted and we ran into each other's arms. Oh, that moment is difficult to describe. I was wrapped in his big, strong arms, and I knew he would never let me go again. And that first kiss. It was AMAZING, saving myself completely for this man to whom I was now married.

After that, it was a cold, happy blur. We had a short ceremony, some dancing, and some food. I do remember that during the ceremony Nate sang once again "Pour My Love on You." It was a complete surprise, and it was very special.

Before too long, we left to go to the place Nate had prepared for me. It was so cozy and romantic inside, with a fire going in the wood stove. We had a romantic first seven days before we went back to Family Week for a huge wedding feast. The first morning was a Shabbat, so we couldn't cook anything and we didn't have everything we needed, so we ended up eating yogurt out of wine glasses with forks.

Nate

Once we had committed to one another in the covenant of betrothal, we were released to fall in love completely. Everything went to a whole new level in our relationship once we were one hundred percent committed.

I think both of us weren't quite sure of the reason for the waiting period, other than the picture of Yeshua leaving and coming back for His Bride. During the intervening months, we began to understand. I started work on our home (a yurt)—preparing a place for my bride. During this time we talked for two to three hours on the phone every night. I would send Katie a love email every morning for her to read when she awoke, and we would text throughout the day. I also downloaded a countdown app and would send her a text every morning, with how many more sleeps we had until the wedding weekend.

It was about halfway through this period that we began to realize what the waiting period was all about. It was about trust: expressing love and endearment without touch, but instead, only by words. It was really a strengthening time for our relationship. It bound us together in a deeper way. We read the Bible and prayed together every day on the phone. It was hard, but it was really good.

We decided not to talk on the phone during the final week before the wedding for several reasons. One, it was getting harder and harder to hang up every night. Two, we wanted to spend more time with our families, and three, we really wanted to focus on being ready. I finished the yurt the day before I was going to go to Kenlake for the wedding. (A yurt is a round Mongolian tent that is built with lattice work and a thick canvas cover.)

I had prepared the place, and now I was off to get my bride. We had everyone come out for a three-day campout, and no one knew the day or the hour except my father. We wanted it to be a picture of Yeshua and His Bride; we don't know the day or the hour of His coming, but we must be ready. So Katie had to be ready for when my father sent me to get her.

On Thursday night, we had a "friends of the bridegroom" party, but I wasn't really "there," knowing that at any time after six o'clock, Dad could say that it was time. I didn't sleep much that night. We all slept in a cabin a few miles from the campground where everyone else was staying.

The next morning when we got up, Dad gave us the plan. The sound system had blown a fuse the night before and I had been working on it fruitlessly until about 11:30 p.m., so that morning someone had to go into town to get another fuse and put it all back together before anything could happen. We decided to send Joshua in to get it, and when he got back, the guys would make the announcement that the bridegroom is coming. This would give Katie one hour to get ready and get to the campground. She was staying in a cabin close by.

Finally, Joshua returned, and all the brothers raised the cry that the bridegroom was coming. We all went to a building nearby, where I was to pick up the white horse (well. . . actually, a palomino) that I would ride to the campground. My brothers were all going to ride in behind me on a trailer, where they would be playing music, but the sound board blew the fuse again, just before we were about to go over. We were running around, trying to get something to work, and in the process I got a big grease smear on my pants. I ran to the bathroom and scrubbed it out as much as possible. We decided to proceed without the sound system and go all acoustic, which ended up working out really well. Dad prayed and then he said, "The time has come." Off I rode to get my bride! The horse wouldn't go fast enough for me, even at full speed; it seemed we were in slow motion. As I rounded the bend in the road, there she was, so beautifully dressed in white. I galloped onto the grassy field where Katie was waiting, my brothers right behind me on the trailer, playing instruments and singing a crescendoing melody. As I rode in, Katie came running to me. I leaped off of the horse and embraced her for the first time. It was an amazing moment. Then we kissed our very first kiss.

We had a short ceremony. We read our vows, drank the cup, our parents blessed us, and I sang a song. We had some hors d'oeuvres, and we were off. I was taking my bride to the place I had prepared for her. We had decided to have our wedding and then seven days later, we would return for the wedding feast. This is an ancient Biblical custom that is believed to date back to Jacob and Leah (Genesis 29). We thought we would be able to enjoy the feast more, and all the company as well, if we waited—and the timing was convenient because most of the guests were staying at the campground for the seven-day Festival of Unleavened Bread. So seven days later, we returned to a grand feast. My brothers had slaughtered the fatted calf. After the feast, there was dancing and celebration late into the night.

We took our first year off, doing everything together. We were blessed in January with a little boy whom we named Chananyah Ben-Tzion. It means God has shown favor to a son of Zion. God has truly shown favor to us.

The Man and the Maid

Written by Brayden Waller for Nate and Katie's Betrothal

Proverbs 30:1, 18-19 (KJV) The words of Agur the son of Jakeh...
*There be three things which are too wonderful for me, yea, four which I know
not: The way of an eagle in the air; the way of a serpent upon a rock; the
way of a ship in the midst of the sea; and the way of a man with a maid.*

In the mind of Agur the son of Jakeh
The way was unknown of the man with a maid
The passion, the purpose of this drama divine
Makes all other riddles take second in line.
What perplexed Agur has perplexed me too,
And the answer remains that I have not a clue
How love's fires lit are like fine dry tinder
That expands to a blaze no forest can render.
From Adam and Eve to the Shulamite girl,
Romance has captured the heart of the world.
A bachelor, once lonely, began a new life
By trading a rib in exchange for a wife,
Not that ol' Adam had a say in the deal,
But his Maker a story was soon to reveal.
This story outstretches the sky in its span—
How a woman was formed to complete a man.
From Eden, this saga was launched to soar
Through time and space till time no more,
How a man was humbled and cut in the side

To supply from himself the needs of his bride.

The first and last Adam were looking for one

Who would share in their dreams and leave them for none.

The mystery is great, but the intention clear

Of the man and the maid in the parable here:

The great deficit staged is a man alone

Who waits to be joined to bone of his bone;

The years of waiting, a helper to meet

Are seen as mere moments when the two are complete.

The goodness and favor that a wife does bring

Makes the virtue of waiting a rewarding thing

There are three, said Agur, too wondrous for me:

The way of these,

An eagle in air, a snake on a rock and a ship on the sea.

The first couple flew high like an eagle in flight.

As they walked with their God, arrayed in His light

Until the serpent so sly came to deceive

The mother of life—the woman named Eve.

The height that you long for your marriage to reach

Will be gauged by the measure of Satan's defeat.

That serpent of old will meet his demise

And the man of the maid will break through the skies

To rescue the bride whose garments were purged

As she went through the fire and spotless emerged.

But till that day, we are reminded well

By the parable your lives live to tell,

So as you go from here, your ship to guide,

Hang on tight and enjoy the ride.

A haven's waiting at your journey's end

When you meet face to face your bridegroom friend.

The journey will really begin at that call,

For *that* romance will be the crowning of all.

A Story Only the Almighty Could Write

Christopher and Emily Fournier

Christopher

I have had the blessing of growing up in a home with parents who love and fear YHWH with all their hearts and who have dedicated their lives to raise the next generation in the love of YHWH, in purity and in righteousness.

When I was young, my father instructed me to, *"Keep your heart with all diligence, For out of it spring the issues of life"* (Proverbs 4:23). My father shared with me that the greatest gift I could give to my future wife would be a pure heart and eyes that were kept only for her. As I began to grow up into young manhood, I came to realize just how much the world desires to keep us from maintaining purity of heart. Since YHWH is the fullness of purity, not only do the pure in heart see YHWH, but all those who see the lives of those who walk in purity see a glimpse of YHWH. For this reason our adversary, the devil, seeks to mar YHWH's name by defiling us. Maintaining a pure heart in a corrupt world is not always easy, but the blessings that it brings are sure and lasting. As I became a young man, I began to be confronted with the temptations that every young man faces. I took to heart the warnings of Solomon, *"Rejoice, O young man, in your youth, and let your heart cheer you in the days of your youth; walk in the ways of your heart, and in the sight of your eyes; but know that for all these [Elohim] will bring you into judgment* (Ecclesiastes 11:9). Like Job, I made a covenant with my eyes that I would not gaze on a virgin. (Job 31:1) I have been very blessed to have a father who has encouraged me to remain pure and who has prayed with me throughout these most crucial years of my life.

Growing up in a conservative family has produced in me strong convictions in many areas in life. When I came to the age when my thoughts as a little boy of staying in my father's house all my life began to give way to desires of having my own family and a wife to cherish, protect, and provide for, I began to realize just how precious a gift it would be to find a young woman who held to the same values as I did. When I was eighteen, YHWH began to reveal to my family and me His truths concerning His Sabbaths, Feasts, and His Torah. I eagerly embraced all of these truths, though I realized that the path of finding a righteous, YHWH-fearing wife was only getting narrower. If YHWH had a wife and family in store for me, then that young woman was now rarer than I had previously thought. I firmly believed that YHWH was not limited, and that if it was His will for me to be married, and if He could make Adam a helpmeet out of his rib, then He could most certainly fashion one for me. If you will care to bear with me a little while longer, you will find out that such miracles do indeed take place!

As a young man I realized that it was my responsibility both to protect my heart and my sisters' in Yahshua, by being chaste in my behavior and not making eye contact with young women. A young woman should never have to struggle because a young man leads her on through flirting with his eyes. True love for our sisters is that we guard and protect them by our modest behavior. We must seek to do and say only that which is pleasing to our Savior. *"As obedient children, not conforming yourselves to the former lusts, as in your ignorance; but as He who called you is holy, you also be holy in all your conduct, because it is written, 'Be holy, for I am holy'"* (1 Peter 1:14-16). *"Flee also youthful lusts; but pursue righteousness, faith, love, peace, with those who call on the Lord out of a pure heart"* (2 Timothy 2:22).

Many years back, YHWH opened my eyes to how destructive the process of dating is. For one, it teaches young people to give their hearts to one another and then to break up. Dating around or going from one girl to another encourages an unhealthy pattern of being discontent in your relationship and in many cases creates a pattern which continues into marriage and eventually leads to divorce. Many young men and women are scarred for life because of the dating game. Marriage is holy, and if we prepare for it in holiness, then YHWH will reward us with the fullness that He intends for marriage. Dating destroys the process of holiness and is a path that produces many broken marriages.

This past year, YHWH had put an increasing desire in my heart that He would be the One to give me my wife. I realized more and more that I only wanted the woman YHWH thought suitable for me. I know that I have much to learn, and I knew that YHWH would be faithful to give me the wife that would make me the man He wants me to be. My greatest desires were that she would love YHWH above all else, that she would be modest in behavior, and that she would be submissive in heart.

Several times this past year, a feeling came over me that I would be getting married within the next year. I ignored the feeling because I could not see how it would be possible. There was no young woman in my life that I felt YHWH leading me to marry. In all honesty, I had no clue how YHWH would ever reveal who He would choose to be my wife. We had met some families with young women that had virtuous qualities, but I did not feel YHWH's peace or leading. In this way, I knew from experience how YHWH would tell me which ones were not for me, but I didn't know how YHWH would tell me which young woman was the one for me. I had faith that YHWH would reveal it clearly when the time would come.

Emily

My family and I were not sure how we were going to go about "finding" spouses for my five siblings and me. When I was about eight years old, we decided that we did not want to follow the world's way of dating. We had seen so many examples of broken relationships that we concluded that dating did not work. We were searching hard for another way. Until about two years ago we had planned to follow the courtship method of finding a spouse. In the spring of 2009, we were introduced to the betrothal process...

There had been several things going on in my family that I thought could make it nearly impossible for my siblings and me to "find" spouses. There were many times I was about to give up, and though I wanted to get married, at the same time I was not sure that I did. After we went through a tough family situation earlier this year, I gave all of my desires and concerns about marriage to YHWH. Little did I know what would happen during Sukkot, about six months after I gave it all to Him.

Christopher

Through a series of events our family decided to celebrate the Feast of Tabernacles in 2011 at Montgomery Bell State Park. I was driving one of our vehicles, and as I drove into the campground, one of the first families I saw was the Massey family. We had met them a couple times over the past two years, but had never really gotten to know them. Little did I know that one of the young ladies I saw as I pulled into the campground was the gift YHWH had chosen for me, nor did I know that this feast would impact the rest of my life. Emily's brothers, Jacob, Samuel, and Isaac, came over and helped us put up our tents and set up our campsite.

Jacob and I became fast friends and spent a lot of time together during the feast. Throughout the week, we talked a lot about Scripture and found out that our families had much in common. On the evening of the first day of the feast we had the Massey family over to our camp for dinner; we had a wonderful time. I immediately noticed that Emily and her sister, Lauren, had gentle and quiet spirits and were modest both in their behavior and in their dress. This blessed me tremendously. I thought that I would casually observe them as they interacted with my sisters throughout the week. At this time, I had no thoughts except that it blessed me to see their love for YHWH and their hearts of purity. Throughout the course of the week, we were at each other's campsites every night. On the third day of the feast, some of the men wanted to go out to our farm and help us work on our house. We were in the process of building our house, so there was lots of work to be done. The whole Massey family volunteered to go and help.

As my family and I have read the Scriptures over the past few years, we have been led to live a more agriculturally-based life. We realized we had become entirely dependent upon man and his system, and this could end in a trap. We desire to live dependent upon YHWH and what He provides us through His creation. We have, over the past few years, begun to farm with horses and have sought to grow as much of our own food as possible. This lifestyle also caused the road to become narrower in my avenue of finding a wife. There are not many young women who would, when it comes down to it, actually like to live without many of the comforts in the mainstream life. It was not until after YHWH spoke to me concerning Emily that I found out that these same things were on her heart as well. But I am getting ahead of myself; let me get back to how it all happened.

I worked with my brother and one of Emily's brothers on our house that morning. After lunch, my dad and some of the men kept working on the house, while my sisters and I, the Massey family, and a few others went to pick field corn that we had grown for our animals. While in the cornfield, I again noticed Emily, yet did not let my thoughts go anywhere. The next night we had the Masseys over at our campfire. We talked and visited until about 12:00 that night. When I went to bed I laid there tossing and turning. Emily's name was going through my head over and over, and there was a great sense of peace that came over me. I first tried to stop thinking about her, yet I was sure that the peace I felt was from YHWH. As I lay there, I felt prompted by YHWH to go speak with my father. So I did. He felt that it was very possible that YHWH was speaking to me, so we poured out our hearts before YHWH and committed everything into His hands.

My father talked with my mother the next day. Together they came to a complete peace about taking the next step. I asked them to talk with my sisters to hear what they thought about my thoughts toward Emily. They know me probably better than I know myself, so I wanted to know if they felt that Emily would be the one for me. They all individually felt a complete peace. The fact that my parents and sisters all felt YHWH's leading in this match gave me great hope that it was indeed YHWH speaking to me.

Emily's father was not there, so my parents shared with Mrs. Massey my thoughts towards Emily and told her that I would like to have both Mr. Massey's and her approval before Emily would know anything about the matter. I feel that it is very important for the sake of the young woman that she would not know that the man is interested in her until the parents agree on the union. It is then her decision. In this way, it spares her from emotional turmoil that could come if one of the parents did not feel right about the union.

Emily

Originally, my family and I were planning to go to Israel for Sukkot the year of 2011, and for a while, we thought that we would most definitely go. Then, at the last minute, things fell through, and it did not work out. After we realized that we would not be able to go to Israel, we were invited to about six different

Sukkot groups that were scattered all over the U.S. and a couple of groups in Canada.

My family and I prayed about it and felt YHWH leading us to go back to Montgomery Bell for Sukkot. We e-mailed the family in charge of the group and told them we would join them again this year. Our family had been told by several other families that we should get to know the Fourniers. We knew of them but never seemed to get a chance to spend very much time with them. In one of the e-mails that we received, we found out that the Fourniers were also going to attend the Sukkot gathering at Montgomery Bell that year. My family and I were very excited to have an opportunity to get to know them.

On the first Shabbat, the Fourniers invited our family to their campsite for dinner. This was the first night that we started getting to know each other. We had no idea at that time what was going to transpire between the two families. While we were at the Fournier's campsite that night, we shared our testimonies, sang, played games, and did lots of talking and laughing. We got along so well with the Fournier family that after the first night we spent nearly every day and evening together. There were many evenings that we would stay up until midnight talking. Throughout the week my brothers were able to develop a friendship with Christopher, and they got to know him fairly well. Though I had no idea at that point what was going to happen, I did learn a lot about what he believed. My brothers were always ready to tell us about everything they did throughout the day.

Little did I know that four days into Sukkot, Christopher had been talking and praying with his parents about the possibility of pursuing a relationship with me. About halfway through the week they talked to my mom about it. My family and I feel that it is important to have both parents' blessing. My dad was not available for Christopher to talk to at that time, so Christopher arranged a time to visit with him to get his permission. I had no idea whatsoever that he had approached them. On the way home we stopped at a friend's house and some of the Fourniers were there. One of the Fournier girls asked me some questions about what I believed, what I thought about various things, and what my favorite things were. I was still completely unaware that Christopher was interested in me. Looking back now, it seems so obvious what was going on during those two weeks. I believe that YHWH had put a blindfold over my eyes during that time so that I wouldn't see anything.

Christopher

A few weeks later, Mr. Massey and his family came to visit us on the pretense of looking at some land that was for sale right near our property. The Massey children all thought that they were coming to look at the property, but my family all knew why they were really coming to visit! After Tabernacles, I immediately began to clear out the spot that I had always talked of building my house on in the future. All my younger siblings became very curious as to why I was clearing "my house spot" all of a sudden. We could not keep the secret from them. I may have been some-what irrational but I had a confidence that YHWH was telling me that she was the one. And if that was the case I knew I had better get busy!

While working on a construction job, there was a Mexican man on my crew. I told him I was working to make money to build my house, because I was probably getting married.

"You mean, you don't know if you're getting married?!" he asked.

"I am asking her father for permission this weekend," I told him.

"Is she pretty?"

"Of course, she's pretty," I said confidently. Then after a moment's thought I told him, "Well, I don't hardly know what she looks like and I haven't ever talked to her."

Of course, he thought I was crazy, yet he was intrigued and I had a chance to tell him about the way YHWH had led me to pursue this relationship.

It was not outward beauty that I was looking for in a wife, although she is the most beautiful girl in the world!!!!! What I saw in her was a beautiful heart and a love and commitment to YHWH. Love is a commitment, not just an emotional attachment. True love must be based upon much more than the outward appearance.

Emily

While we were at Sukkot we found out about a property that was for sale right next to the Fourniers. The property sounded exactly like what my family and I have been wanting for several years now. When we got back home from Sukkot, my family and I had a discussion about the property, and we decided to go back and look at it and visit the Fourniers again while we were there. I thought we were going down just for a visit and to look at the property; I had no idea at all that Christopher was going to ask my dad if he could marry me!

While we were still at the Fournier's place, I was told that Christopher was interested in pursuing a relationship with me. Throughout that day and the next day I did a lot of praying and thinking. After Shabbat dinner and throughout the rest of the night, I had a strong feeling, though it was not an audible voice, that YHWH was telling me that Christopher was the one. I felt such complete peace that my answer should be yes.

There were many character qualities that I had wanted in a husband. Most of these qualities are not things that you would find in most young men. Though I have not been waiting nearly as long as many young women, I still did not think there was anyone out there. I wanted a husband who loved YHWH with all of his heart, soul, mind, and strength; who loved children and interacted well with them; who desired to work from home; and who would lead his family in YHWH's ways. There were many little things that I also wanted in a husband that YHWH has blessed me with in Christopher.

Christopher

I spoke with Mr. Massey on November 12, the day after they arrived, and he and Mrs. Massey gave their approval. Mrs. Massey then took Emily on a walk and shared with her my desire for her. My sister said when Emily came back into the house, she had a stunned look on her face! She had no idea of my desire for her, and now the decision was all hers. I expected it to take her a week or so to give me her answer, but within two days she felt YHWH's leading that I was the man created for her. There was much rejoicing within both our families.

Together Emily and I chose to refrain from all physical contact until the wedding day. Some may wonder, "Why don't you touch if you know you are getting married?" The Scripture says there is an appropriate time and procedure for everything. The physical contact of a lover arouses emotions that are pure and holy in the proper time. But it can also awaken desires before the appropriate time. Consider it this way: Emily is a gift given to me from YHWH. Just like with any gift, there is an appropriate time to open it based upon the benefactor's will. If I were to rashly take the gift and open it before the time determined by the benefactor, would I be showing gratitude for that gift? There would be no gratitude shown, but rather a lack of self-control and a desire for self-gratification. By refraining from physical contact, we were able to demonstrate our love and commitment to each other in that we could look out for the good of the other and not our own desires. The sure foundation of a happy marriage can only be when the man and woman both look out for the best interest of the other and not their own personal interests.

At our betrothal, four months later on March 18, 2012, I offered Emily a cup of wine which she accepted and drank in the presence of many witnesses. In doing this she was saying she would enter into the covenant of marriage with me. Our families blessed and encouraged us from the Scriptures and prayed over us. We had all our family and the adults present (forty-seven people) sign our ketubah as witnesses to keep us accountable to our vows. After eating and singing and dancing, I stood up and read the words that Yahshua spoke to his disciples after He made the covenant with them. *"In My Father's house are many mansions; if it were not so I would have told you. I go to prepare a place for you"* (John 14:2). After saying these words to Emily I turned to walk out the door. Before leaving, I turned to take one last glance at her. I only looked for a second because I felt I had to go. My heart was so full I did not know what to do. I went home feeling so full, yet so empty. My bride was mine now, yet it would be nine long weeks before I would see her beautiful face again. Once home I sat down to write her a letter. The words that came to me were those from Yahshua, *"Therefore you now have sorrow; but I will see you again, and your heart will rejoice, and your joy no one will take from you"* (John 16:22).

Emily

At the betrothal was the first time I saw the chuppah Christopher had built for me. (The chuppah is the canopy symbolizing the man's covering over the woman and the house he will build for her.) It was beautifully made of a carved cedar arch and woven cedar lattice. It made me think of beauty and strength. As I stood under it during the ceremony, I knew my beloved would prepare a place of the same beauty and strength for me.

When Christopher offered me the cup, I took it very quickly. Afterwards all my siblings teased me that I took it way too fast; they weren't sure that Christopher had even offered it to me before I took it!

After Christopher left, my heart was crushed. The one I loved so much was gone and I wouldn't see him again for a long time. The next day I received a letter (by way of his sister) which read, "I love you so, so, so, so much. I will hold you in my heart until I can hold you in my arms. I am yours!" That encouraged my heart. This was the first of forty-seven letters I received in the nine weeks until our wedding. Each one was filled with encouragement and love. I felt like I was receiving a part of him. On one occasion my family and I went to a wedding of friends. Christopher's family was there also, though he stayed back to work on our home. He sent eight letters with his eight unmarried sisters and throughout the day they gave them to me, telling me something from his heart, such as, "You are the most beautiful among women," and "like a lily among the thorns, so is my darling among the maidens." In his letters he compared me to the beautiful wildflowers growing in the woods about the home he was building for me; he told me I was as a beautiful crown on his head. Though I could not see him I felt safe in his love through the sweet and loving words he wrote for me.

Christopher

During the nine weeks of long hours working on our home, Emily was continuously in my thoughts. I wrote letters telling her of the zeal that consumed me. I longed to see her, to touch her for the first time and to hold her; I wanted to let her feel my love and not only hear of it. I now have a better understanding of how YHWH feels toward His Bride as His great and glorious day is approaching by experiencing that special time of waiting for my bride. That long awaited May weekend finally arrived. There were three days in which my father had to choose from for me to get my bride. The time was set for sometime between Friday at 3:00 p.m. through Sunday 12:00 p.m. Even as we do not know the day or the hour of the Heavenly Bridegroom's coming, so neither the bride, groom, or guests knew when my father would choose.

My father chose the time by the Scripture, *"Behold, I come quickly"* (Revelation 22:7 KJV). On Friday afternoon, the 18th of May, my father told me it was time. By 3:30 p.m., Emily's father, her brothers, and my brothers were blowing shofars and announcing the bridegroom's coming. Many people were expecting a time of waiting and were taken aback by the quick arrival. It served as a great reminder that we must *always* be ready, for our Bridegroom is coming!

Emily

The sound of the shofar shocked me. Was he really coming already? I had no idea that he would come so soon! Suddenly time seemed to stop. I knew I had only *one* hour, but that short hour seemed *so* long to me. Everyone else seemed to be taking their time—I was ready to go! We finally got to the place of meeting. I was extremely nervous and very excited. I looked anxiously for him. Then, through the trees I saw a group of young men come into sight. They held torches and there, in the middle was a beautiful white percheron horse! He pranced with animation and held his head high. My heart began to pound as I saw my bridegroom sitting astride that beautiful horse! I think that was the most beautiful sight I will ever see.

As he emerged out of the trees, I moved towards him. Then suddenly he halted the horse, dismounted and broke into a run. I ran to meet him. I don't think anything on earth could have held us apart. We embraced each other, touching for the first time. Being held so close and never having been touched by another man made me feel so secure in Christopher's love for me. Christopher mounted the horse and I rode behind him. Together we rode to the place where the wedding would take place. Under our chuppah, we reinstated our vows that we had shared with each other at our betrothal and we washed each other's feet symbolizing that we desired to lay down our lives for each other. Christopher sang a song to me, called "Arise, My Love" and we danced our first dance together. It was so awesome to feel his arms around me and to be loved by someone so dearly. I had never felt so treasured and prized.

Christopher and I served all the guests at the wedding feast, as it is written, *"Blessed are those servants whom the master, when he comes, will find watching. Assuredly, I say to you that he will gird himself and have them sit down to eat, and will come and serve them"* (Luke 12:37).

Something that I think is very important to YHWH is purity. Because I kept myself pure, I was able to give all of my heart to Christopher. I did not give even a portion of my heart to another man. I also tried to dress and behave modestly. You may have never heard of behaving modestly. Even if you dress modestly, you can still be immodest in your behavior. Some things I tried to abstain from in my pursuit to behave modestly and remain pure are not having long conversations with young men, and not praying with, or having any one-on-one time with them. I also tried not to play group games where there are not any or just a few other girls, nor will I look at a young man in the eyes. Because of this, I admit I was very shy and nervous around Christopher at times. Though I think this is much better than the alternative, it is actually a form of a witness that I kept myself pure. I had never looked at a young man in the eyes before. Christopher, in fact, is the only young man that has probably ever seen the color of my eyes. I was very careful to keep from making eye contact with just any young man, as that could cause feelings to arise that should only be for my husband. I have been extremely blessed by Christopher's diligence in keeping himself pure and am glad for every effort that I have made over all the years to keep myself pure for him.

I would like to encourage all of you young women to wait upon YHWH and let Him show you who "the one" is that YHWH has for you. It is well worth the wait! YHWH has a plan, and His ways are perfect. You may not see how He will work it out right now, but He can make a way when there seems to be no way. Give all your concerns and desires for marriage to Him, and He will bless you. He may not have the same plan for you as He did for me, where in six months He brought my future husband to me. But when it does happen to you, you will know it is of Him when you have a great peace like you never have had before. Through my experience I have learned that YHWH's ways are always best. *"'For My thoughts are not your thoughts, nor are your ways My ways,' says [YHWH]. 'For as the heavens are higher than the earth, so are My ways higher than your ways, and My thoughts than your thoughts'"* (Isaiah 55:8-9). May YHWH bless you as you strive to follow His ways for your life. *"He hath made everything beautiful in His time..."* (Ecclesiastes 3:11 KJV).

Christopher

In all things, YHWH has shown Himself faithful. The years spent waiting and learning to trust YHWH for my future have been well worth it. He has given me a wife whose character and beauty have surpassed all I ever wanted. I encourage you young men to *"Humble yourselves under the mighty hand of [YHWH] that He may exalt you in due time, casting all your care upon Him for He cares for you"* (1 Peter 5:6-7). *"The blessing of [YHWH] makes one rich, and He adds no sorrow with it"* (Proverbs 10:22). *"You will show me the path of life; in Your presence is fullness of joy; at Your right hand are pleasures forevermore"* (Psalms 16:11).

We now have been married for two years and are blessed with a little boy, Benayah, and another little one on the way! We are so thankful for the wonderful ways in which the Father has blessed us and look forward to what He has for us as we continue to serve Him together.

A Word of Encouragement

Steve & Kelly Fournier

(Christopher's parents)

Steve and I would like to encourage all of you young people who desire to be betrothed one day to "trust in YHWH with <u>ALL</u> of your heart." Use this time of preparation before marriage to passionately love your Heavenly Bridegroom. He loves you with an everlasting love and desires to have an intimate, personal relationship with you. Genuine and lasting peace can only be found in trusting our Heavenly Father in every area of our lives. As you trust in YHWH, His peace, which surpasses all comprehension, will guard your heart and mind in Him. Be to your Heavenly Bridegroom what you would one day desire to be toward your spouse. YHWH holds your future in His hands, and when He brings that special person into your life, it will be in His perfect timing. He is the only one who can give you the wisdom you will need in making this life-changing decision.

If there is one thing that we could not emphasize enough to you parents who are entering into this decision-making process regarding potential spouses for your children, it would be that both you and your spouse would be in total agreement and have a great peace before going forward. This is one of the most important decisions that you and your child will ever make concerning his or her future. When a young man comes to us to ask for one of our daughters, Steve will initially ask the young man several questions. If he answers the questions satisfactorily, we will then evaluate his spiritual maturity, personality, strengths, and weaknesses. As the parents, YHWH will give us wisdom and peace on whether or not we should go forward. If we have a peace in our hearts and believe that the young man would fit our qualifications, we will then approach our daughter and let her make the final decision. We would like to emphasize the importance of prayer in asking YHWH: is He leading in this union between your son or daughter and this potential spouse?

When our children were growing up, we could not emphasize enough how important it was for them to keep themselves morally pure. The word *moral* means "practice, conduct, or manners; it has reference to the law of YHWH as the standard by which your character is to be determined" (Webster's 1828 dictionary). Purity or chastity, as applied to young people before marriage, implies purity in relationships and in all interactions with other young people of the opposite sex. It is important for young people to understand that they can flirt with their words, their dress, and even with a glance of their eyes. We want to warn you that flirting is very dangerous and can lead to defilement. 1 Peter 2:11 states, *"Beloved, I beg you as sojourners and pilgrims, abstain from fleshly lusts which war against the soul."* We strongly believe that it is YHWH's will for all young people to keep themselves pure and undefiled, both physically and emotionally, before marriage. *"Flee also youthful lusts; pursue righteousness, faith, love and peace, with those who call on [YHWH] out of a pure heart"* (2 Timothy 2:22).

In today's society, almost every billboard, magazine, or advertisement is seductive. On top of that, with TV shows, movies, and the internet, immorality is all around us. It is very difficult for young people, especially for young men, to maintain moral purity. We need to train our daughters to dress modestly to protect young men from stumbling. We also need to encourage our sons to be like Job and make a covenant with their eyes, *"... Why then should I look upon a young woman?"* (Job 31:1). As parents, it is our responsibility to protect our children, especially our daughters, from immoral men. Immorality is sin and is very destructive in a marriage. Colossians 3:5 instructs us to *"...put to death your members which are on the earth: fornication, uncleanness, passion, evil desire, and covetousness, which is idolatry."* As our older children became young adults, we would pray with them and encourage them to be careful not to give their hearts to anyone who would not one day be the one YHWH would choose for them. We would remind our sons and daughters that their whole hearts were the most precious gifts that they could ever give to their spouses one day. We encouraged them to go to sleep in the area of thinking about getting married until YHWH would awaken them in this area. We would encourage them to use the time of waiting as a time to draw closer to our Heavenly Father until He should choose to bring those special people into their lives. When any of our children had struggles with desires to be married, we would pray with them and encourage them to be faithful in the things that YHWH had set before them during that season of their lives. We also would encourage them to be accountable to us if they had any struggles in this area. Being accountable to someone—especially to your father—is a safeguard for you. We pray that YHWH would give you much wisdom as you enter into this new season of your life in choosing a righteous, YHWH-fearing spouse through the betrothal process.

From the Foundations of the Earth

Aaron and Victoria Hood

Aaron's Story

I was twenty-one years old and feeling like marriage was some kind of mirage—something that today's culture would say is "out of style." But for me, growing up in a family of fourteen children, marriage was the only way to have a family. My parents had grown up with the idea of "try before you buy," and they had suffered a lot of broken relationships and broken hearts from it. They kept me out of that cycle, but they were sure that there had to be another more biblical, less painful way. I grew up in a strong, Bible-believing family, knowing that dating was a dangerous way to find "the one." I definitely felt odd, and I can't tell you how many times I had to answer the question, "Got a girlfriend?" with a long explanation. But I saw how precious few succeeded in finding "the one" with the first girlfriend. The vast majority were those who went through several relationships and broken hearts, as well as being left with scarred emotions. I also recognized how many of those relationships that did lead to marriage ended in divorce.

These observations helped me heed my parents' counsel to try an approach called "betrothal." A few of the young men that I respected, as well as my older brother, had done a betrothal or something close. The blessing and purity blew me away, and the fruit was strong, committed relationships. I decided that this was what I wanted to do.

Maybe I should start by describing how betrothal normally works. I (a young man) see a young woman whom I would like to pursue a marriage relationship with. Before even approaching her, I go to my parents, and we pray about this girl together. If they feel like it is God's will, and would be a good match for me, they allow me to go to her parents, and they pray about it. If her parents also feel it would be God's will and approve of the young man, then the girl's parents ask the girl (so she doesn't feel pressured by being asked directly) and she prays about it and says "yes" or "no." If the answer is "yes," they become legally married, but they don't come together as husband and wife until there has been a period of getting to know one another.

This was the framework I understood when my story began. Age eighteen: time to get married, move out on your own, face the world, and be your own man . . . right? So I started praying about my wife, went and got a job, and bought a truck. I was on my way to being a married man. Wrong! I would pray about a young lady, and after a month or two, decide it was a whim or just physical attraction. I would talk to my dad and he would point out the girl's character, whether strong or weak, and help me look past the outside. *"Charm is deceitful and beauty is vain, But a woman who fears the LORD, she shall be praised."* (Proverbs 31:30)

So a year passed, then two, and I grew discouraged. I said, "The LORD is going to have to send a white dove that will land on my shoulder and tell me who I'm supposed to marry." But the white dove never came. So at age twenty, and no closer to being married, I gave up the idea of being married for awhile, and began to really press in to my relationship with God. So another year passed, and at twenty-one, I felt much more mature and ready for marriage, but was still feeling very far from this "marriage thing."

My dad would periodically check on me to see how I was doing. On our way to work one morning, he asked me if I had anybody I was praying about. As we talked, he softly mentioned, not wanting to pressure me in any way, that Mom had been praying about a certain young lady whom she felt could be the one.

"Do you want to know who?" he asked.

"I guess so," I replied.

"Victoria."

He didn't have to say her last name. I knew exactly who he was talking about. But at the same moment, I felt like I should clarify. "Victoria Waller?"

He went on to tell me that Mom had dreamed that we had married. I tried to think of all the reasons why not, and I came to the conclusion that the only reason was that an angel is not supposed to marry a man.

Our families had known each other since before I was born. Her brothers were some of my best friends. I had spent a lot of time with them, working in Israel and on the road, speaking, for months at a time. I didn't really know Victoria personally, but I did know one thing about her. She was one in a million—hard-working, graceful, strong, and had a great spiritual walk. Let's just say it this way: the only reason I could think of for not marrying her, and the reason I had not considered it before was that she was too good for me. I didn't have a chance. It really encouraged me that my mom thought that I did. Maybe there was some hope after all.

For the next couple of months, I began to pray about this wonderful turn of events. In August, about three weeks after Dad's initial suggestion, Mom and I were returning home from attending the birth of one of Victoria's nieces. As we were driving, Mom broached the subject and asked what I thought about her suggestion. I told her I had been praying about it, and I appreciated that she thought so highly of me. I just wasn't sure if it was even a possibility. She then told me her dream, and how she had been sure for a long time that Victoria would make a great bride for me. I then told her about a time when I had been in Canada with the Wallers when I had unintentionally caused untimely emotions by prolonged eye contact and one-on-one conversations with Victoria. Her older brother, Zac, noticed this and made me aware of what was happening and how damaging it could be if it was carried any further. He had puzzled me by his final remark. "I'm not saying this isn't God's will, only that it's not the right way or the right time." Upon relating the story to my mom, I thought more intently on his remark. At that point, I began to pray more seriously.

We had a Hebrew class coming up in December, hosted in the Waller's home. Mom and Dad, knowing I would like to attend, and that Victoria would be there, asked if I would be able to focus and not give her any hint of my interest. I decided that I would test the waters by at least attending the first week. At the end of the week, I felt I could attend the whole class and still keep myself in check. During that time, I had great opportunity to watch and observe Victoria closely, as we were in a lot of the same classes. I found myself constantly aware of her presence or absence. In my zeal to be discreet, I battled whether or not to voice my thanks for the meals she prepared for us. After returning home, I was immediately questioned by my parents on the status of my heart. I decided to pray seriously about the next step.

Late on the night of December 30th, Mom and Dad said they wanted to talk to me after everyone else had gone to bed. The next day, I was leaving to go to Israel for the pruning, and would be gone for two and a half months. I was anxious to know what was on their minds. As we sat down in the living room, Dad questioned me about whether I still desired to pursue this relationship with Victoria. I thought for a moment and then answered "yes."

Dad continued, "We want you to know that you have our blessing and that we feel it's time for you to approach Mr. Waller." I was excited. This was the farthest I had ever been in pursuing a bride. But the more I thought about approaching Mr. Waller about his daughter, the less hurried I became. Mr. Waller, with his large red beard and strong build, was not too far from matching the look of the Vikings I had seen in history books. Growing up with his sons, I had heard stories of him bench pressing 500 pounds and being on the football team in college, and how, on a school bus he was driving, he had grabbed *two* 250-pound rambunctious teenagers by their shirts and held them to the ceiling to restore order to the bus.

It was with these thoughts that I boarded a plane for Israel for the winter pruning, with a month to prepare for Mr. Waller's arrival. The time passed quickly, with quite a few earnest prayers for courage, but I felt a little closer to being able to broach the subject with him. Opportunities would come and go, leaving me frozen. A week passed this way, and every time I called my parents, their first question was, "Did you ask him?"

"No," I would reply. Finally, my mom gave the advice that I should set a date and ask him. That I did—February 9th. With that resolution, I firmly decided, "If I perish, I perish." And if I did perish, it would be a worthy cause.

On February 9th, Shabbat, I started looking for an opportunity to talk to Mr. Waller alone. This proved to be a difficult task, since we had guest speakers, and many of the men wanted to discuss the Torah portion with him. At one point, an opening arose right after lunch, but I seemed to be struggling with some type of paralysis. I'm telling you, my legs just wouldn't work! Shortly after dark, I realized my time was growing short. It was now or never. Putting one leg in front of the other, each step was deliberate. I walked into the tent and asked Mr. Waller if I could talk to him. "Sure," he said, and followed me outside the tent. We walked to a somewhat secluded spot, off to the side.

Before I lost courage, I plunged in. "Mr. Waller, I need some direction. My parents have given me their blessing to ask you to pray and see if it could be God's will for me to marry your daughter."

"Which one? I have four daughters," he jokingly replied.

Not feeling it was very funny, I said, "Victoria." At that, he became more serious and said that he'd pray about it. I was quite happy to hear that response. He stated that he wanted to get to know me better and that we would need to sit down sometime and talk. I agreed completely. We then prayed together for the Father's will to be clearly evident. As we separated, aside from being extremely relieved that I was still in one piece, I felt very excited at being one step closer to being married.

I immediately called Mom and told her I'd asked. She, of course, asked me, "What did he say?"

I replied, "He said, 'Of course, no!'" Being on Skype, I could see her disappointed look.

"Really?" she said.

"No." I quickly eased her fears. I then relayed to her the whole conversation. Excitedly, she reminded me she would join with Mr. Waller and me in praying and fasting on Sundays. The next morning, Mr. Waller called me aside into his bedroom and asked me to relay to my mother that he wanted to tell Mrs. Waller, and that Mom shouldn't mention anything to her until he had told her face-to-face once he was back in the States. I complied immediately, and relayed the message. Mr. Waller and I began to look for opportunities to talk privately, without arousing the suspicions of the other pruners. This was a difficult task, seeing as sickness was the only exemption from being in the field with everyone else. Also, free time was hard for Mr. Waller to find, in the midst of all his meetings.

Finally, it was decided that I would join him in visiting one of the families in the community. We would leave early, drive to a secluded place, talk for a couple of hours, and then go visit the family. Even this aroused suspicion. As I was preparing to go, several of the guys inquired why I was going. I responded with the only honest answer I could find: "Mr. Waller asked me to come along." I was a bit nervous as we began to talk. He asked me about my plans for the future and what vision I had for my life. I began to relax and feel more at ease. We talked for an hour.

I answered his questions as honestly as I could. Leaving the meeting, I felt at rest in leaving the results to the will of God. We continued to pray, and every Sunday, we fasted together. The rest of Mr. Waller's stay passed quickly, and he left on March 5th without any further conversation. A day or two before I left Israel on March 10th, I spoke to Mom. She told me that Dad and Mr. Waller had had a meeting and that she and Dad would be meeting with Mr. and Mrs. Waller in a couple of days. I was surprised and happy to see how quickly things were progressing.

As our flight left Tel Aviv, I wondered about what would transpire within the next couple of weeks. I figured that upon my arrival, my parents and I would get together again with Mr. and Mrs. Waller to confirm that everyone was in agreement, and hopefully not too long after that, Mr. and Mrs. Waller would ask Victoria. She would then either give her consent or rejection. I was sobered to think that within a month, Lord willing, I could approach the final step to being a married man.

The second leg of our flight, from New York to Pennsylvania, was smooth. In Philadelphia, however, there were only enough seats on the next flight to Nashville for three of the four of us who were flying together (we were on standby). Making a quick decision, Luke Hilton, my brother Jesse, and I got on the first flight, leaving Joshua Waller to catch the next flight, two hours later. After a total of thirteen hours in the air and close to thirty-three hours awake, we landed in Nashville, TN.

My family and the Hilton family were there to greet us. As we walked out to the parking lot after gathering our bags, Caleb and Mrs. Waller, along with the younger Wallers—Olivia, Havah, Britt, Tessa and Mack Tanner—met us there to pick up the wine we had brought for them from Israel. As I hugged Mrs. Waller, I thought for sure that she must know, but she gave no indication that she knew anything. Victoria was not with them. I figured she would be coming later, with the rest of the family, to pick up Josh.

As we left, my family decided it would be good to get something to eat before heading home, so we went to Shoney's and ate lunch. Afterwards, Mom and Dad wanted to take us somewhere we'd never been. It wasn't exactly normal, and being exhausted from traveling, I just wanted to go home and go to bed. On the other hand, I'd been gone for two and half months and figured it would be good family time. We pulled into the parking lot of the Gaylord Opryland Hotel, piled out and made our way into the atrium. We found a secluded spot and were talking and enjoying the scenery when I saw a few of the Wallers heading towards us. I was taken aback and thought, "Wow, they came to have family time at the same exact place!"

Victoria's oldest brother, Brayden, began to jog towards me. Having known and been close to Brayden, I was excited to see him and greeted him with a shout of "Shalom!" and embraced him. Without any further greeting he excitedly and quickly announced, "Shamati sheh ata rotzeh lehitchaten achoti!" (I heard you want to marry my sister).

Flabbergasted, I wondered how he had heard, and who else was privileged with this information. I managed to stammer a reply, "Ken, Be'ezrat HaShem!" (Yes, with God's help!)

Seeing my look of surprise, he added in English, "You have my blessing."

Without even giving me time to process, Zac, Victoria's second oldest brother, stepped in right behind Brayden, and grabbing me by my collar, he proceeded to push me back into the rail and declared, "I heard a rumor that you want to marry my sister!"

Well, whoever didn't know, knows now, I thought, since he said it in English. I responded quickly to keep from being pushed over the rail. "Well, Zac, that wouldn't be a rumor," still not comprehending what was going on.

At this point, Mom stepped in while handing me a bouquet of flowers she'd been hiding in her coat, and gave me the most valuable piece of information I had heard all day. "Victoria said 'yes.'"

Wow, things were making a lot more sense! With that phrase, she conveyed to me three valuable things: (1) Victoria knew I had asked; (2) everyone but me knew; and (3) most importantly, she had said "yes!" So in essence, this was sort of a gauntlet I was walking with her brothers giving their approval of the idea. Caleb came next, and then I saw Victoria for the first time. She was escorted by her brothers Joshua and Nate.

My head filled with one thought. "She said 'yes.' Is this really happening?" Having been awake for so long, I thought it quite possible that I was dreaming. But those flowers were still very real in my hands, and Victoria standing before me was as real as ever. As I moved forward to give her the flowers, I very nearly walked right past Mr. Waller, who was also waiting in line to give me his blessing. He gave me a big bear hug and allowed me to continue towards Victoria.

I knelt on one knee, extended the flowers to her, and said, "Victoria, please?"

Her response was quick and concise. "Baytach," she said, which means "absolutely." I stood to my feet as our families erupted in cheers and shouts of approval.

Thus began a few awkward moments of realizing that there beside me was the woman that I was to spend the rest of my life with, but I couldn't think of the first thing to say to her. I only recognized later the beauty of that moment. The reason the moment was awkward was only due to the fact that neither of us had ever been in that situation before. The love that was to develop between us would be our first. Upon the suggestion to relate each other's stories, both families settled down to hear the chain of events. As the details of the story unfolded, it became very clear that this was God's will.

As I went to bed that night, I thought about our parting glance. I had looked her in the eyes and remembered that time in Canada and thought, "It's the right time, the right way, and it's okay."

Over the next couple of weeks, we began making decisions about the timing of events up to our wedding. We would wait until after Nate and Katie's wedding to announce our plans. The betrothal was to be the 27th of April and the wedding in June.

Awkwardness was no longer a factor, and our emotions began to run high within the first couple of visits. Family Week arrived, and with it daily visits and long conversations between us. As I began to see into this beautiful girl's heart, I discovered a pearl of great price. We talked mostly about our beliefs and convictions and where we thought God was leading us both. At first, I thought it might be impossible to have a lighthearted conversation with this girl. I soon realized that this was the foundation of our marriage being laid.

Family Week passed all too quickly, and by the end, the seed of love had burst forth within us. The time had come that I had to leave. Victoria was standing near our bus talking to a few of my brothers who weren't helping me pack up. Slightly jealous, I walked over to her. She handed me her journal, saying she thought maybe reading it would help me see into her life a little more. As I pulled out of the campground, I was comforted to know that soon I would never have to leave her side again. At the present, it stood that our communication would be thirty minute phone calls in the morning and as many letters as we could write. When I talked with my parents, it was also decided that I could visit every weekend until our betrothal.

The first weekend came. I talked to Victoria on Friday morning and told her to expect me sometime before nine the next morning. I talked it over with Dad, explaining that it being Shabbat morning, I wanted us both to get some rest. I asked him what he thought I should do. He quickly stated, "I'd be there as early as I could if I was you!" Now he was talking my language! I was up and left my house by 5:30 a.m. I arrived on her doorstep at 6:30 sharp. I didn't exactly feel comfortable enough to burst into the Waller's house at such an early hour, so I sat on their front yard swing and read the Torah portion for the day. I then looked at my watch. Seven o'clock—still too early. I decided to try and serenade her awake by playing my guitar. I increased the volume as the time got later. Finally, at 7:45, she emerged, sleepy-eyed and hair in disarray. She obviously had just awakened and rushed out to see me. Laughingly, she asked how long I had been there. As I told her, I handed her a bouquet of yellow roses.

The weekend passed too quickly, as always. There never seemed to be enough time. Another couple of weeks went by, and each time we parted, it seemed as if our emotions had reached a new level. On one of my visits, the plan was for all of us to lead worship at a conference nearby. After the worship time had ended, many people we hadn't seen in awhile came, and, upon congratulating us, asked to hear our story.

I got a call from Dad, and he told me that I needed to return sooner than I had planned. Upset, but knowing there was no other choice, I told Victoria I had to leave. She seemed greatly disappointed. As I said goodbye, I realized that the next time I would see her would be at our betrothal. We pulled away and my brother, Samuel, told me there had been tears in Victoria's eyes when he had told her "bye." I regretted even more having to leave. At that point the time couldn't pass fast enough until our betrothal. I stayed up late a few nights preparing our chuppah but I never had any trouble rising early the next morning to talk to Victoria.

I arrived late in the afternoon to the park where the betrothal was to be held. As I pulled in, Victoria exited the door of her family's cabin. As our eyes met, the reality of the moment sank in. I was getting betrothed to her the next day! I began to visibly shake, overwhelmed by all the feelings inside me that were stored up until this very moment. We rushed about, trying to get ready for Shabbat. I started putting the chuppah together with some help from a few of the guys. The rest of the family arrived and hastily joined in the Shabbat preparations. We had a very special Shabbat, and electricity was in the air for Victoria and me. Oblivious to anyone else, we talked late into the night—under supervision, of course. Eager for the next day to come, and sleep being the easiest and fastest solution, I drifted off to sleep without hesitation. The morning broke dark and rainy, but the sun shone in my heart. Victoria, upon my invitation, joined my family for breakfast.

My main goal before the betrothal was to have a private talk with Mr. Waller about the acceptable level of affection I could show Victoria at the ceremony. I had thought that he would be rather strict with his daughter, so you can imagine my surprise when he displayed no reservations at the idea of me kissing her! I was severely taken aback, as I had assumed only the holding of hands would be allowed. He then explained that he had never been in this situation in which I found myself. He thought I should talk to some of Victoria's brothers and my brother Levi, who were married, to get their opinions, due to their experiences. The end result was that I decided to hold her hands and even allow a side embrace. I would wait until the wedding to kiss and fully embrace her.

The time came, and everything was prepared. With only immediate family present, I waited near the chuppah for Victoria's grand entrance. She arrived in a long white dress, simply wrapped with a blue sash. Her eyes shone with light, like two deep pools of water. Her hair was down and curled. She was so beautiful, and time stopped. The ceremony was short and to the point. As Victoria stepped under the chuppah, I reached both of my waiting hands for hers. I thought she would faint. I wasn't in much better shape myself. We began with reading our ketubah to one another. We played songs we had written for each other, washed each other's feet, and had our families speak blessings over us. Just before the blessings, I wrapped my arm around her shoulders, enveloping her with my prayer shawl, symbolizing my desire to be a spiritual covering for her. You could have knocked us over with a feather. Love had been awakened in our hearts. The meal afterwards was joyful and festive. The others celebrated carefree, while Victoria and I were drinking in every moment together, knowing the time of separation was nearing. All too soon, I was putting the ring on Victoria's finger, promising to prepare a place for her. With the family looking on, I held her face with both my hands. She had tears in her eyes as I tenderly said, "I love you," and left. I couldn't look back. It would be seven weeks until I saw her face again—on our wedding day.

Although I had much preparation to do, and stayed very busy working with my dad, the time passed painfully slow. I would wake up at 4:30 a.m. to read my Bible and pray for an hour before calling Victoria at 6:00. We would discuss the portion we had read, pray together, and then hopefully have a few minutes to chitchat before heading to work. I would again call Victoria at 9:00 p.m., and we would talk about our day for another thirty minutes, finally going to sleep at 10:00. Thus, I spent the majority of my days, counting down until the wedding. About two weeks before the wedding, my dad and I were talking and he began to explain how he felt like he better understood the Father's heart. As he had watched the way my anticipation caused me to be totally focused on my bride and our wedding day, he realized how Yeshua must also be—and even more—passionate for His Bride and wedding day. My father wondered if the Heavenly Father ever felt forgotten, as he had, during this process.

The initial preparation had finally begun. I threw myself into the fray with vigor. Family and friends helped me prepare for the day I had been awaiting. We had rented a campground for the weekend of June 14-16. The idea was to make a clear picture of the "ready or not, here I come" reality of Yeshua's coming. The wedding could be any time during those three days. The LORD had provided a place not far from the camp for me to stay, and Victoria would stay in the camp with the guests, waiting for the shofar's blast. I had positioned watchmen at the camp and warned them to be alert for the signal I was to give one hour before my coming.

Friday, the day had come. The final details had fallen into place and all was ready. Most of the guests had arrived, and plans were made. A friends-of-the-bridegroom party was held, and all the men came to a cookout to celebrate with me. A diehard tradition was upheld, and I was thrown into the lake against my will by Victoria's and my brothers. I fought like a wildcat, but to no avail. The water cooled my spirits and we had a great, rowdy time, many joining in the water spray. Upon hearing that the same tradition had been carried out with Victoria by the girls on the other side of what I thought was the same lake, I started swimming, humorously acting like I would swim the lake to get to her. We dried out by playing volleyball. Because many had Shabbat to prepare for, the party broke up about an hour before dark. My family and I had Shabbat dinner, together with a few friends.

When all had died down, I got ready to go to bed. Dad and a few of my brothers were also bunking down in the next room, in case Dad decided to go at any time during the night. Then the guys would be there ready to jump at a moment's notice. I told my dad goodnight, not expecting to sleep much. He said, "Don't go to sleep yet; it's time to go get your bride." I looked into his face a full minute, trying to see if he was serious. His expression didn't change and he added, "The wedding will be at midnight." Whether he was joking or not I didn't know, but he didn't stop me as I quickly got dressed. My brothers jumped into action in a matter of seconds, grabbing the fireworks that we were to alert the watchmen with. The friends who brought the horses my dad and I planned to ride were saddling them as we jumped into our vehicles. The sky lit up as we alerted the watchmen across the lake. I could faintly hear the shofar blasts through the night, waking the camp on the other side.

We made our way to the place where we were to finish getting dressed, and Dad and I were to mount the horses. The horse that I was riding seemed to feel the urgency that was pulsing through my body, and it pranced in the darkness. As I grew comfortable with my mount, I realized that this was the last step. Memories flooded my mind, and love filled my heart. My brothers, singing, jogged easily beside me. I hung back and allowed my dad and brothers to precede my entry. My horse again trotted in circles, anxious to follow the others. I heard a roar as the waiting crowd momentarily thought Dad on his horse was me riding in. I gave the horse its head and galloped full steam into the campground. Another shout arose as the horse slid to a stop. The field was brightly lit, and my eyes swept the crowd looking for one face. There she was. I started walking towards her, but then paused to fix that moment forever in my memory. We ran into each other's arms, oblivious to the world around us. We kissed for the first time. I felt as if, in that moment, I truly began to live.

Victoria's Story

March 5th, 2013: Dad and Britt (my brother) were coming home! We were all in a hurry trying to get the house clean and welcoming. We wrote "Welcome Home" messages on the front porch windows and hung a banner over the driveway. Finally, we drove to the airport to pick them up. After hugs and kisses, we returned home. From all outward appearances, it seemed to me like any other return from the pruning.

That night, as Mom and Dad were preparing for bed, Mom nonchalantly asked him, "Did anyone talk to you in Israel?" Dad knew exactly what she was referring to, and replied, "I'll tell you all about it in the morning." That was the wrong thing to say if he was planning on getting to sleep anytime soon. The lights went back on, and Dad proceeded to tell Mom that yes, a young man had approached him about me. Mom's first reaction was "Oh man, we can't tell him 'no.'"

The next evening, Dad told us he had to go meet with "Mr. Mark." We were a little sad because he had just gotten back from being gone for six weeks, and we would have liked to have had some family time. Nevertheless, he is a very focused man, and we figured he was meeting with Mark Cornelius about Israel.

That Shabbat, we had a great, leisurely day, staying home and relaxing. As Shabbat was coming to an end, Dad came into the living room, where several of us were sitting and talking. "Hey Sherri, come, I want to take you on a date," he announced. The thought crossed my mind, "What if someone asked in Israel and Dad is going to tell Mom about it?" As it turned out, my fleeting thought wasn't too far from reality. In fact, the date was to include Mr. Mark and Mrs. Anita Hood, and it was my future they were discussing.

We were already in bed when they returned that night. Sunday morning found me in a hurry, making up for time I had lost in an alarm malfunction. I was getting breakfast and packing food to be gone for the day. We had planned to spend the day helping my brother, Nate, on the home he was preparing for his bride. Mom called me from the laundry room that was adjacent to the kitchen saying, "Toria, come to my room." My heart immediately skipped a beat as I wondered what I had done. Then it occurred to me that maybe this was it!! At that, my heart began to pound. As I rounded the corner, my suspicions were confirmed when I saw Dad also standing by the bed. There was an expression of sobriety on his face. I followed Mom and sat on their bed, wrapping my arms around my knocking knees and stabilizing my beating heart. I raised my eyes to meet Dad's. He cleared his throat to begin. My sisters were sleeping peacefully. Unbeknownst to them, our world was about to change. The floodgates of tears were about to be released.

"Someone approached me in Israel." Dad paused as I processed.

I raised my hands to my face to suppress the squeal of growing emotions welling up in my very being, not knowing the day I had dreamed of and looked forward to was so near. All I could think was, "WHO?" I didn't have a clue. Just a week earlier, Nate and I had been stripping bark from cedar posts and talking about his bride and their upcoming wedding. I had asked him how to know for sure that someone is your life companion. I felt I didn't know a man, that, if he asked that day, I wouldn't have to pray for at least a month about. And here I was, about to be confronted with the question that would forever shape my future.

I looked to Mom, who asked, "Do you want to know who?"

"I think so," I replied.

Dad looked me squarely in the eye and said, "Aaron Hood."

In a matter of seconds, scenes flashed through my mind—his godly character and obvious desire to be a man of God were my first thoughts. These were followed by the realization that he had witnessed almost every embarrassing, ridiculous thing I had ever done. These moments of reflection brought a resounding peace within me, as I realized that he knew me for who I really was, and still wanted to spend his life with me! I vocalized my heart, "Well, I guess there's only one answer to that question."

Mom said, "Yes or no?"

"YES! But I guess I need to pray about it for a couple days." Walking out of the room, I had to collect myself and act as if everything was normal, so as not to arouse the suspicions of my brothers and sisters.

I awakened the girls, and also my brothers, Britt and Mack Tanner. We finished packing and were soon on our way. I was in a daze, and could not concentrate on anything but THE decision at hand. I thought back to when I had just been coming into my teen years and didn't know how to deal with the thoughts of romance that invaded my mind.

Our families, the Hoods and Wallers, had known each other for over twenty years, and it seemed as if Aaron was constantly around. When I was fourteen, he went on a month-long speaking tour with us, and then proceeded to fly to Israel to spend another three months with our family. During this time, especially, I realized that I was going to have to get my thoughts under control. I had to tell myself that Aaron was probably not going to be my husband and it would be very destructive for my future if I allowed myself to spend time fantasizing about someone else's husband. So I tried to take my thoughts captive and to guard my heart with an iron shield, but there were times when the iron seemed to crack and the thoughts still invaded. At one point on that tour, I had a girl tell me that she liked Aaron, and being young and very immature, I responded, "What if *I* like Aaron Hood?" I later went to her and told her I had no business talking about such things and asked her to please forgive me.

The years went by, and the struggle went on. I would tell myself, "Just be normal; it doesn't have to be so awkward." One such time, after I had turned seventeen, several of the Hoods (including Aaron) came to Canada to help host a Family Week. During that time, Aaron and I began to talk more than usual making more eye contact, which caused more of a battle in my mind. My very protective older brother, Zac, noticed this, and consulted with Mom and Dad. He proposed that Dad talk to me, and he himself would talk to Aaron. Dad took me for a walk and challenged me to be careful that the motives of my heart were pure. He said that if I heard tomorrow that Aaron was getting married, I should feel no jealousy. I had been telling myself that Aaron's attention wasn't affecting me, but in reality, it was consuming my thoughts. I decided that no matter how awkward it was, I would stay as far away from guys as possible—especially Aaron Hood. I then put into practice something I learned from my sister-in-law, Tali: whenever the thoughts came in, I would immediately start praying for Aaron's wife, whoever she was. In that way, I could disconnect myself from being that person.

When I turned eighteen, I realized, "WOW, God has delivered me!" I no longer felt bombarded by thoughts towards Aaron. In a conversation I had with my sister, Olivia, I told her I felt free for the first time in years. Unbeknownst to me, that was right around the time that Aaron began to pray about marrying me.

Now, here I was, three months from turning nineteen, very happy and comfortable with my life. I loved my family more than anything in the world, and yet one of my greatest desires was to be a wife and mother. I walked down to the creek while everyone else was eating lunch. Sitting there on the bank I prayed, "God, if this isn't Your will, please show me." I didn't hear an audible answer, but I felt at peace.

That night when we arrived home, I told Mom and Dad, "I think this is God's will. I've no idea what I'm stepping into, but I think I'm ready."

"Are you ready to tell your siblings?" Mom asked. Olivia and Havah were out milking the cow. I decided to bring my exciting news to them first.

They looked at me very suspiciously as I approached them. "Well, somebody asked and I said 'yes!'"

They looked at each other with an expression that read, "Our suspicions have been confirmed," and then asked, "Who is it?"

With great excitement, I replied, "Aaron Hood!" They were shocked! Neither of them had any idea that Aaron was interested in me. (They told me later that my trying to act as if nothing was happening was to no avail. By the end of the day, they knew someone had asked; the only question was "who?")

Mom quickly began making calls to gather the family. In no time at all, the entire family had congregated in the living room, aside from Joshua, who was flying back from Israel with Aaron. The rumors and guesses had already begun, in the short time since the summons. "Is it Joshua?" was the common question.

"Well," Dad said, giving me the floor. All eyes were on me in expectancy. I told everyone the news with great enthusiasm.

Brayden was the first to react to the news. "Nobody but Aaron!" he declared excitedly. The rest of the family joined in with unanimous approval.

Now we had to decide how we would break the news to Aaron. We decided on a big party at the airport. I called Mr. Mark and Ms. Anita to let them know my decision. Both were overjoyed and after agreeing to keep in touch about the details for the next day, I hung up the phone. I lay in bed that night and realized what I had done. I had just made the decision to leave my family, who I loved dearly, for a man I barely knew. I cried myself to sleep, hoping love would come quickly.

Morning came, and with it, the reality that this wasn't a dream. I kept myself as busy as I could, comforting myself with the thought that once I saw and talked to Aaron, I would feel more at ease. The plan changed several times through the course of the morning; the final one was to pick up Joshua from the airport, then meet up with the Hoods at the Opryland Hotel. As we approached the hotel, my body shook with excitement and nervousness. My five older brothers took their positions escorting me in. Brayden, Zac, and Caleb walked with their wives in front of me, while Joshua and Nate each hooked one arm in mine and walked on either side. Britt and Mack Tanner were directly behind. The rest of the family followed close after.

The time was beautiful. At first, I couldn't bring myself to look Aaron in the eyes—the emotions were too strong. I had never experienced this before. As Aaron knelt before me, my heart beat rapidly. I found myself saying the word I had rehearsed so many times in the past twenty-four hours, "Baytach" (Hebrew for "absolutely"). I managed to look into his strong blue eyes as I accepted, with shaking hands, the flowers he held out to me. As we left the hotel, Aaron walked beside me, making attempts at small talk. I really didn't mind the awkwardness. I had seen my brothers go through this phase in their relationships. I knew, looking back, we would treasure these endearing moments.

We saw each other off and on during the next few days. One of the times, we met up at my grandparents' house to tell them the news. I met Aaron in the kitchen after shy hellos. We walked into the living room and sat down next to each other. We were wanting to see if they would notice anything out of the ordinary. Aaron engaged in conversation with Poppa, as the rest of the family fought back laughter. "Well Poppa, I want to tell you something," Aaron said at last, "Victoria and I are getting married." Poppa just about fell out of his chair. He was unsteady as he stood to hug us.

"I've been waitin' for this," Nana said, beaming happily. We prepared to eat lunch and I fixed Aaron a plate. Aaron's younger brother, Jesse, looked skeptical when I handed Aaron the plate.

"That's weird," he said.

Five days later was Aaron's twenty-second birthday. Calling not being an option because of an agreed-upon arrangement, I decided to make him a shirt for Nate and Katie's wedding to match the rest of the brothers. We stopped by and dropped off the shirt on the way to Family Week. With it, I left the first of many notes. I didn't see Aaron again until he came riding in with the rest of my brothers, accompanying Nate, who was coming to get his bride. Aaron was as handsome as ever. My eyes met his steely gaze. My heart leapt as I realized he was looking for me.

On the walk to the ceremony, a girl asked how it felt to have my brother, only eighteen months older, get married. "Who knows; you could be next," she said.

"That's a scary thought," I replied nonchalantly.

At the reception, Dad called Aaron up to make his announcement. I stood nearby holding my breath as Aaron began, "I'm getting married!" Aaron paused to build suspense.

Cheers and applause erupted, but quickly died down as someone shouted, "To who!!?"

"Victoria Waller!" he declared. I jumped and squealed excitedly. It was really happening. Aaron came to my side and gave me his coat (it was chilly). We stood together as everyone came to congratulate us and give us blessings.

We spent as much time as possible with each other the whole Family Week. Aaron would come down to our campsite and sit on the swing, or I would walk up to his family's bus and we would talk. By the end of Family Week, I was sure of one thing: I was falling in love! We left a few days after Aaron and his family did. I was amazed that already, I felt lonely without him. As we were leaving, I looked back at the campground with anticipation for the next time.

Friday, April 26th: The house was in an uproar of preparation. For me, the time couldn't pass fast enough, yet the impending separation made me grasp for every moment. We all arrived at the park where the betrothal was to be held in the early afternoon, and began to get ready for Shabbat. I ironed my dress, first off. I really didn't know when Aaron would get there, so I was trying to hurry but be relaxed at the same time. I then started the salad for dinner, the entire time glancing out the window, waiting. I decided to practice my song for Aaron. I played it through a couple of times. Where the keyboard was set up, I couldn't see out the window.

Suddenly, everyone started looking outside and smiling at me. He's here! I went out to meet him. He showed me the chuppah. It was beautiful! They began setting it up right away. Shabbat was coming! Aaron asked me to head up the decorating of the chuppah. It was really sweet how he wanted me to feel a part of things. I'm a dreadful decorator, but with the help of everyone, it turned out lovely. Shabbat dinner was really nice. My sister, Olivia, really worked hard and pulled the whole thing off. Aaron and I got to talk until 11:30 p.m. or so. Shabbat morning, I woke early but rolled around in bed until seven o'clock and then got a shower and read a bit. Aaron came with his younger brother, Noah, and invited me over for breakfast. The whole day was beautiful. Each time I looked into Aaron's face, I tried to memorize each feature, so that I would be able to see him when I closed my eyes for the next seven weeks.

Finally, the time came. I put on my sister-in-law Becca's wedding dress and the girls curled my hair. As we were walking out our cabin door to go to the Hood's, Dad asked me if Aaron had told me what he was planning as far as touching during the betrothal. He said he had told Aaron that he figured, biblically, it would be fine for him to kiss me, but to ask my brothers what they thought. I wasn't quite sure if I was ready for that. As I walked into the Hood's cabin, I felt a secure peace. Aaron stood on one side of the chuppah and I stood on the other. His parents blessed him, and he went into the chuppah. My family blessed me, and I walked into the chuppah. Aaron held his hands out to hold mine. Before, I had wondered what that moment would feel like. Aaron said it perfectly. I felt at home. I didn't automatically feel butterflies. I felt safe. We read our ketubah and drank the cup. We made a salt covenant. Then Aaron played me his song while Olivia put a head covering on me. The song was beautiful! I sang him my song. Ms. Anita then handed Aaron his tallit. He took it and wrapped it around his shoulders while explaining that since his tallit symbolizes his prayer life, he wanted to cover me with it. At that point he opened his arm to me and enveloped me with the tallit. My stomach flipped as he drew me near. I felt like I never wanted to leave that place. The rest is kind of a blur to me. It was really special.

Everyone came up and blessed us. Then the party began! We took a bunch of pictures. Aaron and I walked arm and arm over to our cabin, where a beautiful meal was waiting. The night was lovely. All the family danced their hearts out. Aaron and I danced to a few songs, but mostly we sat on the couch nestled next to each other. I've never felt so overcome with love in my life. I love Aaron Hood with all that I am. The time then came . . . he had to leave. He gave me a ring as a seal to our covenant, and I gave him one. We prayed for each other. He held my face with his strong hands. I wanted so badly for the moment not to end, but I knew it had to. Tears filled my eyes as I watched him go. I had to keep telling myself that forty-nine days wasn't really that long.

The days between our betrothal and wedding were filled to the brim. My first priority was to decide on a pattern for my wedding dress and to order materials for it. That accomplished within the first week, I tackled the next project: Aaron's shirt and vest. With great uncertainty, I cut out the shirt, wanting it to be perfect, but unsure of my capabilities. Nate and Katie planned a canoe trip to have some fun family time before I got married. After borrowing two canoes, we loaded up in our big red bus and headed to Nate's yurt on the edge of the river. We camped out in the bus that night. Then, early in the morning, we dragged our canoes down to the water. We made it fifteen miles down the river that day, only flipping twice and losing most of our food. We camped that night huddled around a fire in a swampy cove. Being close enough to civilization, I found reception and called Aaron. When I got back to the family, I found them laughing and reliving the events of the day while trying to dry out their drenched blueberry bagels over the fire. The next afternoon, we rowed our canoes to the closest dock as we neared the Tennessee River. Being plum tuckered out and fried by the sun, we collapsed on the dock.

After arriving home, I was again bombarded by the preparations that still lay ahead. Being a very task-oriented person, I made myself a list so I could stay focused. Over the next few days, the list seemed to be growing more than diminishing. My days revolved around the times of 6 to 6:30 in the morning and 9 to 9:30 at night, during which Aaron would call. It soothed my heart to hear his loving voice. Our emotional intimacy grew daily; we could freely express our hearts to each other without physical attraction being a distraction.

My sister-in-law, Becca, hosted a bridal shower for me. I was strongly encouraged by all the mothers and wives who readily gave their counsel.

Aaron had to come pick up the camper he and I would live in for our first year. So we decided that I would go spend the day with his family, and he would spend the day with mine. My sisters, Olivia and Havah, accompanied me to Dickson, the halfway point between our homes. We had to carefully plan out our exchange so as not to see each other. Samuel and Hannah, Aaron's younger siblings, escorted me to Clarksville, and Olivia and Havah accompanied Aaron back to our house. I had a great time visiting with Aaron's family. It helped me understand Aaron's life and family in a deeper way.

Samuel drove me back, along with Micah and Eli. The ride was boisterous as they told me of their plans to start a quartet, blaring the music they envisioned singing. We reached the meeting place about thirty minutes ahead of Aaron. We relaxed, talking and joking, until Samuel got a call from Aaron asking where we were, to which Samuel replied, "In the parking lot."

Aaron exclaimed, "I'm pulling in right now!"

"I'm not joking," Samuel insisted.

"Well, get in the store NOW!" Aaron commanded, not enjoying the moment as much as Samuel was. "I'm closing my eyes. Take a run for it!" This we did, barely avoiding failure.

Safely inside the store, I thought: "To anyone looking on, this would seem crazy! Here I am, yards from the man I love passionately, and instead of running into his arms, I'm not even looking in his direction."

One week before the wedding, my family and I went down to Texas to host a Zion's Sake Conference. As the van drove out of our driveway, I began questioning my sanity. We had finished all twenty of our siblings' wedding garments, but Aaron's and mine were still lacking the finishing touches. I also hadn't even begun packing, but just like everything else, I figured it would all fall into place when the time came. While in Texas, Aaron's dad decided we could talk longer than our allotted thirty minutes, which news was received with great appreciation.

When we returned home, we swung into action. While discussing wedding plans, one of my brothers suggested we think of a way to make the bride's entrance more dramatic. Ideas began forming, the first of which was to stage a battle between the Waller and Hood men. Then my brothers would feign defeat, and as a gesture of peace between tribes, I, the daughter of the chief, would be given as wife to Aaron, a prince of the Hood tribe. My brothers, unwilling to accept defeat—even in jest—went on to the next idea. One idea led to the next, until they finally decided on constructing a palanquin to deliver me to my beloved. I, not concerned about the details of the day—only that it would come quickly, gave my consent. So they set to work.

Thursday morning found us in a scurry of packing, repacking, and then packing again. We set out, and stopped a few times along the way to get the remaining items for our honeymoon. We arrived at the campground shortly before dark. I retired to bed soon after supper, wanting the time to pass as quickly as possible. Morning dawned bright and clear; I felt rejuvenated. Sitting down, I began finishing my dress hem and embroidered the last stitches on my waistband. Havah came in—just the person I was looking for. I wanted her to draw a design on my sash. She insisted I come join all the girls gathering outside the camper. I told her I would be there in a little bit; I really had to finish my dress. Seconds later, Olivia appeared, saying, "All the girls are waiting for you!" She urged, "The guys are with Aaron, and the girls want to party with you!" I reluctantly set down my sewing and followed her out the door. Around one hundred girls were assembled, and they all cheered and began congratulating me as I stepped down from the camper. Suddenly, Olivia and Havah charged, hoisting me onto their shoulders. They began running down toward the lake. The rest of the ladies pursued, laughing. Miraculously, we made it down the hill and to the water's edge unscathed. With Liv and Hav's last ounce of strength, they threw me in and plunged in after me! We splashed, laughed, and played together before heading up to prepare for Shabbat.

That night, Ms. Anita climbed into the camper and pretended to hug me goodnight. "I'm your wakeup call; the wedding's at midnight," she whispered to me. At midnight! My girlhood dream was coming true. Two hours, and I would be in Aaron's arms. Joy coursed through my being. Ecstatically, I got up and began to get ready, along with my sisters. I had thought I would only have one hour to prepare. Given the extra hour, I had time to enjoy those once-in-a-lifetime moments with my family. When I finally heard the shofars blow, one hour later, I stepped outside our camper door, dressed and ready.

As I made my way to the waiting palanquin, I felt much calmer than I had expected as I was hoisted onto my brothers' shoulders. Surrounded by my family, the procession wound its way, singing jubilantly, to the place where Aaron would come to meet me. I watched the road we were approaching, intently straining my eyes for any movement that might be my beloved. Dad held my shaking hands as I waited anxiously. Music filled the night air. "Ruach ve'hakalah omrim bo" ("The Spirit and the Bride say come"), we sang. I then saw what looked like a flashlight in the darkness coming closer. I stood to my feet clapping, exhilarated with the moment. I could hear the hoofbeats of a horse, and then saw men running toward us. My brothers slowly set the palanquin down, and I was able to step gracefully out. Confusion gripped me for a mere second. Whoever it was that was riding the horse had stopped and dismounted, but Aaron was nowhere to be seen. Just then, a sound came that sent my heart sailing. The pounding of another horse's hooves galloping through the darkness. I could see him at last, his hair ruffled by the wind as he was rapidly approaching. I began running, arms spread wide, and was caught in his tender embrace.

Dreams Awaken Love

Caleb and Kendra Waller

Caleb's Story

I first met the Lupinacci family four years ago at a Passover Seder. We hit it off really well, but I never thought much of the possibility of Kendra being my wife one day. Because my brother, Brayden, married Kendra's sister, Tali, our families spent a lot of time around each other, and that was always fun—but my interest in Kendra started in October 2010 during the grape harvest in Israel.

One day, I was talking with one of the vineyard owners, who expressed to me that he could use my help on a project. I was honored that he would ask me, but at the same time, I realized that it would be a big commitment and I would need to spend a lot more time in Israel. This sparked a prayer in me: "Father, I know that You would not want me to work here alone, and You did not create man to be alone, so if this is Your will, either make a way for my family to stay here, or give me a wife!" Little did I know how quickly He would answer that prayer.

That night or the next, I had a dream. In the dream, I was sitting in this man's vineyard, having a picnic, and across from me sat beautiful Kendra. I extended my hand to her; she looked at me, smiled, and put her hand into mine. This is where I would say the beginning point was for me. Needless to say, I woke up that morning a little dazed, having not ever really thought about Kendra being a potential wife before. In my mind, I pulled up my list of standards that I had set for what I wanted in a wife, and she fit everything on the list perfectly! I thought to myself, "Why did I not see this before?"

Now, I would like to explain something. With dreams, you have to weigh them. I would never say that just because you had a dream about someone, that this is your answer. No way! You have to put a lot of prayer into it, and you also have to have the right authority structure involved (i.e., parents). If I had gone to my dad after the dream, and he did not agree with it, the whole thing would have stopped there.

I wanted to be accountable on this, so I shared the dream with Brayden that following weekend. He was excited at the possibility. I didn't have time to think about it much because it was the middle of the harvest, and I had a team I was responsible for, which kept me busy. But I kept it in the back of my mind. At that time, Kendra was attending a Hebrew school in Jerusalem and would come and spend the weekends with us. It seems that the Father had kept me from noticing her until then because I wouldn't have been able to contain it. In His perfect timing, He showed me who the love of my life would be. For that, I am so thankful!

Everything stayed the same for about a month—until Kendra finished her school and came and stayed at the HaYovel base, where I was stationed. Now I was around her every day, which was fun, but this was a big test for me. How was I going to act normal around her and not show any interest, whatsoever? At this point, I had shared with Mom and Dad my interest in Kendra. They also had a good feeling about it, and they began to pray about when I should pose the question to her father.

In November, I returned to the States, leaving Kendra, Brayden, Tali and their daughter Yael, who would all be returning a month later. I got busy with HaYovel work—phone calls and making plans for the next trip that spring. I felt it was best to leave it up to Mom and Dad as to when I would proceed further. I would just wait until then and try to keep myself as busy as possible in order to keep my mind off of it. I was doing really well until January.

In January, we started an intensive Hebrew class, where we studied eight hours a day. Having just spent three and a half months in Hebrew school, our teacher, Brayden, was ready to go full steam. Kendra came and joined the class!! So there I was, trying to focus on Hebrew and spending eight hours a day in the same classroom with the lady I felt that God was leading me to marry. After a week of this, I went to Dad totally exasperated, and told him that Kendra needed to go home, because it was too difficult to be around her, and I could not be myself when she was around. Dad's response took me by surprise. He said, "Well, if you are sure that she is the one, why don't you go talk to Mr. Kenny right now?!" I sat there speechless for a minute, looking at Dad to see if he was really serious. I had not been expecting that at all!

So I stood up, straightened my collar, and with the most confidence I could muster, I called Mr. Kenny. I asked him if he could help me with something; he said "sure." So I told him I would be over in little bit to pick him up (the Lupinacci family was spending a couple of nights at my grandparents' house, which is a quarter of a mile down the road). I picked him up and posed the question. After talking with Mr. Kenny, I remember driving back and thinking, "I have just jumped off the cliff. There is no turning back; I am either going to fly or fall!"

Now, I could do nothing but wait. And it was the longest weekend I have ever experienced in my life. Mr. Kenny talked with Kendra the next evening, and to my great relief and excitement, she was ecstatic.

Two weeks after the "yes," I flew to Israel for three months. Kendra was at the airport to see me off. It felt a little awkward, saying "bye." It wasn't that I was in love with her; it was just a feeling of wanting to spend as much time with her as possible, which if I had tried to explain, I couldn't. These feelings were all new to me. I had never felt so drawn to a lady before. So, to avoid as much teasing as possible from the ten other guys I was traveling with, I quickly pulled my mind back to checking in my bags and getting ready to board the plane.

The next stage, I would call the "awakening of love." My parents felt that at this stage, leading up to the betrothal, it would be good for us to write and just talk one day a week, so the emails began to go back and forth between us. I remember the first Skype call; it was kind of short, still very meaningful, but it was hard to get off, knowing it would be a whole week before we could talk again. By the next week, the conversation lasted five hours, but they seemed to be just a few minutes. By the end of the three months in Israel, all the twenty-four hours in that one-day-a-week conversation were well used.

When I landed at the airport and saw Kendra, I knew that our relationship had skyrocketed. When I looked into her eyes, I could . . . well . . . *something* had changed!

We were soon wrapped up in planning our betrothal—a royal party with over three hundred guests. We had decided to have our betrothal in the States and the wedding in Israel six months later. You will find in some of the other stories in this book that they decided to separate until the wedding, but we felt (along with the counsel of our parents) that we would still see each other, but we would not touch until the wedding. The touching guideline was set in place so that we could focus more on connecting spiritually and emotionally, to build a strong foundation for our marriage. I would encourage other couples to consider not touching before marriage, because when it comes to physical contact, it is hard to know where to draw the line—especially if you have a long wait.

I soon found that the physical draw was creating a conflict. I sought counsel from my married brothers, who told me that my feelings were valid. I was created to have this desire for Kendra, but the sacrifice of waiting would be rewarded on our wedding day.

We had ten months from the day she said yes to the time we married. We could have gotten married sooner, but we both felt strongly that we wanted to get married in Israel. I can't tell you how many times I asked myself why we decided to wait that long, but we held our resolve and waited.

After we were married, I was thinking about what those ten months had taught me. Throughout my whole life I had pushed the limits, which in some cases might be a good thing, but in others it can cause trouble. That brings me to this point.

One day I was sitting next to Kendra and I thought, "We are not supposed to touch; I think I can scoot a little closer without touching her." I could tell Kendra liked me being a little closer, and I was enjoying it too. I didn't touch her, but got mighty close. I could tell later that day that something was wrong with Kendra; she seemed to want to distance herself from me. I was hurt. Had I said something? Done something? What was it? She had to go home before we had time to talk. For hours, I went over everything that we had said during that visit; what was it? When I called her the next day to ask about it, what she answered struck me to the core. She said, "I don't trust you." She wasn't mad at me; she just felt like I had not protected her when we were sitting on the couch, so how could she trust me in other areas if I was not going to stand on what I said I would do? It then became my goal to build Kendra's trust in every way possible, to show her I was a man committed to my word and the standard we had set.

The wedding day was beautiful, with our ceremony held at Psagot Winery. I woke up that morning thinking, "The day has finally come, after what seemed like an eternity." I remember running into Kendra's arms for the first time, feeling like a champion. The rest of the ceremony was a blur, and then we were off for a romantic honeymoon in Israel.

In finishing my story, if I could leave you with one thing, it would be this: the world is full of weak men who can't stand against their fleshly desires, thereby making women feel threatened, insecure, and unprotected. For me, the greatest thing I can be is a MAN whom my wife can trust and love.

I am now a father, with two beautiful little girls who never cease to amaze me. My relationship with Kendra is growing deeper every day. I am so thankful to the Father in heaven for His bountiful blessings in my family's life.

Kendra's Story

When I was growing up, I always knew that when it came time for me to get married, God would reveal to me who my husband was going to be. I did not want to rely on my own understandings or feelings. This was something way too big for me to figure out. So here is another testimony of how faithful the God that we serve really is.

Our story starts in 2007 when we first met the Wallers. My family was going to a Passover Seder that was hosted by the Waller family. Little did we know how this family would impact all of our lives. As we pulled into the parking lot of the church where the Seder was being held, a young man of sixteen (whose name was Caleb Waller) happily greeted us. My first impression of him was that he was really friendly—and that was it. I was seventeen, and wasn't even thinking about marriage at this point. It wasn't until about two years later that I ever thought about the possibility of Caleb being my future husband. I was still finishing high school and I knew, at that point, that I had a lot of growing up to do before I could enter into marriage.

Almost two years after that Passover Seder, Brayden Waller (the Waller's oldest son) asked to marry my oldest sister, Tali. They decided to get betrothed before their wedding. It was hard saying goodbye to my sister (we were all really close), but I knew she wanted to get married. I was so happy to see the holy example that they were setting for us. It was the night before their betrothal when I began having thoughts toward Caleb. That evening, both families had gathered together for a time of worship. After this time, Caleb stood up to get some tea and then suddenly, his face went pale and he fainted. The family immediately gathered around him and began praying. I felt a strong inclination to pray for him. As I began to pray quietly in the Spirit, I began crying. When I went to bed that night, I had the thought for the first time: "Could Caleb be my husband?" As I slept that night, I had a dream about Caleb. I woke up from the dream with a sense that it was a warning to keep my heart in the right place. I had learned that it says in Song of Solomon 8:4, "I charge you, O daughters of Jerusalem, do not stir up nor awaken love until it pleases." I knew that this "charge" could not be ignored, so over the next two years, I had to be active in taking captive my thoughts about Caleb because I did not want to awaken or stir up love before it pleased. I wanted to have my heart so guarded that if I was to get news that Caleb was going to be getting married to someone else, I would be able to enter into joy for him. I knew that I had to trust that God would work everything out in His perfect timing for my life.

During this two-year period of trying to guard my heart, my own family and the Wallers spent a lot of time together because our families became closely connected through the marriage of Brayden and Tali. A year later, my other sister, Angela, got betrothed and married to Samuel Spear. I was the last one at home; both of my sisters were deeply in love and happily married. It seemed like the reality of marriage was becoming more and more real as I kept being surrounded by it. Therefore, the struggle to keep my heart pure became more heated. In order to keep myself in the right place, I chose to keep myself busy and occupied.

During this time, I made two trips to Israel, spending a total of eight months there, learning Hebrew, and also spending time in the vineyards with HaYovel (the ministry that the Wallers have in Israel). This put me in a lot of situations where I was in very close proximity with Caleb. Sometimes, we were even living in the same house together (along with thirty other people). Caleb would say that during this period, he thought I did not care for him at all. I was, in fact, trying to avoid him like a plague because of my struggle with having thoughts for him. I would still have short conversations with him, but I was always very guarded.

It wasn't until January of 2011 that things changed. Caleb talked to my father about why he believed I was to be his wife. My dad said that it was alright with him (he had been praying about Caleb for me for awhile), and that he would talk to me about it. Before my parents told me about Caleb's interest in me, they prayed that I would receive confirmation from the Father. The same night that they prayed, I had a dream that Caleb and I and our parents were sitting around the living room, planning our betrothal. I had had other dreams about Caleb, but this one was definitely different. I really felt a peace about this one. The next day when my parents told me that Caleb believed that I was to be his wife, I knew immediately that he was to be my husband. The Father had been preparing my heart for this, and the dream that I had had the night before was the confirmation that I needed. The news of his asking came as a great relief to me. Finally, I did not have to struggle with having thoughts towards him.

After we all came to this realization together, my parents and I sat down with Caleb and his parents. During the meeting, we decided that both Caleb and I felt led to get married in Israel during the harvest. This meant that it would be ten long months of waiting. I don't think either of us realized how long and hard that would be. We had to keep encouraging and reminding each other of how glorious it would be when we could finally consummate our covenant with each other on the same mountains where our God had made covenant with our forefathers.

The betrothal period was a great journey of getting to know each other more and building trust between us. Every day, I am more and more in awe of how perfect this man is for me. And God created me to walk with him the rest of my life! God truly is the perfect matchmaker.

A Final Word

We hope you have been blessed
by these betrothal stories. We hope they have
enriched your spiritual understanding of
being betrothed to Yeshua.

If you are interested in betrothal
as the way you want to start your covenant with
your future spouse, keep in mind
the gravity of entering into covenant
with someone, and keep your focus on Messiah.
May He guide you so that your experience will
be another illustration of His great love for us,
and of the fast approaching day when we will
be presented pure and spotless to Messiah!
What a glorious day it will be!
Yeshua desires us so much that
He paid the price with
His own blood
to make that day possible.

*I go to prepare a place for you. And if I go and prepare
a place for you, I will come again and receive you to
Myself; that where I am, there you may be also.*
John 14:2-3

*"Trust in the LORD with all your heart, and lean not
on your own understanding; in all your ways acknowl-
edge Him, and He shall direct your paths."*
Proverbs 3:5-6

Betrothed

is available at:

hayovel.com

olivepresspublisher.com

amazon.com

barnesandnoble.com

christianbook.com

deepershopping.com

parable.com

and other online stores

Store managers:

Order wholesale through
Ingram Book Company or
Spring Arbor
or by emailing:

olivepressbooks@gmail.com

CPSIA information can be obtained
at www.ICGtesting.com
Printed in the USA
FFOW04n0253030415
12374FF